AF149857

# TIME
### AND
# CHANCE

*Justice Mohta*

# TIME
### AND
# CHANCE

## V. A. MOHTA

RUPA

Published by
Rupa Publications India Pvt. Ltd 2019
7/16, Ansari Road, Daryaganj
New Delhi 110002

*Sales Centres:*
Allahabad Bengaluru Chennai
Hyderabad Jaipur Kathmandu
Kolkata Mumbai

Copyright © V.A. Mohta 2019

The views and opinions expressed in this book are the author's own and the
facts are as reported by him which have been verified to the extent possible, and
the publishers are not in any way liable for the same.

All rights reserved.

No part of this publication may be reproduced, transmitted,
or stored in a retrieval system, in any form or by any means,
electronic, mechanical, photocopying, recording or otherwise,
without the prior permission of the publisher.

ISBN: 978-93-5333-460-4

First impression 2019

10 9 8 7 6 5 4 3 2 1

The moral right of the author has been asserted.

Printed by Parksons Graphics Pvt. Ltd., Mumbai

This book is sold subject to the condition that it shall not, by way
of trade or otherwise, be lent, resold, hired out, or otherwise circulated,
without the publisher's prior consent, in any form of binding
or cover other than that in which it is published.

*In the administration of the Almighty, like human administration, virtues and vices are not always proportionately rewarded or punished.*
*I gratefully dedicate this book to the Almighty for all the partialities showered on me, although I have no idea of who or what, that Almighty is.*

V.A. Mohta

# Contents

# Foreword

M.N. VENKATACHALIAH
*Former Chief Justice of India*

These eminently readable memoirs of Justice (Retd) V.A. Mohta have in their title the familiar ring of the former British Prime Minister James Callaghan's autobiography *Time and Chance*. But the savour of Justice Mohta's recollections is different both in context and content. The common thread is that both believe in the Ecclesiastics, that the race is not always to the swift, nor the battle to the strong; but 'Time and Chance happeneth to them all'.

Justice Mohta, an esteemed personal friend and a respected colleague in the judiciary is a model of judge and gentleman. The account of the journey of his life recorded in these pages can be a precious treasure for any young lawyer. I have read every page of this beautiful biography with great interest and profit.

Herold Laski, in his tribute to Justice Holmes, described the hallmark of a great judge. A great judge must be a great man. He must have a full sense of the seamless web of life, a grasp of the endless tradition from which he cannot escape. He must be able to catch a glimpse of the ultimate in the immediate; of the universal in the particular. He must be a Statesman as well as jurist; thinker as well as a lawyer. He must have a constant sense of essential power and yet be capable of humility in its exercise. He must be the conscience of the community and not of its dominant interests. In being supremely himself he must yet be supremely selfless. He has to be in the great world and yet aloof from it, to observe and to examine without seeking to influence.

These are indeed stern and exacting tests but they set out an ideal and a goal. A system which produces such great judges can really be proud and feel some real assurance about its future. 'True most judges', in the words of Justice Holmes, 'had no wings and were not thunderbolts but very honest and hard working judges'. Justice Holmes once said, 'both sceptic and the worshipper alike agree—that if American Law were to be represented by a single figure, that figure would be one alone, and that was John Marshal'. An American judge said that to see his Chief Justice preside over the court was like witnessing 'Toscanini leading an orchestra'.

The fairness and incorruptibility of the English judge was a proud English reputation. Judges, as someone said, are often mistaken, sometimes imprudent, occasionally stupid but always incorrupt and incorruptible. Justice Rehnquist once remarked that when he first joined the court he felt as if he was entering a monastery. Louis Nizer spoke of a leading trial lawyer who went to the Bench and when asked how he liked his new duties, he is said to have confessed: 'I am quite not sure. The trouble is I do not know which side I am on!' A lawyer in England who accepted a judgeship, after an experience of the hard work it entailed, is said to have lamented: 'I thought slavery had been abolished in England!'

Indian Judiciary has produced many eminent judges of remarkable judicial stature. Some are well known and famous; a few of them remained hidden from limelight. These sentiments come to my mind when I think of Justice Mohta and his ilk.

In my fairly long acquaintance with Justice Mohta, I have no hesitation to say that he was among the finest judges I have had the privilege to know. Justice Mohta was a great gentleman. The charming thing about the narration of the events of his life are his interesting references to many personalities, particularly his interaction with the eminent lawyers Ram Jethmalani, Motilal Setlevad, A.K. Sen and others, that have a personal touch. There are other personalities like Mohammad Rafi, Naushad Ali, even Harshad Mehta, whom Justice Mohta had occasion to meet. He recounts his travel in the same flight with the famous 'King-Kong' (known as the man-mountain of Europe) and how he lost count of the eggs he consumed during the late night flight.

Justice Mohta became judge in April 1979. The invitation to him to join the Bench is an interesting reflection on the gracious manner in which the Chief Justice of Bombay High Court dealt with the matter and the mast gracious and dignified manner in which the invitation was extended. When Mohta sought time to consult his well-wishers, the gracious Chief Justice Deshmukh gently prodded Mohta to count the former also among his well wishers. Mohta also wanted to know whether he had the prospect of being Chief Justice. The response of the Chief Justice was most modest and gracious. It is another matter that 'Time and Chance' ensured Sri Mohta's place amongst a galaxy of great Chief Justices.

Justice Mohta was a judge of great sagacity and wisdom. More than all he was a humane judge as the summer midnight order of 1982 as the vacation judge of the Bombay High Court—where the matter concerned the hutment dwellers who faced convenient eviction—indicates. In that case, the lady lawyer whom the author described as 'fire-brand,' waited late into the night outside the judges official residence till Justice Mohta returned after watching a Marathi play. He was a self-confessed Marathi theatre buff. Every one knows who the 'Fire-Brand' is, but very few know that inside this fire brand dwells a gentle and sensitive soul.

The book is full of many interesting anecdotes. There is a reference to D.M. Pritt's answer to the question put to him: 'Which lawyer do you rate as the best in the world?' He answered: 'Your Attorney General—Setalvad, whose short and terse submission on law as well as facts and sense of dignity is unparalleled'. Mohta recalls an interesting interaction with Motilal Setalvad. There is a grateful remembrance of Sri Athalye, Mohta's Senior at Akola.

After demitting office as Chief Justice, Justice Mohta resumed his legal practice in the Supreme Court in 1995. He has authored a learned treatise on the Law And Practice of Arbitration' Justice Mohta fondly recalls his association with Ram Jethmalani. The admiration seems mutual. It would appear that Ram Jethmalani, when asked as to whom he considered as his 'worthy opponents' is said to have quipped: 'My friend Ashok Desai, one lawyer called Mohta'. He's not so well-known unfortunately, but he's very good'. In these memoirs this 'very good lawyer' emerges, despite his eminence as a man of law, as a simple and honorable man who looked at the world around him with wide-eyed wonder.

These memoirs of Justice Mohta amply reward the reader and show how great success in the legal profession and as a judge can go along with charming humility and graciousness.

—M.N. Venkatachaliah

# Note

'*Babuji*, you have a long way to go!' and one would immediately hear him saying 'Are you a friend or not? Don't wish me such a fate. I want to go with my dignity intact.'

On 14 May 2018, *Babuji* made his last appearance before the Supreme Court of India where he practised for more than two decades after retiring as the the Chief Justice of the High Court of Orissa. He left for Nagpur where he would usually go every summer. On 3 July 2018, he died as he would have wished, with his boots on and dignity intact. His last rites were performed in Nagpur where friends, family and well-wishers gathered in huge numbers to pay their last respects.

As a mark of respect Full Court References were accorded to him by the Supreme Court of India, the High Court of Orissa and the High Court of Bombay. Two of the speeches made at the References are included in the book.

To honor his legacy his portrait was unveiled by the Hon'ble Chief Justice of India, at a function organized by the Supreme Court Bar Association to recognize eminent senior members of the Bar for their contribution to law. He always advised us, 'success is the result of a combination of luck and effort. Luck is beyond one's control, so there is no use bothering about it. Effort is one's own. Therefore, concentrate on it.' He led his own life on this principle.

Towards the end of his life he analysed the luck and chance factor that were beyond his control and revisited his storehouse of memories—some cherished, some insignificant, some painful, but most of all, the meaningful ones that gave his life the significance it had.

It is unfortunate that now when the book is finally complete, he is not here to see it. Perhaps this is the playing out of 'Time and Chance.'

This book is his journey, as he penned it.

—Devansh Mohta

# Preface

Autobiographies are life stories of great people narrated by themselves to enlighten the future and enrich the past. This is not an autobiography in that sense, as I am neither vain, nor naive enough to think that the story around my life can either inspire anyone or add to history. These are simply jottings made in the dimming light of my sunset hours to tell readers that luck plays a great part in the so-called 'achievements' of life—only, its percentage may differ from person to person. In my case, good luck has played quite a significant role.

Blessed with an affectionate family and a loving circle of relatives, I have luckily always been able to bask in the goodwill of a large number of personal and professional friends. My seventy-fifth birthday celebrations in Delhi in 2008 provided the ideal platform to recount anecdotes on the familiar theme of luck and fate. Some of my listeners on that day have been coaxing me to write the story of my life. I had hesitations: The truth is that most of us are sure that we are generally accurate about our perceptions of others; but when it comes to inward attention, subjectivity overtakes reality.

My eldest grandson Devansh who lives in Delhi, had presented me with a gold-bordered notebook with the following inscriptions on its front page:

Dearest Babuji,

write, please, so that we know;

write, please, so that we remember.

Love,

Devansh

3. 7. 2010

I was then busy in writing the second edition of my book, *Trademark, Passing Off and Franchising*. Soon after the final script was dispatched to the publisher in early 2012, Devansh ganged up with another of my grandsons, Nakul, who also lives in Delhi, to apply sustained pressure so that I wrote the story they wanted to hear. I decided to succumb to their demands; perhaps also, to my aroused vanity. (Who says that no element of vanity is involved in writing about oneself?) So, I set about tracing old files, arranging papers in order and used them extensively to alert my memory during the summer recess of 2012. I started sorting out the events of some interest in my life, focusing mainly on the crossroads and turning points. It was a fascinating exercise.

In the Hebrew Bible, as a part of Ecclesiastes, it is stated: 'I returned and saw under sun, that the race is not to the swift, nor the battle to the strong; neither yet bread to the wise, nor yet riches to men of understanding; nor yet favour to men of skill; but time and chance happeneth to them all.'

How true!

After a close and honest analysis of my life, and of many others whom I happen to know, I am convinced that even in the administration of God, good deeds and sins are not always proportionately rewarded or punished. I am grateful to God for all the favours He has showered upon me.

This chronicle is of value to me for one more reason—it provides me a platform to publicly acknowledge the debts due to several known and some unknown well-wishers, the repayment of which is not on the realistic agenda. I thank them with all the sincerity at my command, for showering so much affection and goodwill upon me.

On my eighty-first birthday
26 April 2014

# I

# THE BEGINNING

## ROOTS

I am a child of fortune. Born in Akola, a town in the Vidarbha region of Maharashtra, on 26 April 1933, to Shri Aidanji Mohta, the scion of an extremely wealthy and reputed business family, and Smt. Hirabai, I have lived a robust life, rich in experience and fulfilment.

We are Maheshwaris, a minority Vaishya community from Khandela, Rajasthan. Although our small population has spread throughout India and even abroad, occupied in business and intellectual pursuits, we remain close to our traditions and are proud of our long and fascinating heritage. We are the followers or 'wari' of Lord Shiva, who is also known as Mahesh, and an enthralling legend surrounds the origin of the Maheshwaris. We are told that Maharaja Khadak Singh, the popular ruler of Khandela, had twenty-four maharanis, but no child. To fill this void, he performed a big yagya or prayer ceremony, and soon after, Prince Sujan Kuvar was born.

Maharaja Khadak Singh's joy, however, was short-lived. Sujan Kuvar was influenced by the Jain religion and greatly impressed by its philosophy. He not only lost faith in Hindu gods but also started hating them. He destroyed Hindu temples and had them rebuilt as Jain temples. A keen hunter, he once came across

Hindu sadhus performing yagya at Suryakund while he was out hunting with seventy-two Rajputs (Umraos). He ordered his men to destroy the ongoing yagya.

Enraged by this act, the sadhus cursed the Prince and the seventy-two Umraos, transforming them into stone statues. Consequent to this shocking incident, Maharaja Khadak Singh committed suicide and his maharanis became satis. The wives of the seventy-two Umraos then approached the saints for forgiveness and mercy. Impressed by their devotion and love for their husbands, the saints advised them to approach Lord Mahesh and Goddess Parvati and impress them by continuously chanting the Akshay Mantra.

Shiva and Parvati, pleased by their piety, had compassion for these devoted wives who had lost their husbands through no fault of their own, and restored the stones to their human form, but ordered the Umraos to relinquish their weapons and convert from being Rajputs (warriors) to Vaishyas (traders). While the Umraos were taking a purifying bath in the pond after regaining human form, their bows and arrows melted and coloured the pond, which was named Loh-Gal and is in existence even today.

Lord Shiva also demanded that this new and revitalized community be named after him and so the 'Maheshwaris' came into being, blessed by Lord Shiva with higher growth prospects in business and trade. This is how our ancestors adopted scales in place of weapons, and how new Maheshwari Khaps (last or family names) came into being. With the passage of time, more family names were added to the list.

The community did not breach the condition laid down by Lord Shiva, but some Maheshwaris feel that Lord Shiva could have done better in terms of fulfilling his promise of blessing all members of the community with high growth! No doubt there have been industrialists such as the Birlas, Bajajs, Biyanis, Dhoots, etc., in the community, but the vast majority of Maheshwaris are comparatively poor.

Our ancestors migrated from Jaisalmer to the Vidarbha region in present-day Maharashtra, hundreds of years ago. Jaisalmer is a town in the Thar Desert of Rajasthan, near the Indo-Pakistan border, and its nickname is 'the golden city of India'. 'Jaisal' was the name of its founder king and 'mer' means hill fort. This town had strategic significance and was a halting point on the traditional trade route traversed by Indian and Asian merchants on camel caravans. The route linked India to Central Asia, Egypt, Arabia, Persia, Africa and the West. The main source of income of the town was the levies on caravans. With emerging ports like Mumbai and sea trade replacing traditional land routes, the glory of Jaisalmer faded, as did its main source of income. After all, it was the driest place in India and had hardly any vegetation. One can but surmise that these were the catalysts for several families—mainly of traders—to migrate to other parts of India.

Jaisalmer stands on an old ridge of yellowish sandstone crowned by a fort within which lie a palace, several ornate Jain temples and finely sculptured houses. Its massive sandstone walls are a tawny colour during the day, turning a magical honey gold as the sun starts setting. That is why it inspired Satyajit Ray, the famous film director and producer, to use it as the setting for a detective novel, which he later turned into a famous film, *Sonar Kella* or Golden Fortress. Today Jaisalmer is one of the most popular tourist destinations in India, not only for its fort but also for the magnificent and elaborate yellow stone 'havelis' and libraries depicting Jain heritage and housing some of the rarest manuscripts and artefacts of Jain tradition.

## VIGNETTES AND MEMORIES OF MY FATHER

My father, Shri Aidanji Mohta, had vast business interests including the export of cotton to Japan. The centre of his commercial activities was the town of Akola, in the Vidarbha region of the present-day state of Maharashtra. He was a devout Gandhian, a forward-looking social reformer and a keen sportsman with a special interest in football. Even as a child, I was aware of the great respect my father commanded in the social and commercial life of Akola. Our family home was an old three-storied house with six huge carved wooden pillars imported from Burma. It had been built by my grandfather Shri Sangidasji in the heart of Akola.

As a child I was told that it was the first three-storied building in that small town, and one of the local sites visited by people from nearby villages. The ground floor of this mansion was the hub of our family's business activities while the first and second floors were our residence. In addition to this, the family owned several open plots, hundreds of acres of agricultural and horticultural land, and houses in Akola, Buldana and the neighbouring town of Khamgaon where the family also had a cinema hall. We administered our lands from Village Nimgaon, to which, I may incidentally mention, the very eminent Delhi High Court Chief Justice Shri V.S. Deshpande belonged. My family had a large number of servants, stocks of gold and silver ornaments and bars of bullion that were occasionally taken out. Our wealth was evident to all, and even we children were aware of it.

Akola was also a political hub, mainly because of the presence of the great political and social leader of all-India fame, Shri Brijlalji Biyani, known as 'Vidarbha Kesari' or Lion of Vidarbha. He was a great freedom fighter and an intimate associate of national leaders such as Mahatma Gandhi, Sardar Patel and Jawaharlal Nehru. He was also a forward-looking person devoted to social causes and fiercely advocated the removal of objectionable customs in the community, like the 'parda' system that kept women under the veil and socially out of sight. He was a great Hindi writer, author of several books and editor of *Matrubhumi*, a weekly published from Rajasthan Press in Akola. During the freedom struggle, Shri

Biyani was imprisoned several times and in free India, he was appointed as finance minister of the state of Madhya Pradesh, of which Vidarbha was then a part.

He led the movement for the formation of a separate state for Vidarbha comprising eight districts, with Nagpur as its capital. It is worth noting that the States Reorganisation Commission (known as Fazal Ali Commission and headed by Justice Fazal Ali, a judge of the Supreme Court of India) recommended the formation of a separate state of Vidarbha. This recommendation was largely based on the research material supplied by Shri Biyaniji and his studied and logical statements before the Commission. That the Government of India did not accept this part of the Fazal Ali report is another matter. My father was very friendly with Shri Biyaniji, for whom he had great admiration and regard, and our family were regular visitors at Rajasthan Bhawan, his residence-cum-business premises.

The late Dr Smt Sarladevi Birla, wife of the famous industrialist Shri Basant Kumarji Birla and the proud mother of the late Shri Aditya Birla, was the daughter of Biyaniji. She was then a college student in Pune and visited our house whenever she was in Akola. She was an extremely pleasant, affectionate and popular person whose visits to our home were pleasant times for all. I remember that she had once come to our house wearing a black georgette sari and my father, who was very fond of her but hated the colour black on women, asked her not to wear black at least in his presence. Her fondness for our family made her graciously accept this advice. We were indeed fortunate to be the recipients of her love and affection.

I have some vivid recollections of my short association with my father. Always dressed in khadi with a white dhoti, a long starched white coat, a dupatta and a rose coloured starched khadi pagdi that was held in place by several pins placed in its peculiar and innumerable folds, he never stepped out of the door of the house in any other dress. While at home, he kept the turban on a small table meant exclusively for that turban. No one was permitted to touch the table or the turban that sat upon it. I was not aware of this instruction and one day, out of curiosity, I went near the turban and noticed innumerable pins. Unseen, I removed some of the pins, inadvertently loosening its innumerable folds.

A while later, I heard my father roar in anger as he tried to find the culprit who had touched his turban! I did not dare admit my guilt but my nervousness aroused his suspicion. Under his gaze my nervousness grew and I started weeping as I admitted my transgression. Fortunately my plea—that I was not aware of the instruction and had just been curious—satisfied my father, who pardoned me with a warning against ever going near the turban in the future. Although I escaped corporal punishment this time, I was not always so fortunate. On another occasion, my plea that my crime was without *mens rea* [not intentional], was not accepted. The incident was this: my father, my mother and I were playing cards in the drawing room. My mother played a '10', my father slapped down a 'Jack', showing he had scored a point over my mother, and I threw down a higher value card, a 'Queen', exclaiming in excitement, 'here is the randi', which is how my friends and I described the card, being unaware of the real meaning of the word! My father turned red as he looked at me in shock and then gave me a resounding slap. I started crying and protested that it was unjust to punish me just because he had lost the game! Suddenly, my father burst into laughter and told me that the punishment was for describing the card in filthy terms and not because he had lost the game! That is how I learned that the correct word for the card was 'Queen'.

Although my memory is not usually sharp, for events of my childhood, and specifically those related to my father, it is crystal clear. For example, I vividly recollect his fondness for watermelon: every evening a whole watermelon covered with a cloth wrung out in cold water was kept ready for him, and he would fan it with a hand fan for expeditious cooling before cutting the fruit in two and then relishing the cool sweetness of its flesh.

I also remember a room in a dharamshala rest house in Nathdwara[1] where the family had stayed and also the gallery of a similar dharamshala in Kankroli[2], which adjoined a lake on which small planes occasionally landed. When Kamla and I visited Nathdwara and Kankroli in 1992, I tried to locate these two dharamshalas. I was then a sitting judge of the Bombay High Court and was in a position to make some unreasonable demands! Since I did not know the name or exact location of the dharamshalas, which are abundant in both these towns, I requested a tour of all the dharamshalas and ultimately located them. I was delighted to visit the dharamshala at Nathdwara and see the mango tree under which my brothers and I had sat with our parents in the evenings, and equally delighted to climb the difficult staircase at Kankroli dharamshala, which we had scurried up one hot afternoon when my father took us to see a small aircraft landing on the lake.

My father was bedridden for many years in the last phase of his life. He suffered from severe bronchitis and paralysis of the tongue. My mother devoted all her time and energy to looking after and caring for him. It was during my father's illness that Shri Brijlalji Biyani was released from jail after undergoing long imprisonment for participating in the Freedom Movement. A huge crowd had gathered on the streets of Akola to welcome him. Soon after his welcome procession was over, Shri Biyaniji came to our house to see my father. They embraced each other with tears in their eyes. At night, Shri Biyaniji was to address a meeting being held in his honour at the Cotton Market. He

---

[1]The town of Nathdwara in Rajasthan is famous for its temple dedicated to Lord Shrinathaji and said to have been built in the fifteenth century.
[2]Kankroli houses the Dwarkadhish Temple, also built in the fifteenth century.

was a scintillating speaker and his meetings always had a huge attendance. On learning of this event, my father insisted on being carried out to the gallery in the front of our house from where he would be able to listen to Shri Biyaniji's speech.

It was just a few days after this that my father breathed his last at the age of sixty-two. So shocked was my mother on his demise, that she intermittently started having fits. This ended the brief, halcyon period of my childhood. My father left behind a widow, my mother Hirabai, two married daughters Kesharbai and Gulabbai, and four sons—Khushalsingh (aged forty), Vithaldas (aged eleven), Vallabhdas (me; aged eight) and Laxmansingh (aged three). Khushalsinghji was my stepbrother and was adopted by my father's younger brother, the late Shri Tolaramji. He lived and carried on business separately in the nearby new three-storied house. At the time of my father's death, Vithaldasji was studying in middle class, I was in primary and Laxmansingh, whom we all fondly call 'Lala', was just a toddler. What misfortune for him to have lost his father at such a tender age.

The events of this terrible loss are vividly etched in my memory. My father's passing away at midnight, the huge crowd that assembled in front of our house the next morning and the route we walked in the funeral procession are still real for me. Whenever I had occasion to go to the cremation ground after this in Akola, my eyes would be drawn to the exact spot where he was cremated. It all remains clear in my mind. When my mother left this world in 1976, I saw to it that she too was cremated at the same spot.

My father had asked Shri Dhanrajji Bisani, whom we called Kakaji, to look after us; a duty he performed very sincerely and affectionately, looking after all of us during not only our childhood but also when we were adults. His guidance to our illiterate mother was invaluable and he advised her like a true well-wisher and mentor, helping her to manage our properties and affairs.

One afternoon, shortly after my father's death, my elder brother Vithaldas and I noticed that the large portrait of my father was missing from the wall in the drawing room where it had pride of place. We asked Kakaji about this disappearance. He informed us that a public condolence meeting was being held for our father at the New Plaza talkies and that Shri Biyaniji was presiding over this meeting. My father's portrait was being used by the organizers as a sign of homage and grief at my father's passing away.

As the meeting would have started by that time, my brother and I decided to rush to the venue without even pausing to change out of our school uniform, which was a half-sleeved shirt and shorts. The theatre was full. No one recognized us and we stood near one of the gates along with some other persons, spectators to this awe-inspiring event. The emotions in the theatre were poignant. Shri Biyaniji could not even complete his speech for sobs overwhelmed him at the loss of my father. There were some other speakers, whose names I don't recollect, but amongst them was one Shri Shivji Bhai, a respected Gujarati cloth merchant, whose shop was near our house. The substance of his speech had a lasting impact on me. He recounted that he had one day seen my father in an unusually agitated and angry mood stride past his shop. On enquiring about the root of this agitation, my father told him that he had suffered huge losses in business and had sought legal advice from Shri Mahajani, an advocate. Shri Mahajani had advised him to file for insolvency considering the extent of his losses. This was unpalatable to my father. He fought with the lawyer for giving such sordid, albeit practical, advice and left his office stating that should the occasion arise, he would consider it less dishonourable to sell his children than to accept a degrading option such as insolvency.

Shri Shivji Bhai's speech strongly influenced my youthful and impressionable mind. My father was a noble and self-respecting individual. I was proud to be his son and determined to uphold his honourable values.

For a number of years my father visited my dreams, guiding me at crucial moments of my life. Until this day, I can honestly say that I have never allowed any person or occurrence to tempt me to compromise my self-respect, regardless of the importance of the person or the attractiveness of the temptation. Everything has a price in life, but I do not regret the price I have paid. Surprisingly, while chronicling the journey of my life, I find that I have gained much more for adamantly adhering to this value than what I have lost.

Even after our father's demise, Shri Biyaniji's love and affection sheltered us. I was the recipient of his advice and encouragement for a long time even after I became a lawyer. I would seek his blessings every year, during a Diwali visit to his home. Sometime in 1965, he shifted to Indore. During this time, his friends and admirers decided to publish a book, titled *Biyaniji—In the Eyes of His Friends*. During one Diwali visit, he informed me of this development and asked me to contribute an article about his association with my father. I had never written an article before and I informed him about my inexperience, admitting at the same time that I had many memories about his association and meetings with my father. He asked me to write about those meetings. On his insistence, I noted down what I recollected and sent that write-up to him at Indore, on receipt of which he wrote me an appreciative and encouraging letter suggesting I develop the art of writing for which I had the potential. He also suggested I should shift to Nagpur for practise. The seeds of desire to practise writing, and also to start practising law in the Nagpur High Court, were sown by him through that letter dated 31 October 1965, which he had written in Hindi. I have preserved that letter as a valuable document and it is appended at the end of this book.

## JUVENILE OFFENCES

I must confess to some early transgressions. As a child, I was extremely fond of milkshakes. Green 'khas' and pink 'gulab' (rose) were my favourites. Kunj Bihari Hotel at the corner of the main road near our family home displayed the rose and green coloured bottles of milkshake, tempting me beyond reasonable limits! One summer afternoon I developed an irresistible urge for these delicious treats and demanded four annas from my mother to purchase one glass. She refused to give me the money, saying it was unhealthy for children to consume cold drinks on hot afternoons. I could not control my desire and when she left the room, I opened the almirah that had a drawer where small change was kept. I was lucky. There were some coins in the drawer out of which I picked up a four anna coin and rushed to the hotel. I drank a bottle of rose milkshake and approached the counter for payment but no one was at the till. I waited for some time with the green khas milkshake bottles staring at me. With every second that I waited, my desire to drink that khas milkshake increased. Finally, I picked up a bottle, drank it up, placed the coin on the counter and hurriedly escaped from the hotel.

Thus, within the short span of a few minutes, I had committed the two offences of theft and cheating, of which only I had knowledge and henceforth always felt guilty about. Several years later, when I was a lawyer in Akola, I was able to expiate my sin. The son of the old owner of the hotel approached me for advice in a rent control case against him. When he asked me about my fee, I told him the amount that I usually charged but when he started to pay, I refused to accept payment. Astonished, he asked me why I would not take the money. I told him that I owed his family some amount and narrated the incident of my criminality. He started laughing and replied that in that event, and if I insisted, he would deduct 25 paisa from the fees and recover the old dues for my satisfaction. I did not agree, as I told him that the interest accrued over a period of at least twenty years would also be considerable. There was no repayment of the debt, but I did get the satisfaction of atonement of a crime.

## A CHANCE MEETING WITH DILIP KUMAR

Guilt at my theft subsided substantially when I read about the early life of famous film star Dilip Kumar, who, in his youth, had committed similar crimes! Dilipji would steal money from his father's fruit shop in Crawford Market, Mumbai, for the purpose of enjoying a drink at the famous fruit juice centre known as Badshah Cold Drink House, situated just across the road from the market.

I accidentally met Shri Dilip Kumar and his wife Saira Banu at the Taj Mahal Palace Hotel in Mumbai during a wedding reception hosted by the late Shri Gulam Vahanvati (later Attorney General of India), who was then the Advocate General of Maharashtra. I told him that there was something common between him and me as we were both juvenile offenders! Perplexed by the comment, the couple asked me what I meant. I narrated the incident about my theft and told him that I had read about his thefts for the same purpose. Dilip Kumar just smiled.

## EDUCATION

I received my primary education at Municipal School No. 2 in Akola. When I was in class four, our teacher Shri Mankar Guruji had to go on leave for two days. He appointed me class monitor and left me in charge during his absence. Before he left, I asked him how I should handle one of my classmates, a bully who terrorized our class. This bully was often scolded by Shri Mankar Guruji and had once even received a whack with a scale on the palm of his hand as punishment. Guruji, being in a hurry, advised me to do what he did. So, when I received a complaint from one of my classmates that the bully had misbehaved and beaten him, I tried to intervene, in my role as monitor. My efforts were in vain and the bully carried on with his obnoxious behaviour. I therefore hit him with a scale to prevent further aggression.

On Guruji's return, the bully complained about what I had done. Guruji was annoyed at my exceeding my authority and asked me to explain my actions. When I told him that I had merely done as he had instructed, i.e. followed his example, everyone including Guruji and the bully laughed heartily. The episode ended there, but not without a warning to me. Although Guruji's fondness for me did not decrease, perhaps because he was satisfied about the absence of *mens rea*, I got my first lesson in the proper exercise of delegated power.

For secondary education I was admitted to the New English High School, established in 1927 by the Akola Education Society. In my days, it was a small institution running classes at two different places, one of which was rented, the other being a semi-permanent structure. I vividly remember being the butt of everyone's mirth when in class six, Shri Mandaogane Guruji asked us to write an essay in Marathi on the subject 'My House'. I described our ancestral three-storied house saying that we carried out our business activities on the ground floor, had our residence on the first floor and the top floor was vacant. When Guruji read out the last sentence to the class, he asked me whether the description of the top floor was correct. I bravely asserted 'yes' without realizing the catch! My classmates teased me relentlessly for that admission, which they insisted implied that my head was empty! The teasing was harmless and did not offend me, as I was not a dull student but generally stood first or second in the annual examinations. My competitor was one Sitaram Agarwal. We both lost our positions when an extremely bright new boy named Shankarlal Moyal joined us in class eight. He continued to excel through life, and, after retiring as Labour Commissioner in the state of Madhya Pradesh, now practises law in Indore. We remain good friends and are in close touch even today.

The Akola Education Society, which was formed by eminent and social-minded citizens of the town, including my senior Shri A.S. Athalye, has spread its wings since my school days. It now has a chain of schools and colleges in Akola and nearby places including a college of law. Professor P.D. Mandaogane, who was my schoolmate, is presently the president of the Society, which, under his able and dynamic leadership, has become a multi-faculty institution providing education from kindergarten to graduation.

After matriculation, I was advised to pursue a degree in engineering, as there was ample scope in that field. I thoughtlessly joined the science (maths) course and it took me a long time to realize that mathematics was not my cup of tea. I struggled to complete my Intermediate Science course, which I did, though not in the first attempt. I then applied for admission to the Birla Engineering College, Pilani, where I was put on the waiting list. Assuming I would get admission in Pilani (which I did not), I carelessly missed the last date for admission to colleges in Nagpur University and so risked losing a year. Fortunately, this was averted. My relative, Trilokinath, was doing his MA from DAV College, Kanpur, affiliated to Agra University. He told me there was no last date to apply for admission in colleges affiliated to Agra University and the only criterion to appear for the university examination was a minimum of 75 per cent attendance in classes over a period of two years. Therefore, I joined the first year BA class in DAV College, Kanpur, perhaps the biggest college of Agra University, with over five thousand students. The college functioned from 7.00 a.m. to 10.00 p.m. and imparted education in faculties such as arts, science and commerce. There were in all ten classes of seventy students each. I was admitted in the last class 'J'.

I stayed with Trilokinath in his room at the huge and notorious DAV College hostel. Situated on the banks of the Ganga and adjacent to the famous Green Park where cricket test matches were and are played, the hostel housed several aged persons amongst its population of approximately nine hundred. These 'students' gained admission in various courses and then deliberately did not clear their exams so they could use their student status to get convenient accommodation at nominal cost in the industrial city of Kanpur. Some were known bad-hats whose reputation made even the police reluctant to enter the hostel, and because of whom it was nearly impossible to get a rickshaw to it. Many students would refuse to pay the rickshaw-puller his fare and if the poor man demanded it, inmates of the hostel would unite and chase him out of the hostel. The only way of securing a rickshaw was to hire it for the 'kacheri' [or court], which was at some distance from the hostel, get down there and walk to the hostel, hoisting along whatever baggage one might have. Some courageous rickshaw-pullers did enter the hostel, but only if payment was made in advance.

The alleviating factor for living in the hostel was that it had been the hiding place of famous Indian revolutionaries like Chandrashekhar Azad and Bhagat Singh during the Freedom Movement. Paltu, the old barber frequented by the hostellers, enlivened our haircuts with proud tales of their exploits and of his interactions when he had shaved some of them. Although the college has illustrious alumni like former Prime Minister Shri Atal Behari Vajpayee, both the hostel and the college were indisciplined, indecent places. The one-and-a-half years I spent there were both embarrassing and uncomfortable.

Perhaps leadership could have mitigated the ills of this institution, but unfortunately, that was not to be. I recollect our principal's visit to the hostel one evening after examinations were over. The students chided the principal—who both set and examined history papers for the MA exams in universities throughout Uttar Pradesh—because his indications of probable topics on which questions would be asked had been wrong, and so the college was likely to lag behind the SD College with which there was constant competition. The principal assured the students that they had no need to be worried as all the answer papers would be examined by him!

## MARRIAGE AND HOLY HONEYMOON

I was married on 20 June 1953 at the age of twenty, which according to our old family standards, was a late marriage since a boy was expected to marry soon after attaining adulthood. My wife Kamla was then doing her matriculation. She was beautiful and belonged to the renowned family of Shri Laxminarayanji Innani from Washim, in district Akola.

The practice of going on a honeymoon did not exist in my family but instead, soon after our marriage, my wife and I accompanied my mother on a pilgrimage to Puri (in Odisha) and Rameshwaram (in Tamil Nadu)—two of the four dhams, or important centres of pilgrimage, that the scriptures command every Hindu to visit. At Puri, my mother had a heartfelt darshan (audience) of Lord Jagannath, his sister Subhadra, and his brother Balabhadra, but at Rameshwaram, to our great surprise, she would go no further than the door of the famous Shiva temple. When asked why she wouldn't enter the temple, my mother said that a Vaishnav woman was not supposed to have darshan of the shivling; so though she wished to fulfil her duty as a Hindu by visiting the dhams, she could not betray her Vaishnavite traditions. My mother's attitude disturbed me as I felt it lacked a wide understanding and open mind. But then, I remembered her true qualities: her genuine religiosity and sagacity; her courage and fortitude that had enabled her, despite being illiterate, to rear her minor children and handle our family wealth with great ability during her widowhood. I realized that her reluctance at Rameshwaram was not born of malice, but merely because of the conservatism of the time to which she belonged.

## MID-AIR WITH KING KONG

On the return journey from Rameshwaram, we stopped in Chennai where I received a telegram from my friend informing me that although I had passed my BA examination, the result had been withheld because I had not cleared the compulsory Hindi language paper. Since the last date to fill the form for that examination was the very next day, I became extremely tense. The problem seemed insurmountable. How would I reach the university office at Agra in time to meet the deadline? The relative with whom we were staying advised me to fly to Delhi by the night Dakota mail service of Indian Airlines and from there take the Punjab Mail to Agra so that I could reach my destination by about 10.00 a.m. on the day required. And so I undertook my first air journey.

Imagine my excitement when this experience was further enlivened by the presence of the internationally renowned wrestler King Kong, who was seated a few rows ahead of me! Two seats had been merged into one for the large star who consumed a mountain of snacks despite the late hour at which we were travelling. I tried to count the number of eggs he ate, but was unsuccessful because of the speed with which they disappeared from the plates!

In those days, the night Dakota flights were also a postal service operating from Mumbai, Delhi, Kolkata and Chennai—all via Nagpur, where the passengers deplaned and were shuffled to different flights for their respective destinations along with the mail for each city.

The long and the short of it is that I reached the university office on time, signed the form and register and returned to Chennai via the same route, thereby securing my result. In course of time, I became a graduate with a Bachelor's degree in Arts. I went on to study law, completing the first year of the LLB course from Government Law College, Nagpur, and the final year of the LLB course from the newly established Law College in Akola under the aegis of the Berar Education Society, Akola, of which I was destined to become president after some years.

## REPUDIATION OF FAMILY BUSINESS

My elder brother managed the family business and agriculture while I pursued my college education in Nagpur and Kanpur. Unfortunately, the business suffered heavy losses. To cover the losses and preserve the family reputation, my brother sold much of the family's gold and ornaments. However, the losses continued unabated. Dhanraj Kakaji apprised me of this unpleasant and grim situation when I went to Akola during a vacation. He told me that appearances were being maintained, but the family was in debt to the bank and the moneylenders from whom substantial hundis or deposits had been taken. Kakaji asked me to take charge of the situation as the family reputation was at stake. I was stunned. I contemplated this news and realized I was totally unsuited to conduct the business. My only recourse was to close it down, pay off the debts and save the family honour. I needed to work fast and discreetly arrange for cash without creating a panic amongst our creditors. I consulted close friends and well-wishers, took them into confidence and sought their guidance. They too advised me to move swiftly and arrange for finances without further delay. I was keen to repay the loans with interest at one go so that the closure of the business could be announced and executed without any loss of prestige.

The only avenue open to us was to start selling the property—movable and immovable—and, if possible, arrange some short-term loans from close relatives and friends. I confided my problems to my closest friend, Dr Uttam Chand Jain, who was my lifelong confidante till his demise. Dr Jain was a renowned medical practitioner and president of the famous Janta Homoeopathy College, Akola. I was aware that gold could be sold easily and quickly and hence the first thing I did was to take my mother into confidence. Although distressed, she valued the family reputation and so graciously handed over all her gold and ornaments for sale. Since my brothers and I were all married, we approached our wives. They too magnanimously contributed a part of their streedhan[3] to the pool. I gave the ornaments to Dr Jain and asked him to sell them immediately. Although a better price could have been obtained in Mumbai, we could neither afford the delay nor the possibility of this news leaking out. Dr Jain discreetly and expeditiously disposed of the gold and in a short span of two or three days we had the money from the sale. I was also able to secure some personal short-term loans from relatives who kindly helped us out and so we were confident of our ability to repay the creditors. Fortunately, the value of our properties, which included agricultural lands, garden lands and houses, was greater than the debts we owed.

As soon as the money was credited into the Central Bank of India, Cloth Market branch, Akola, Dhanraj Kakaji helped us to prepare cheques for the creditors, covering the principal and the interest amount. He also took care of informing them about the decision to close the business and requesting them to collect their cheques from the shop. This news led to commotion in the market and incessant inquiries from well-wishers, acquaintances and others. Within two to three days we shut the business down

---

3Personal jewellery, etc., gifted to a bride at the time of marriage.

and were debt free. What a relief that was! Although the speed with which we moved was very costly in monetary terms, it saved and indeed enhanced, our reputation.

We were free from mercantile debt. What remained was repayment to friends and relatives and in course of time, we cleared these by selling a large portion of our agricultural lands, establishments and houses. The patience and fortitude of all these people was truly admirable, as not even once was there a whisper of demand from them. I will always consider myself lucky in having relatives and friends who had, and continue to have, full confidence and faith in me. Yet, for all the good things that have happened in my life, the day the last demand draft of ₹20,000 to repay our relative in Agra was dispatched, remains my happiest and proudest day. Debt-free at last! The only properties that remained unsold were the three-storied family house in Akola, the cinema in the nearby town of Khamgaon, and agricultural lands and an establishment in village Nimgaon. Colossal business failure became the first turning point in my life.

# II

## PROFESSIONAL AND SOCIAL LIFE IN AKOLA

### MOVING ON: MY EARLY DAYS IN THE LEGAL PROFESSION

Circumstances left me no choice but to seek my fortune through ways that did not require monetary investment. Since I had a degree in law, this was the obvious avenue for me to explore. Therefore, I obtained a Sanad to practice law and started my search for a senior lawyer with whom I could be associated. Rao Bahadur Shri A.S. Athalye, alias, Kakasaheb, was the most famous lawyer not only in Akola but in the entire region. He was gracious enough to grant me an appointment to meet him at his Ramdaspeth bungalow. When I introduced myself and disclosed the purpose of my visit, Kakasaheb, who had known my father, was surprised to hear that someone from our family was opting for a profession in law. I was candid in my explanation to him and to his son, Shri N.A. Athalye, alias Balasaheb, who was also an advocate and present at the meeting. Kakasaheb told me that I was welcome to join their office as a fourth junior. My relief and joy at this opportunity were unbounded, although he informed me very firmly that juniors in his office were not paid. Since Kakasaheb repeated that statement, I assured him that despite the circumstances under which I had sought devilship with him, I had no expectation or desire for remuneration at that point. And so, the next day, I joined Kakasaheb's office. In course of time, I was the recipient of genuine love, encouragement and admiration from both Kakaseheb and his son Balasaheb, who in his own right was an astute lawyer specializing in labour laws and was subsequently appointed directly as District Judge with seniority of ten years.

Knowing the Bar was overcrowded, I asked Kakasaheb about the likely prospects of a new entrant in such a competitive field. I was surprised to hear that he too had asked this question of his father-in-law (who was his senior) when he shifted to Akola after resigning from the post of headmaster at the famous Aryan High School in Girgaon, Mumbai. He said, this is an age-old question that has been asked by every new entrant to the Bar. He gave me the same answer he himself had received—namely, that luck plays a part in every field, but a person who is passionate about his profession, willing to work hard and has the patience and financial depth to wait for the fruits of success, is unlikely to fail. I found Kakasaheb's words both encouraging and convincing.

As I mentioned earlier, the void left by my father's death was deep. I dreamt of him frequently even after I crossed middle age and his invisible hands guided me at every crossroads of life. To a great extent, Kakasaheb filled the vacuum left by my father's death. He was my guide and mentor not only in my professional life but also in the personal sphere. In all my years, I have not come across a lawyer better than Kakasaheb in the art of drafting or explaining the basic principles of law. I remember he recommended I should read Brooms' *Legal Maxims,* which I found invaluable throughout my career. Even when I started independent practice after about three years, I continued to take Kakasaheb's advice. One such guidance by him was the other turning point of my life, more about which later.

## MY SENIOR: SHRI ATHALYE

On 19 December 1986, approximately seven years after I became a judge of the Bombay High Court, Hon'ble Shri Justice V.D. Tulzapurkar, then a former judge of the Supreme Court of India, chaired a public memorial for the late Kakasaheb and his son, the late Balasaheb, at Pramilatai Oak Hall, Akola. I was privileged to be invited to speak at this function by the Athalye family. I spoke from my heart as I remembered my mentor. Some excerpts of my speech are reproduced here:

It is my proud privilege to pay tribute to the memory of those whom I revered most in my life—late Kakasaheb Athalye and Balasaheb.

Kakasaheb's career was a saga of struggle in his earlier life and distinguishing achievements in its culmination. While being educated at Wilson College, Mumbai, adverse circumstances compelled him to approach the principal, requesting for time to deposit the requisite fee. The principal told the young man, 'Mr Athalye, your career is more important than recovery of fees'. So overwhelmed was Mr Atahalye by the helpful and generous attitude of the principal that no young man in need of money for education ever returned empty-handed from his house. He was always accessible to those in need of either advice or bounty.

There is no dearth of self-made men, but few remember their humble beginnings and endeavour to ensure that others do not suffer from those disadvantages which they themselves had suffered. Kakasaheb was one of those exceptions. Generosity of heart was his speciality.

Sometime in 1961 or 1962 I had the good fortune of meeting the doyen of the Indian Bar, Attorney General Motilalji Setalwad. When he learnt that I was from Akola, he remembered Kakasaheb and told me that he was an able lawyer who had wasted his talent in a mofussil and that had he been in Mumbai, he would have been one of the leading lawyers even there.

Kakasaheb's speciality was commercial law. His attitude towards courts, opponents and litigation was extremely fair. He never hesitated to help settlements. Indeed, he always encouraged them and thus rendered real legal aid throughout his life. He was unquestionably the brightest star ever seen on the horizon of Akola Bar.

By dint of sheer brilliance and high values, he attained honours in public life and so also, wealth. Riches and honours did not spoil him nor did they disrupt his simple and plain living. His service in public life of this region was unparalleled. To give the long list of the positions he occupied in this gathering at Akola is an exercise in futility. All the positions came to him unasked. He was not a person but an institution, a legend in his own lifetime. He was a student of Barrister Jaikar who, in his autobiography, has made a fitting reference to him.

Balasaheb Athalye was naturally a chip of the old block. How could he be different? Extremely brilliant and frank, he was a fine orator—in English as well as in Marathi—it was a treat to listen to his address in the courts. Like a skilful general, he surveyed his terrain, found the strategic spots to attack, prepared his ammunition with thoroughness and fired the shot with accuracy. He rarely missed the target. Labour law was his specialization. He was at the peak of his practice when he left the profession and joined the judiciary at great personal monetary sacrifice, much against the advice of Kakasaheb.

My association with Kakasaheb was so intimate that for me, impersonal analysis of his personality is nearly impossible. He was so warm and affectionate to me that I always felt that I got at the age of twenty-eight what I missed since the age of eight—fatherly affection and guidance. He gave me all the encouragement and valuable tips at a time when I needed them most. I shall ever remain grateful to God for creating circumstances that brought me in contact with him.

## CONSCIOUS ETHICS: LAYING THE FOUNDATION OF MY PROFESSIONAL ATTITUDES

From the beginning of my legal career, I had vowed to maintain integrity whilst advising those who came to me for consultation. I can proudly say that I have kept that vow till this day. It has given me great satisfaction, besides standing me in good stead in myriad ways, not excluding monetary. That may sound ironic considering my first year's income was the disappointing figure of ₹550!

I recall that at a party to celebrate the settlement of a long-standing dispute in court, a lawyer dealing with the litigation, although reluctant, was persuaded to speak. He said, 'As a general rule, I never speak unless I am paid. But on this occasion I give you three words of advice free: "litigate, litigate, litigate!"'

Abraham Lincoln's advice to young lawyers was just the opposite. He said, 'Discourage litigations. Persuade your neighbour to compromise whenever you can. As a peace-maker, a lawyer has a superior opportunity to be a good man. There will still be business enough.'

My experience is that Abraham Lincoln was correct not only morally but also in his conclusion about business. People are more willing to pay hefty fees to reliable lawyers who have established reputations of giving genuine advice, including the advice to avoid litigation. Such advice saves them avoidable costs, misery and the growing uncertainty involved in the litigation. This reputation, though not easy to build, is extremely rewarding. Besides the economic benefits, it builds invaluable goodwill and gives great mental satisfaction. I have with me even now the original wills of several old clients, friends and relatives, for the purpose of their smooth execution. More than fifty years of association with law as a junior, as a judge and as a senior advocate after retirement, have confirmed my belief that conciliation is the best method to resolve legal disputes. Legal process, by its very nature, is lengthy and costly. In addition is the growing uncertainty of the result, which, recent trends and developments show, is almost bordering on a gamble. I have spoken at many public functions and contributed several articles in national and international newspapers and journals on this disturbing aspect of our judicial system.

## MY FIRST COMMERCIAL CASE

My legal career gained momentum after I won a controversial civil suit in Akola. The suit was for damages and the defendant was accused of failing to make timely delivery of a consignment of pulses, which he had verbally agreed to sell. The plaintiff was a retailer and the defendant a wealthy but cantankerous manufacturer, known in the market for unfair practices— especially when the agreement was not reduced in writing, which was not uncommon. He was a regular litigant and a fighter with a record of invariably succeeding in the courts. Although the claim was not large, the case had assumed significance in the business circle of the town. Rates had risen, and that, quite simply, was the reason for the breach of contract. As the claim depended upon oral evidence, both parties entered the witness box and the defendant, who was overconfident, almost met his Waterloo during the cross-examination.

A table showing the continuous rise in the monthly rates prevalent in the market was filed on record and the case was fixed for oral arguments. Unfortunately, on the day of arguments, the court noticed that the said document was not proved. However, the senior judge, Shri G.V. Deo, appeared to be convinced about the breach and the falsity of the defendant, but was stuck with the question of proof of damages. I realized that it was a lapse on my part and I was feeling guilty about it. I relied upon absence of cross-examination of the plaintiff on the aspect of increase in rates. The judge stated in open court that the defendant was a liar and he would grant time to the plaintiff to prove that document in case an application was made. Realizing my predicament he remarked in a lighter vein, 'Don't worry, bring any witness. There are many readily available in the court premises, I promise to believe him.' Everyone was laughing, but not me. After a pause, he called the stenographer and passed an order: 'Arguments heard. Suit decreed with costs. Reasoned judgment tomorrow.' As he rose, he looked at me and said, 'Very well done.'

I relate this incident not to make a point regarding right or wrong, but to demonstrate how the attitude of a judge can affect a case. Hon'ble Judge Shri G.V. Deo did not allow the procedure to come in the way of doing substantial justice. His kindness in saving a junior from embarrassment and at the same time encouraging him was a gesture I have never forgotten till this day and kept in mind even during my tenure as a judge

## A PRINCIPLED FIGHT: CHALLENGE TO FIVE-RUPEE FINE UP TO HIGH COURT

Mayur Hotel in the mofussil town of Washim had a paan counter on its premises. Although Mayur Hotel was registered under the Bombay Shop and Establishment Act, the so-called paan counter was not, and hence the magistrate had imposed a five-rupee fine on the owner and directed him to get a separate registration for it. The fine did not perturb the owner, but he was very agitated by the verdict that the hotel and the paan counter were two independent entities. He engaged me to challenge the said order. Hence, a criminal revision challenging the said order under the then prevailing Criminal Procedure Code, 1898, was filed and it came up for hearing before the District and Sessions Judge Akola, Shri M.A.R. Khan (who was later elevated to the Bench of the Bombay High Court).

As he was initially reluctant to refer the matter to the High Court, given that the fine involved was meagre, it took strong argument to convince Judge Khan, himself a paan enthusiast who chewed one of these delicious delicacies as he heard me argue that paan was nothing but one of the common items of food for sale in all mofussil hotels of the area. He reluctantly acquiesced and referred the matter to the High Court, recommending quashing of the order as per the law then prevailing.

Some years later, the reference came before Hon'ble Shri Justice D.G. Palekar at the Nagpur Bench of the Bombay High Court. When the matter was called, the government pleader— Shri G.R. Mudholkar—came rushing in with his after-lunch paan still in his mouth. During the course of the hearing, when the government pleader opposed the reference, Justice Palekar wittily asked Shri Mudholkar, how it was possible for him, sitting on the Nagpur Bench, not to accept this reference? According to the learned judge he could not refuse to take judicial notice of the deep-rooted practice of chewing paan even in the courtroom in the Vidarbha area! There was a brief silence before everyone burst out laughing at Justice Palekar's tongue-in-cheek remark, and the reference was accepted. Justice Palekar, who was later elevated as a judge of the Supreme Court, remains one of the most dignified judges of my acquaintance. I was fortunate to have appeared before him in his various capacities of District Judge at Akola, High Court Judge at Nagpur and as a judge of the Supreme Court in New Delhi.

When he was a District Judge in Akola, Justice Palekar once showed the members of our Bar a finger on his left hand that had the marks of several pinpricks on it. Apparently, whenever the Hon'ble Judge felt sleepy on the dais, he would prick himself with a fine pin to keep awake, especially after the lunch break!

## FORFEITURE OF PROPERTY AS MODE OF PUNISHMENT

My profession as an advocate and later as a judge led me to ponder sundry ethical and social issues. One such issue arose when I represented the son of a ghee merchant in Akola. This ghee merchant, a wily businessman, owned a huge property. He had, perhaps with wise forethought, inducted his young son into the business and thereafter showed on record the young man to be the owner of the business. Since the business entailed dealing in adulterated ghee, which is an offence under the Prevention of Food Adulteration Act, it is not surprising that retribution finally caught up with him.

Municipal food inspectors, after giving prior notice, had taken samples of the ghee the merchant was supplying. On the given day, the inspector had taken samples and sent them to the public analyst for his report. Now, as the young owner informed me, the food inspector had taken samples from a particular tin, in which pure ghee was kept for the purpose of inspection. Despite the careful management of the sample, the public analyst's report showed the sample as being adulterated and consequently, the municipality lodged a case against the son in which he was convicted and sentenced to undergo imprisonment for six months and to pay a fine.

The son challenged the conviction in the High Court and engaged me to plead his case. To my astonishment he had confessed not only the nature of his business, but also the modus operandi whereby a particular tin containing pure ghee was kept for the specific purpose of providing samples to food inspectors, whenever a stage-managed raid, of which the municipal officers would give him prior notice, was conducted. Consequently, he was sure that the report would be in his favour, but unfortunately the second deal was not successful and the food analyst gave an adverse report.

The matter came before Hon'ble Shri Justice B.N. Deshmukh in Nagpur. The merits were not such as to lend themselves too much argument. However, I prayed for leniency on the grounds that the accused was a young man and recently married. While the Hon'ble Judge had noticed his youth, I thought it proper to also point out that he was a novice in the business that was, in fact, being carried out by his father. Justice Deshmukh was a kind and considerate judge. He adjourned the matter for two weeks and asked me to ensure the presence of both the father and son in the court on the date of hearing. On the given date, the innocent son and the cantankerous father were present.

Justice Deshmukh heard the pleas and after some time indicated to me that he proposed to impose a fine of ₹20,000 and sentence to imprisonment on the accused up to the rising of the court—in case the fine was actually paid. The accused son and I felt very happy, but the old man did not agree and started bargaining in the courtroom. I asked for some time and the matter was adjourned for hearing after recess, during which period the accused son and I tried to convince the old man to comply with the order without bargaining.

The old man asked me to negotiate the amount of the fine, which I declined. The old man said in that case, he would himself request a reduction of the fine and if the request was not granted, the son would undergo the sentence, since, in his words, 'In any case within six months he is not going to earn more than ₹20,000!' After the recess, the inevitable happened and the revision was dismissed. The hapless young man had to undergo the sentence to save his father the ₹20,000. This, and many other cases, made me wonder whether imprisonment was actually a deterrent for offences linked to earning money illegally.

Perhaps the real deterrent would be forfeiture of the property earned through such anti-social endeavours. Some observations of the Supreme Court in the case of *Shobha Suresh Jumani Vs. Appellate Tribunal, Forfeited Property And Another, 2001 (5) SCC 755* are not only worth reproduction but also worth considering by the lawmakers, if at all they have the time or inclination to look into this aspect seriously:

It appears that for controlling the cancerous growth of corruption, apart from further deterrent provisions, illegally acquired properties by means of corrupt practices could be forfeited under the provisions by suitable amendment in the Act. The question whether the time is ripe for such amendment or not is to be decided by the legislature. However, we cannot turn our eyes from the fact that because of the mad race for becoming rich and acquiring properties overnight or because of the ostentatious or vulgar show of wealth by a few or because of change of environment in the society by adoption of materialistic approach, cancerous growth of corruption and illegal gains of profits have affected the moral standards of the people and all forms of governmental administration.

It is to be mentioned that under the Indian Penal Code, various punishments are provided in Section 53 which include forfeiture of property and Sections 61 and 62 provide sentence of forfeiture of property. However, Sections 61 and 62 were deleted by the Indian Penal Code (Amendment) Act, 1921. But considering the situation prevailing in the society, it appears that the said provisions are required to be reintroduced so as to have a deterrent effect on those who are bent upon accumulating wealth at the cost of the society by misusing their post or power. We hope that the legislature would consider this aspect appropriately.

## ABORTIVE MOVE TO JOIN SUBORDINATE JUDICIARY

In the journey of life there are many roads one thinks to travel and at times the road that appears the most appealing may not be the one on which our destiny is written. Such was an experience in the early years of my career, when my feet were set on the path of being a lawyer but my financial success was meagre and the road appeared rough. District Judge Akola Shri N.D. Kamat, a kind and gracious judge who went on to become Registrar of the Bombay High Court and then a judge of the Bombay High Court before retiring as Lokayukta of Maharashtra, was hearing a first appeal titled *Gulab Vs. Sonabai.*

The case involved the twin points of Hindu law and Transfer of Property Act. As counsel, I was naturally thoroughly prepared and was very happy and encouraged when the Hon'ble Judge complimented me in open court. My interactions with Shri Kamat continued in the same positive vein on other occasions when I appeared before him. Then one day he called me to his chamber during the lunch break and, after some pleasantries, informed me that the government had invited applications for the post of civil judge junior division-cum-judicial magistrate, a post for which he suggested I should apply. The suggestion thrilled me and without any loss of time, I went in pursuit of the job. I collected the application form and filled it out. The application required character certificates from two well-known persons. I decided to request my senior, Kakasaheb, to vouch for my character and also requested another senior and highly respected lawyer, Shri Y.R. Dongre, for the same. Shri Dongre promptly gave me the required certificate along with his blessings, but Kakasaheb appeared less forthcoming. He stared at me with a somewhat surprised look and asked me to return the next morning to collect the certificate. Accordingly, I went to him and found the certificate ready on his table. He handed it to me and my joy knew no bounds.

With much to do before the submission of my application, I hurried to leave, but was halted by Kakasaheb asking me to sit down and discuss something. Kakasaheb strongly disapproved of my plans to change my career path at this stage and asked me how I had neglected to consult him before taking such a decision, considering I habitually sought his advice. In Kakasaheb's analysis, my future as a lawyer was bright, albeit the start appeared slow and unpromising. He also felt that the level of judicial service I sought was unsuitable, as there would be many administrative and hierarchical hurdles that were unlikely to suit me. Kakasaheb's advice left me perplexed and confused: I had tremendous faith and respect for him and also great confidence in his wisdom. He was a father figure not only in the Bar but also in society. Telling him that Shri Kamat had advised me, I left the final decision to Kakasaheb. He spoke to Shri Kamat on the phone and conveyed his views. I was feeling slightly embarrassed, but Shri Kamat asked me to go by Kakasaheb's advice and I abandoned the idea of applying for the post in the judiciary. Despite the dark clouds that choked my career in the beginning, Kakasaheb's advice proved to be like divine intervention, which changed the course of my life. Did 'time and chance' not happen again?

## LOSS OF AN IMPORTANT CLIENT

A leading commercial banker-cum-hundi broker of Akola had transferred many of his pending court cases to my office. Now, as it happened, a very old dispute between a textile mill owner and the banker's family was referred to the Arbitration Tribunal comprising three eminent and respectable merchants of Akola, who had no previous experience of arbitration proceedings. The chairman's son, Shri Narayandas Khandelwal, one of my well-wishers, requested me to help the tribunal to conduct the arbitration and also to draft the award. I informed them that I represented one of the parties in some cases, a fact with which they appeared to be familiar but did not see as a limiting circumstance since they had already discussed this with both the litigants. It was rewarding to know that everyone concerned had faith in me and I agreed with pleasure. My assistance was required only to ensure that the proper procedure was followed and to draft the award. When the tribunal concluded the hearings and reached its decision, I was requested to prepare the award based on its decision. I was also requested to keep the award a secret till the tribunal declared it, which it wanted to do that same evening.

I went home and started preparing the draft by hand in my bedroom on the first floor of our house. As I was about to conclude this process, my uncle, Shri Dhanraj Kakaji, came and told me that my client, the banker, was downstairs and wished to meet me urgently. I went down to my office, which was on the ground floor of our house, and on meeting me, my client immediately asked about the conclusion in the award. I told him that everyone would be informed about it within a few hours and requested him to wait till that time. He angrily informed me that he was aware of this and did not want me to tamper with the decision, but only sought the privilege of information, which, as a client, he believed was his right. I did not agree. He lost his temper and told me he would withdraw all the cases entrusted to me if I did not comply. I told him the files were available in the office and that he could take them whenever he wished. While leaving the office he told me that his court clerk would come to collect the files. The clerk came within a few hours and took away the files. My erstwhile client was so angry that he would not even acknowledge my presence when our paths crossed in the court or on the street! However, fairness demands that I mention on the positive side that he advised a close relative of his, who did not live in Akola, to engage my services in an important litigation known as the Laxmi Bank fraud case. In course of time, his anger waned and his trust and confidence in me was such that I dealt with all his legal problems and cases, from top to bottom.

## LAXMI BANK FRAUD CASE

The State of Maharashtra had filed a criminal case under Sections 405, 409 and 477 (a) of the Indian Penal Code against various officers and functionaries of Laxmi Bank including the managing director, chairman, secretary, general manager and branch agents of M/s Laxmi Bank Ltd. Cases were also filed against certain merchant account holders of the bank. The chargesheet was filed sometime in 1962 and the trial was conducted and concluded by the additional sessions judge, Akola, Shri G.K. Patankar.

Shri Gopaldas Mohta, a mill-owner, was the managing director and chairman of the bank and his munim, the deceased Shri Surajmal Sanghi, was the general manager. Shri Bhikulal Agarwal was the secretary. The merchants accused included well-known people—such as Shri Durgaprasad Saraf, Shri Ramnarayan Mor, Shri Agarwal—from Nagpur and the nearby town of Tumsar. There were in all fifty-seven accused, out of whom about ten or eleven were acquitted in the trial. Shri Surajmal Sanghi died even before the trial commenced. The accused office bearers of the bank were arrested and for a considerable time, were refused bail. Shri Gopaldas Mohta and Shri Surajmal Sanghi were put behind bars in Akola Central Jail. Shri Surajmal Sanghi was permitted to have a hernia operation in Mumbai after which he expired in hospital. There was loose talk in the market about his committing suicide by consuming a shard of diamond after the operation. Shri Bhikulal Agarwal had turned approver and was examined as PW no.1.

The prosecution's case was that the bank had to recover a sum of approximately sixty lakh from Shri Gopaldas Mohta's firm M/s Rekhchand Gopaldas in its banker's account. The accused persons entered into criminal conspiracy to commit a breach of trust in respect thereof, and committed the offence of falsification of accounts pursuant to a conspiracy. Accused no.1, Shri Gopaldas, committed breach of trust by dishonestly converting to his own use the said 'chose-in-action' with the aid and abetment of office-bearers of the bank by making false entries in the banker's account during some period in 1948, and thereby wiped out dues as having been received. The breach of trust lay in closing or squaring off the dues by making false credit entries, resulting in the bank's losing the right to recover its dues from the firm of M/s Reckchand Gopaldas. The breach of trust thus committed resulted in a shortage of cash in the Akola branch of the bank, which shortage was dishonestly concealed from 1948 to 1960 by resorting to various methods, necessitating falsification of accounts.

The initial indulgence was by the original conspirators, including the chairman, his munim, who was his general manager, the assistant secretary, etc. Others such as bank agents and private merchant-customers joined and participated in the conspiracy from time to time. The basic charge against the customers was that they had indulged in showing false transactions of receiving loans in the beginning of the accounting year and showing repayments just before the closing period of that year, thereby using their black money as white. The additional sessions judge, after a long-drawn trial, including the lengthy and brilliant cross-examination of the approver by a famous criminal lawyer Shri Ram Jethmalani, held that the prosecution had established the charges against accused no.1 the managing director and chairman, no. 2 the secretary, no. 3 the honorary agent, the general manager deceased the Shri Surajmal Sanghi and the Assistant Secretary Shri Bhikulal Agarwal (the approver), and no. 4 the agent of Akola head office branch.

Merchants of Tumsar and Nagpur were closely related to my banker client, who had withdrawn his cases from my office in anger. They were represented by a senior lawyer from Nagpur,

Shri V.K. Sanghi—the father of the late Shri G.L. Sanghi, well known senior advocate of the Supreme Court. The banker client had contacted me after a long time and after some friendly talk introduced those relatives and told me that they were interested in engaging a lawyer from Akola to assist Shri Sanghi. He frankly told me that they were interested in selecting a junior lawyer who could be trusted, and that was why he had approached me on their behalf. I was surprised at this proposal by him but was very happy to receive the offer, and in my heart of hearts, I also appreciated his gesture of forgetting the past and showing large-heartedness. The fee of ₹100 per day was fixed. The trial went on for more than a year, ending in 1966.

## RAM JETHMALANI: A WELL-WISHER

During the Laxmi Bank fraud case, I had the privilege of observing Ram Jethmalani's prowess in the courtroom as well as interacting personally with him during the many months he spent in Akola to conduct the cross-examination and deliver the final arguments. Indeed, I count my lifelong friendship with Ram as the greatest personal benefit that accrued to me from the trial. His large-heartedness, daredevil attitude and intellectual vibrance infuse every aspect of his life. There is much to be learnt from him about law as well as life. I recall he once asked me about my background and career and during the course of the dialogue, he threw a surprise question at me: what would I do with the sudden receipt of fees of ₹20,000?

I replied emphatically that I would put the windfall in the bank. 'Wrong attitude,' he said, and suggested I should instead use these funds to visit Japan! I was speechless. His logic was that one should learn to develop confidence in one's capability and take risks. This is the more certain road to success. In the course of our conversation, he disclosed that barring a well-furnished flat in Mumbai, the only other valuable asset he had was a diamond necklace for his wife. Rather than squirrelling away his earnings for a rainy day, he had full confidence in his capacity to earn at any time. This is a story from about 1965, when he had not attained his present status. Hats off to his confidence and daredevil attitude, which enabled him to live life king-size, practising what he preached throughout his life!

My association with Ram was renewed after eight years at the Bar Council of Maharashtra and then again in 1995, when I became a member of the Supreme Court Bar Association, New Delhi after my retirement as Chief Justice of Orissa High Court. As a judge of the Bombay High Court, I had the good fortune of listening to him as a leading counsel mainly for the detenues under the laws relating to preventive detention, of which he was not only a master but indeed maker in the Supreme Court. I also had the privilege of working with him in some cases after restarting my practice in the Supreme Court in 1995. One such case related to the affairs of a controversial stock broker Harshad Mehta, whom I once had occasion to meet in my office at Delhi in connection with his matter in the Supreme Court.

More than half a century has passed since I first met Ram and in these fifty years I have passed through many phases in life, but his love and goodwill for me remain unabated. I am touched by Ram's fond and partial references to me in private as well as public as the following excerpt of an interview he gave to a law journal, *Apex Court Reporter 2006*, shows.

**Q.** Among your contemporaries whom do you consider your most worthy opponent in Court?

**A.** Well, I have never had any worthy opponents to state correctly, except in some rare cases. Because my opponents on the Criminal side will usually be the Govt Pleaders, public prosecutors. There were hardly any. But, at the Bar, even today, in the Supreme

Court, there is a galaxy of good lawyers who argue considerably well. Very worthy opponents. My friend Ashok Desai, one lawyer called Mr Mohta. He's not so well-known unfortunately, but he's very good, Harish Salve, Venugopal, Parasaran, Fali Nariman are all good lawyers.

## HARSHAD MEHTA: A STOCK BROKER BLESSED WITH STRONG FAMILY TIES

I had a long conference with Harshad Mehta and his brothers about his version of the role he played in the business of stock trading, right from his humble beginnings in a small house in a suburb in Mumbai—where his widowed mother had shifted from Raipur (Madhya Pradesh) with four children in search of some avenues of livelihood. What is worth mentioning about him and his family is their unity. Not only during the phase of phenomenal success, but also during the sudden and terrible fall, the four married brothers with their wives and children lived on one floor of a house with their mother, whose word everyone accepted as a command. While the going is good this is easy, but when it is not, unity often becomes fragile. Added to this was the fact that though three brothers were in business, one was a reputed medical practitioner.

## BRIEF INTERACTIONS WITH MOHAMMAD RAFI AND NAUSHAD ALI

During my days in Akola I was fortunate to encounter golden-voiced singer Mohammad Rafi. I was on an Indian Airlines flight from Hyderabad to Nagpur on my way to Akola after attending the marriage ceremony of the younger brother of my friend. By my side sat a person with a very sweet and smiling face, which reminded me of Mohammad Rafi, whose fan I have always been. I suppose my staring must have embarrassed him. However, I finally opened the dialogue and told him that he bore great resemblance to Mohammad Rafi, the great singer. He gave a smile and told me that his name was also Mohammad Rafi and after some time he proceeded to reveal that he was the original. My excitement and joy knew no bounds. What a privilege and good luck, I exclaimed!

As we conversed, he was good enough to not only tell me the purpose of his visit to Hyderabad, which concerned his TV business, but also shared the story of his entry into the world of music in Mumbai. What a fascinating tale it was. He was a street singer in Lahore when another great singer and legend, Shri K.L. Saigal, accidentally heard him singing at a street corner where people had gathered. Impressed by his exceptionally sweet and sonorous voice, Saigal stopped, called him home, and after having a phone conversation with the famous music director Naushad, arranged to send him to Mumbai. Shri Naushad heard his audition and immediately realized his potential as a singer. Rafi Sahab's first recorded song, which made him famous, was the song narrating the life story of Mahatma Gandhi—'Lo suno Bapu ki yeh amar kahani'. Great merit no doubt, but what became crucial was the role of time and chance. All God's grace, he rightly exclaimed.

Some years ago I also encountered Naushad Ali at the Delhi airport. I asked him why one didn't hear much of his music any longer. He sadly commented that the quality of songs was deteriorating. When I told him of my encounter with Mohammad Rafi and Rafi's remembrance about him, he smilingly confirmed Mohammad Rafi's version.

## SMT. MRINAL GORE'S GRAND ESCAPE FROM AKOLA DURING THE EMERGENCY

Smt. Mrinal Gore, who recently passed away, was a well-known socialist leader and one of the many persons against whom the preventive detention order was issued during the National Emergency. As was the modus operandi of the day, she too had gone into hiding, moving from place to place in different attire.

One day as I was resting in my new bungalow, 'Sankalp', a friend from Akola Bar, Shri Garge, a sincere socialist and a thorough gentleman, spoke to me on the phone, saying that my car was needed urgently to send someone to Nanded (Marathwada). He told me that the passenger would look like a Sardar, but was, in fact, Mrinal Gore. She had been hiding in a hospital in Akola, but needed to move as the police was searching for her. I complied without hesitation. 'Sardarji' came in a rickshaw along with a driver; my car was taken out and 'Sardarji' and the driver proceeded to Nanded in the middle of the night. Smt. Gore was not arrested either on the road or at Nanded. This incident has always given me satisfaction, as my friend reposed confidence in me during this risky exercise.

## MEMORABLE CAR TRIP TO KASHMIR IN REVERSE GEAR

The joys of youth are such that nothing seems impossible and no deterrent is sufficient to divert from the goal. My friends Dr Uttam Jain, Yashwant Athalye, Prakash Khelkar and I decided to take a road trip to Punjab and Kashmir. Our steed was to be an old Fiat car and we were to be our own drivers. Yashwant and Prakash, ardent and tireless drivers, were the spirit and leaders of the trip and we set off in fine fettle to enjoy our outing. While travelling from Kulu-Manali to Srinagar via Pathankot, the third and fourth gears of the car jammed. There was no difficulty in driving the car on the flat road, but the car refused to climb certain parts of the high hills and we were really stuck as there were no mechanics who could carry out repairs in the area. But then, Prakash and Yeshwant had a brilliant and original idea. It was that three of us should get out of the car whenever there was a steep hill and the driver should slowly drive the car up the hill in reverse gear with the other three pushing, if necessary! This unusual exercise was quite successful, though tiring.

It was a long journey up the hill and after about an hour-and-a-half when we reached our destination for the day, we were met with yet another situation. There was a school at the top of the hill and the teachers and students observing our approach were convinced that we were part of a film crew and were shooting an exciting adventure scene! They had prepared a delicious high tea for the 'heros' of the film! Imagine their disappointment and our embarrassment when instead of the glamorous heros, heroines and film crew they expected, they were met only by our tired and ugly faces! It was a long circuitous track and they had eagerly watched our ascent. However, the children, their teachers and we had a great time with high tea, which fortunately was not withdrawn.

## BHRIGU SAMHITA

My friends and I planned to visit Hoshiarpur on our way back from Kashmir. The city is known to house a large portion of the Bhrigu Samhita, an astrological classic in Pali, believed to be written by the sage Bhrigu during the Vedic period, and encompassing predictions on future lives and depiction of the past. Legend has it that Bhrigu Maharaj compiled lakhs of horoscopes of people born in different ages and the entire science of astrology is rooted in this database. Samhita means handwritten leaves of the lord and the Bhrigu Samhita is said to be written on bhoj patras (barks of trees) copied onto paper with the help of scholars, though the quality of the paper has become delicate and the ink has dimmed. The complete original Samhita is not available as the invaders of our country plundered large parts of it stored in Nalanda University. A small percentage of the original horoscopes remain and are scattered throughout India.

A pandit, whose name I no longer remember, was the custodian of these ancient writings. I had read about the Bhrigu Samhita in the book *Untold Story* by General B.N. Kaul, blamed as the person responsible for the debacle of the Indian forces in the China–India war in 1962, where he describes his visit to Hoshiarpur along with General J.N. Chaudhuri in the following words:

> I was staying with Chaudhuri at Jullundur in 1958 when he told me he wanted his fortune read by a celebrated Bhrigu (an astrologer of sorts) at Hoshiarpur, about an hour's run from Jullundur and whether I could come with him. Accompanied by another officer, we went to this pandit who told Chaudhuri to his great delight that he would rise to be the Army Chief one day. He correctly forecast some events in my life also.

At my suggestion, Prakash, Yashwant and I had carried our horoscopes on the Punjab–Kashmir trip but Dr Uttam Jain had not. We reached the given address and found a large hall with ample tables and chairs for people to sit and verify if their original horoscopes were available. The original horoscopes, reported to have been found by the ancestors of the panditji of that place, were said to be grouped and packed region-wise based on the place of a person's birth. The relevant bundles would be brought from the house across the road and the interested person would search for his/her horoscope. We started the exercise of searching bundle after bundle of horoscopes inscribed on worn-out old papers that were placed before us. In the evening just before closing, I located a paper (which looked comparatively fresher), bearing a horoscope similar to mine. I was delighted.

There was another lucky person, a military commander, who also located a horoscope tallying with his own within the bundles. We requested the reading of our horoscopes from the original bhoj patras that the pundits claimed were in their possession but were informed that Bhrigu Samhita may not be read after sunset. We had to wait till the next morning for this. The military commander and his wife argued with the pandit to have the reading done that evening as they urgently needed to depart for Chennai and therefore could not wait till the next morning. But panditji was adamant that the rule could not be broken. However, he also told them they should not worry about their son's health in Chennai and that he would soon recover. The couple was astounded at the pandit's knowledge of their reason for visiting Chennai. They reverently touched his feet, convinced about the seer's genuineness since they had not disclosed the fact of their son's illness. My friends and I were also perplexed and dismayed by panditji's power. We naturally discussed all this in the resthouse where we were staying. I also indicated, but without any suspicion at the time, that the paper on which the tallying horoscope was inscribed appeared comparatively fresher than others in that bundle.

As people browsed through the bundles of loose papers, there would be desultory conversations between people, exchanges of information about families, hopes, desires and dreams. Panditji too would converse with people, asking occasional questions and narrating the story of how his ancestors accidentally found the bundles of the Bhrigu Samhita on the banks of the Sutlej river. Apparently, these were only a miniscule part of the Bhrigu Samhita prepared by the sage. He also said that those bundles were kept in the huge godown behind their residential-cum-commercial building across the road and that the family performed a puja to these bundles every day. That evening, at our insistence, we were taken to that building. In the front room sat panditji's old father, who was introduced as Vaidyaji, the famous horoscope reader. The four walls of the room were lined with several almirahs full of medicine bottles and powders. In the godown that lay at the back of the house, we did see a large number of heavily packed bundles.

The next morning, after reading the commander's horoscope, they took me to the first floor over the hall. I sat down and panditji took out a polythene packet of old palm tree leaves on which my past, present and the future were written in Pali. As he started to read I too could identify some words. The opening part of the horoscope stated that this 'prani' i.e. individual, would have the good fortune of finding this kundali on such and such day (which happened to be the previous day). Surprisingly it also mentioned that on that day he would be accompanied by three persons, one person by name 'Pra', the other by name 'Yash' and 'ek anya prani' (one more person). References to these insignificant matters in Bhrigu's horoscope struck me as odd and I wondered why the names of only two accompanying persons were mentioned and not the name of the third person. The story of my previous birth, where I was born and the vocations I had pursued were all mentioned, but of course I had no means to ascertain the truthfulness of the contents. Then started the story of my present life with mention of the past, up to that day. The name of my wife was written as 'Kamalakhya' and the first letters of names of my three sons Anoop, Narendra and Sanjay were also written.

Whenever I tried to ask a question, panditji said he could not explain anything but could only read what was written. He turned a few pages and then started reading my future when he suddenly stopped, showed me a leaf that appeared to state that after the age of forty-five, I would have a serious illness and that to know my fate post that illness, I would have to perform a particular puja. So saying, he closed the packet! I was astonished at this illogical turn of events. Why would a great sage like Bhrigu do this? However, I asked the cost of the puja, which he said was, 'about ₹20,000'. He also told me that the military commander had agreed to perform the puja that day itself and I could join in case I desired.

By now, I had serious doubts about the genuineness of the

whole exercise. The comparative freshness of the paper I had found in the bundle appeared suspicious. The entirely insignificant details such as the date on which I would find the horoscope; the number of persons accompanying me at that time; mention of two of their names and the absence of the third name, which I should mention was that of the friend who had not brought his horoscope, all made me doubt the veracity of what the pandit had said.

The sage Bhrigu also appeared in a somewhat greedy light for halting his revelations about my life at forty-five unless I performed a puja! However, I paid the ₹20 fee for searching the horoscope and returned to the resthouse where I gave my friends an account of the horoscope reading. What was mysterious was finding the correct names of my wife and sons in the horoscope and the correctness of my past till the previous day, which panditji had no means of knowing.

We packed up and started our return journey to Delhi. Inevitably, discussions turned to the 'horoscope experience'. We recalled that a petrol pump owner near Hoshiarpur had guessed that we were searching for Bhrigu Samhita and told us that while several persons from distant places had found their horoscopes, there was no record of any local having found his horoscope. Circumstantial evidence about the fakeness of the horoscope read to me was weighty, but the correct disclosure of my past and the names of my wife and children remained an unsolved mystery. Perhaps we had gone to the wrong address in Hoshiarpur since there are centres there that claim possession of the original Samhita.

I narrated the whole experience to several friends and relatives. One or two older people told me that there is a science and/or magic called 'Karna Pishachya', the practise of which allows experts in the science to know what another individual knows. It made me think of my childhood in Akola, where some boys would ask others to think of the name of some flower and would then guess what they were thinking of, which guess was generally correct. Was panditji's prediction about luck on my horoscope pure guesswork or just a figment of the imagination? Perhaps the following modus operandi may have been used.

First select two or three customers out of the group in the hall, prepare a paper depicting the concerned horoscope, use some chemical to quickly age the paper and, in the later part of the day, slip it into one of the bundles of old papers of that region.

Next, during the night, inscribe Vaidyaji's reading of the horoscope on old palm leaves in Pali and also add to it some verifiable statements gleaned from conversations either overheard or some other method so that the authenticity of the ancient horoscope gains instant acceptance.

Finally, charge only a nominal fee, such as ₹20, for inspection and charge heavily to perform a puja to look further into the future of the chosen individual once faith in the genuineness of the horoscope and fear about a grim future has been generated.

This seems to me to be the only logical explanation for the comparative freshness of the paper on which my horoscope was discovered. It also explains the following: (a) why it was not shown during the course of the day; and, (b) the unusual mention by Bhriguji of the date of the horoscope's discovery by the person concerned and the names of the persons in whose company it would be found. Above all, it explains the unusual and deferred greediness of the great sage Bhrigu for not depicting the crucial part of one's future after a serious illness unless a costly puja was performed!

## SHIFTING FROM ANCESTRAL HOUSE

My brothers and I had partitioned the joint family property shortly after the family debts were cleared. To my elder brother, Shri

Vithaldasji, went our agricultural land and village establishments including houses and fields, while I got the cinema in Khamgaon and my younger brother Laxmansingh got the Akola family house. My elder brother shifted to our village, Nimgaon, and Kamla, I and our three sons, Anoop, Narendra and Sanjay, moved to a rented house in Alsi plots, Akola, where we stayed for about five to six years. Soon after, my elder brother's children Saroj, Ajay and Sarita also came to live with us in the rented house. Kamla must have told all the children not to refer to each other as cousins, which I later learned created some confusion amongst their friends as there was only a two-month age difference between my son Narendra and nephew Ajay—which made their friends ask how two brothers could be born within two months of each other!

I shifted my office from the family house to a rented place in Tajnapeth. Initially the only transport I had was a 'Hind' bicycle, though this was soon exchanged for an old Lambretta scooter, and later still a second-hand Hillman car costing ₹6000. My younger brother stayed in the family house along with his three children, Rajiv, Shaila and Swati. On becoming a lawyer, Laxmansingh shared my rented office in Tajnapeth and in course of time started an independent practice with an office in the family house. Our mother stayed with each of her three sons depending upon her wishes.

The rented Alsi plot house, though double-storied, was very small. It had two bedrooms, a kitchen and a dining room on the ground floor and one room and a terrace on the first floor. The front room was used as the drawing room during the day and our bedroom at night. In 1967, I purchased a 6000 square feet plot on Gorakshan road, Akola. My legal practice was gaining momentum and I regularly went to Nagpur for High Court work twice a week. I had a great desire to start practice in Nagpur and, eventually, planned to shift there. Every week I would go to Nagpur by the midnight Dadar–Nagpur Express and return to Akola either by the Howrah–Bombay Mail (now the Howrah–Mumbai Mail) or the Nagpur–Dadar Express, which reached Akola at about 3.00 a.m. My house was about a forty-minute cycle-rickshaw ride away from the railway station. The final straw in a tiring exercise! After a few years, it became too taxing for me. Family exigencies did not permit me to leave Akola and so my younger brother shifted to Nagpur and started his legal practice, which he continues till this day.

After the enactment of the Maharashtra Land Ceiling Act and the Maharashtra Debt Relief Act, there was a spate of litigations relating to the validity of those enactments. Lawyers, including myself, earned a lot in those cases. Hence, I was able to construct a bungalow on the plot. When my bank balance rose to ₹1,00,000, I took a decision to start construction of a bungalow whose estimated cost was about ₹1,50,000. As the estimated period for completion of the construction was one year, I was quite hopeful of earning sufficiently to make up the deficit. Our bungalow 'Sankalp', so named because I had decided to construct it only from my own earnings, was now under construction. My friends would jokingly remark that a more appropriate name for my house would have been either 'Ceiling' or 'Debt Relief'! The architect of my elegant two-storied house was Shri G.W. Athawale and the contractor was Shri B.M. Modi. The total cost of the building came to ₹1,76,000. The housewarming ceremony took place on 11 October 1973 and my family and I were soon installed in our own home.

I had decided to reduce my trips to Nagpur and had happily settled down in the new bungalow. I even purchased an old Fiat car for ₹19,500. However, while performing the puja for our housewarming ceremony, our panditji publicly informed me that I did not seem destined to stay in Sankalp for a long period. I informed him that I had constructed the house with the intention of settling permanently in Akola, and in course of time, handing over the office to my eldest son Anoop, who was keen to become a lawyer. There was no question of my moving from this house! But, for all my protestations, it appears the prediction was correct, as subsequent unexpected events will show.

Sankalp was a happy family home. In addition to my mother and our own three sons, my nephew, Rajiv, a school-going boy, stayed with us for some time, as did Kamla's brother, Dilip. Kamla looked after all of them and continued to be in complete charge of the family and its affairs leaving me free to devote my time and energy to the profession and occasionally, to social commitments. Subsequently, my two sons Narendra and Sanjay shifted to Nagpur for their higher education and stayed with my younger brother and his family for a number of years. Sankalp remained our primary home for about six years till my elevation as a Bombay High Court Judge in 1979.

## PRACTICE IN MOFUSSIL HIGH COURTS AND SUPREME COURT WITH DIGNITY

I was, in truth, a mofussil lawyer practising in Akola and the surrounding areas. I was not a regular member of any High Court Bar Association, though I appeared at least once a week in the High Court at Nagpur. Occasionally I had appeared in the high courts at Mumbai, Jabalpur, Indore and Chennai. In those days juniors were generally treated courteously and encouraged by the judges, a trend that unfortunately is disappearing in some courts these days. Perhaps the ever increasing and unbearable load of cases in today's courts is one of the reasons. Nonetheless, I see no justification for their humiliation. I have never swallowed an insult in my life, not even from the judges, irrespective of their position or seniority. The rare occasions when I was offered such treatment remain deeply imprinted on my mind.

As a young lawyer, I had a matter in Nagpur before a judge who had been elevated to the High Court from the judicial service.

On the first day of his sitting on the Bench, I was arguing a criminal revision against three convictions under the Companies Act: the first for failure to hold the annual general meeting; the second for failure to submit balance sheets therein; and the third for not submitting three copies of those balance sheets to the registrar. The matter was called at about 11.30 a.m. and my argument was that first and foremost, the annual general meeting could not take place for reasons beyond the control of the director; second, that since no meeting could be held, the question of submitting the balance sheet did not arise; and lastly, since the balance sheet was not submitted, its supply to the registrar was not possible.

While I was still arguing, the clock struck twelve and the judge suddenly told me that he was adjourning the matter and in future, I should come fully prepared. I replied that I was prepared. Then the judge told me that he was adjourning the matter for half an hour and in the meanwhile, I should study the case thoroughly. Completely befuddled by this strange behaviour, I reiterated that I was fully prepared. I had no idea why he was insisting on adjourning the matter when I was fully prepared. Seeing my desire to argue, the judge remarked rudely, 'This is the High Court not a mofussil court'. He knew that I was from Akola since he too hailed from that place. I lost my head and instantaneously replied, 'It is not my first day in High Court.' The Hon'ble Judge lost his temper and suddenly went inside his chamber. My opponent, the government pleader, Shri G.R. Mudholkar (brother of Hon'ble Justice J.R. Mudholkar—judge of the Supreme Court of India), explained that the judge was annoyed because he had his habitual smoke in the chamber at noon, a fact of which I should have been aware. He advised me to apologize to the judge when he returned to the courtroom at 12.30 p.m. Following this advice, once the Hon'ble Judge was again seated and looked at me, anticipating an apology, I unwittingly said, 'Sorry, I did not know.' The courtroom was packed with members of the Bar, as is always the case when a new judge sits in the court. Everyone laughed at my reply but not the judge. However, I must mention that he heard me patiently, though the revision was dismissed.

There was also a Supreme Court Judge at whose hands I met with discourtesy. He tended to dismiss matters even before arguments started. Once, when I requested a hearing before the passing of orders, he told me that he would first dismiss the matter and then hear me. The stenographers were always ready in court and he dictated the usual order 'dismissed' and called for the next case. The following dialogue then ensued between the Hon'ble Judge and me:

**Me:** What about promise to hear?

**Hon'ble judge:** Okay, start.

I argued and concluded by expressing gratefulness.

**Hon'ble judge:** What for?

**Me:** For the unusual courtesy and grace shown in hearing the matter even after the decision was given.

**Hon'ble judge:** Are you being sarcastic?

I remained silent but standing. After a pause, the next case was called. I left the courtroom. Outside, many lawyers who had been victims of the judge's rude behaviour in that court congratulated me for standing up to the judge!

## JUSTICE P.N. BHAGWATI: A BRILLIANT AND CONSIDERATE JUDGE

There have been and are many kind and considerate judges who deal humanely with junior lawyers. One such judge and his courtesy deserve mention. Shri Justice P.N. Bhagwati, a judge of the Supreme Court, was a vacation judge in summer. I had an urgent matter before him that involved dispossession of several evacuees from their allotted plots in Akola. Our advocate on record was Shri Sardar Bahadur whose younger son Shri Vishnu Bahadur (presently working as advocate-on-record, and who like his father has a reputation as a sincere and reliable lawyer), was in charge of the case. It was Justice Bhagwati's last day of sitting as a vacation judge and there was a heavy rush in the court. Despite sitting overtime, the board could not be finished and to our disappointment, our matter did not reach. At about 6.00 p.m. the board was discharged for the day, when several senior lawyers, including Shri A.R. Antulay, (ex-chief minister of Maharashtra) who was then practicing as senior advocate in the Supreme Court, pressed for their matters to be taken up. Another vacation judge was to sit on the bench the next day, but everyone wanted their matter to be heard by Justice Bhagwati, who expressed regret and rose.

Since I had undertaken a twenty-four hour train journey from Akola to Delhi for the matter and had a return reservation for the following morning's Punjab Mail, I was really nervous. Realizing my predicament, the ever-helpful Vishnu Bahadur suggested I should meet the Hon'ble Judge in his chamber and explain my problem. I did not dare but he insisted and took me to the judge's chamber. I was surprised to find we easily gained access. I presented my problem to the judge who asked me to estimate the time I would take for arguments. I was certain of being able to finish the argument within a short period. He consented to hear the matter at his bungalow after an hour. Vishnu took me to his bungalow where we juniors were very well received in his office. Within a few minutes, Justice Bhagwati arrived and opened the brief. He took about seven to eight minutes to peruse the papers and then looked at me saying, 'Yes.'

I narrated the basic facts, which took perhaps five minutes, and showed the judge the Gujarat High Court judgment reported in *Gujarat Law Reporter*. In minutes, the matter was admitted and a stay of dispossession granted. My joy at the result was great, but more overwhelming was my joy at the Hon'ble Judge's behaviour towards a junior mofussil lawyer.

After demitting office as Chief Justice of the High Court in 1995, I started my second innings as an advocate in Delhi and was also doing arbitration work. One such arbitration case was *Reliance Industries Limited Vs. Ispat Alloys Limited* in which the chairman of the Arbitration Tribunal was Justice Bhagwati, and members appointed by the parties were Justice K.J. Shetty, a retired judge of the Supreme Court and myself, a retired Chief Justice of Orissa high court. I had not appeared before Justice Bhagwati after my above pleasant experience in Delhi but as a co-arbitrator with him, I was able to observe his courtesy to everyone he met. His behaviour and quick grasp of commercial law were truly impressive.

## MAHARASHTRA DEBT RELIEF ACT, 1975: ITS VALIDITY AND IMPLEMENTATION

I was fortunate to be part of several important litigations in original courts, high courts and also the Supreme Court during the 1970s. One matter that stays in my memory related to the validity of a very progressive legislation—the Maharashtra Debt Relief Act—the objective of which was to wipe out the debts of marginal farmers, rural artisans, rural labourers and workers. The country was yoked under the Emergency in which fundamental rights were suspended. Inevitable recourse had to be to Articles 301 and 304(b) of the Constitution of India, relating to the freedom of trade, commerce and intercourse in the territory of India and restrictions there upon in public interest. The hearing went on for over a month in the Bombay High Court, during which time I was almost continuously in Mumbai, serving as a lawyer for the Maharashtra Money Lender's Association. As was expected, the moneylenders lost the case in the High Court despite a valiant struggle on their behalf by the cream of the Indian Bar. However, they were able to obtain an interim order of stay for twenty-one days to move to the Supreme Court.

The judgment was challenged in the Supreme Court. Vacation Judge Hon'ble Justice S. Murtaza Fazal Ali continued the interim order and the matter was finally heard by the Constitution Bench comprising Chief Justice A.N. Ray, Justices M.H. Beg, P.N. Bhagwati, V.R. Krishna Iyer and S. Murtaza Fazal Ali. As expected, the judgment of the Bombay High Court was upheld. I vividly recollect the lead submissions of senior counsel Shri Fali S. Nariman. As soon as Shri Nariman rose, Chief Justice Ray remarked that he (Shri Nariman) was representing the exploiters. Shri Nariman in his usual sarcastic style turned to look at the back of the courtroom and replied that some of them were also sitting in the visitor's gallery and then turning to the dais asked, 'May I start the submissions?' There were a few seconds of silence in courtroom no.1 and thereafter his submissions started. The moneylenders lost the appeal. An excellent thought-provoking and realistic unanimous judgment, *M/s Fatehchand Himmatlal and Others Vs. State of Maharashtra*, (1977) 2 SCC 670, was authored by Justice V.R. Krishna Iyer, the prophetic concluding part of which is worth reproduction.

> The legislation we uphold is an added responsibility on the State. It shall be vigorously enforced with sympathy for the victim class, lest the progressive measure proves a paper tiger. The cadres charged with enforcement must have right orientation, correct grasp and social activism, if the law is not to leave a yawning implementation gap. Heroics in court and hortation in the House must be followed by effective enforcement in the field. We state this not because the State is not in great

earnest—it is—but because many a welfare legislation in the country reportedly remains a cloistered virtue or slumberous in effect. The finest hour of the rule of law is when law disciplines life and matches promise with performance. On this note of hopeful valediction we wind up.

The apprehensions voiced proved correct. As usual there was utter failure in the Act's implementation.

## MYSTERIOUS DISAPPEARANCE FROM SHRI A.K. SEN'S RESIDENCE

Prior to the hearing in the Bombay High Court, the moneylenders tried to add as many eminent lawyers to their defence team as possible. Some petitioners decided to engage senior advocate and former union law minister from Delhi, Shri A.K. Sen. The moneylenders made an appointment to see him and so we went to his bungalow on Raisina Road in New Delhi. When our team arrived, Shri Sen was busy with a judge of the Rajasthan High Court in his chamber and we were asked to wait. After a considerable period, we walked out of the bungalow for some fresh air. As we stood by the main gate, a lady unexpectedly approached us, introducing herself as Smt. Sen. She appeared to be tense as she shared her concern for Shri Sen's health. She said that he had been advised not to leave Delhi. Mumbai and Parsi food—which Shri Sen was extremely fond of—did not suit him, but she feared he would not refuse the brief from Mumbai. So saying, she went away, having beseeched us with folded hands not to engage her husband as she knew she would be powerless in dissuading him from going to Mumbai. The clients sought my advice on what to do. I suggested that they should not add the bad omen of a curse from a lawyer's wife to the many difficulties they already faced in the case. We returned to Mumbai without engaging any senior, but the story does not end here.

Later, when I was a judge in Mumbai, Shri Sen, who was union law minister once again, visited the Bombay High Court. The Chief Justice had invited them for lunch, and during the course of introductions, I told Shri Sen that I had had the privilege of meeting Smt. Sen earlier. On being asked how and where, I narrated what had happened a few years before at the gate of his Raisina Road bungalow. Shri Sen remarked, 'Oh! Now I know the mystery of the sudden disappearance of clients whose engagement I had decided to accept.' We all had a hearty laugh.

## MEETING WITH ATTORNEY GENERAL, SHRI M.C. SETALVAD

I had a great desire to meet Shri M.C. Setalvad, Attorney General of India. I had heard much of him from my senior, who obviously held him in great respect, and with whom perhaps he had some personal contact. Lawyers at the Bar spoke well of Shri Setalvad. I had once also read an interview of the internationally famous barrister, D.M. Prit, who appeared in various courts of the world, in which his response to the question, 'Which lawyer do you rate as the best in the world,' was, 'Your Attorney General Setalvad, whose short and terse submissions on law as well as facts and sense of dignity is unparalleled.'

I had an intense desire to meet this doyen of the Indian Bar. God sent me that opportunity sometime in 1963 when I had gone to Delhi from Akola as a junior instructing lawyer in the case of *Akola Electricity Supply Company Vs. J.N. Jarare & Ors*, AIR 1963 SC 7121 = 1964 (2) SCR 513. The electricity company had challenged the award of the industrial court at Nagpur framing a scheme for gratuity at a time when the company had declared closure. The matter was heard in court no. 3 by a bench comprising justices P.B. Gajendragadkar, K.N. Wanchoo and K.C. Dasgupta.

Shri Setalvad addressed the court for about ten minutes, weighing each word in stating the proposition that such schemes cannot be ordered to be framed at the time of closure of a business and that was not only the basic labour law principle, but also the settled legal position. The court called upon the respondent's counsel to show how the award was sustainable, to which the counsel raised an objection to the effect that no case law in support of the proposition was cited on behalf of the Company. I vividly recollect Justice K.C. Dasgupta telling him, 'Attorney General Setalvad is a fountain of purity and we accept his statement about the existing legal position as final.' Not more than fifteen to twenty minutes were required to dispose off the matter.

I was looking for and had expected the lucky moment of meeting Shri Setalvad in the conference on the day prior to the hearing, but was disappointed since no conference was held. The matter was over on a Friday and I remained in Delhi over the weekend. On Sunday morning while driving down Race Course Road in a taxi, I noticed a nameplate, 'M.C. Setalvad', on the gate of one bungalow. I gave in to temptation, stopped the taxi, and entered the gate. I introduced myself to his personal assistant (PA), saying that I had a desire to meet Shri Setalvad, just to pay my respects, and clarified that he did not know me personally. The PA seemed reluctant to entertain my request for a meeting on a Sunday but gave in to my plea and asked me to write down my name, address and purpose of my visit. I put down all the requirements on a piece of paper. After about half an hour, I was called inside Shri Setalvad's chamber. He looked at me closely and, keeping the paper on his table, indicated that I should take a seat.

I have reconstructed, to the extent possible, the early part of our conversation, which went somewhat like this:

**MCS:** Vallabhbhai Mohta. So you are a Gujarati?

**Me:** No. I am a Rajasthani.

**MCS:** What an enterprising community.

**Me:** What is the difference between Gujarati and Rajasthani communities in the matter of enterprise?

**MCS:** No doubt, both are enterprising, but there is a significant difference. There is almost always at least one Rajasthani family in even the remote villages of India, but this is not so in the case of Gujarati families. All right. How many years as a lawyer?

As I answered and expressed my gratitude to him for the privilege he graciously granted to a junior mofussil lawyer, he told me that he was happy to meet a young lawyer on Sunday for no legal work, but asked me why I was keen on meeting him. I told him that my senior, Kakasaheb Athalye from Akola, often spoke about him. He immediately remembered Kakasaheb and remarked that Athalye was a very competent lawyer with clarity of thought and felicity of language and that had he practiced in Mumbai—a place to which he originally belonged—he would certainly have been one of the leading lawyers of the Mumbai Bar. After a brief silence, Shri Setalvad asked me whether I was related to Shri Shivratan Mohta of Karachi, a well-known industrialist. Denying any relationship, I added that had I been so, I would not have become a lawyer! Shri Setelvad also asked me whether this was the first time I had seen him. It was, in fact, the fourth time I had seen Shri Setalvad and I recounted the previous three occasions—the first when he was delivering a convocation address in the Nagpur University; the second when he was addressing the Justice Chagla Commission in the public hearing in an enquiry against Haridas Mundhada; and third, in the Supreme Court, the previous Friday in the Gratuity Scheme case.

I was curious about a photograph that hung on the wall behind his chair and he told me that it was a photograph of his senior Shri Bhulabhai Desai, who was his father Sir Chimanlal's junior and was to Setalvad as Athalye is to me. He fondly and respectfully talked about his senior's love and affection for him.

He recounted how he had once protected him from the anger of his father, Sir Chimanlal.

Senior took junior's side and when junior's father angrily asked him to make a choice between Chimanlal and Motilal, Bhulabhai responded that it was a very difficult choice indeed, but if making a choice was inevitable, his answer would be 'Motilal'.

Emboldened by Shri Setalvad's graciousness, I asked him about reports of Prime Minister Jawaharlal Nehru protecting the Union Finance Minister, Shri T.T. Krishnamachari, in the Mundhra scandal. He answered that Nehru genuinely thought that it was a government policy matter in which no *mens rea* was involved, and that the Attorney General as a lawyer of the government was expected to support the client. On that aspect, there was some difference of opinion between the two, but he hastened to add that Nehru was a great prime minister, having some values and when the Attorney General's role in the Chagla Commission was being criticized in the Parliament, Nehru had strongly defended the attorney general despite his difference with him on the subject. Nehru said that the criticism was unfair since the attorney general had done what he genuinely thought was his public duty. Shri Setalvad also told me that he had in fact offered to resign from the post of attorney general, but the prime minister had firmly declined to accept. What a prime minister! What an attorney general!

That memorable and lucky meeting ended with a cup of tea. As soon as I returned to Akola, I rushed to my senior's house to tell him the whole story. He was naturally very happy.

## PHOTO AND SOME TIME WITH SHRI JAWAHARLAL NEHRU

As he was for crores of Indians, Jawaharlal Nehru, one of the chief architects of modern India, was my hero too. From the time I was a child, I had an earnest desire to see him and have a photograph taken with him. I heard of his practise of meeting groups of visitors in the morning at his residence on Teen Murti Marg, New Delhi. Sometime in the early 1960s, I decided to take a chance to fulfilling my desire during a visit to Delhi. I made a phone call to the prime minister's residence. His PA, one Shri Khanna, came on the line and I disclosed my desire and sought his help. He asked me to meet him early the next morning at the gate of Teen Murti House with my identity card. Nehru would be meeting some groups at 9.00 a.m. in the lawns of the bungalow for about an hour, during which time there could be a photo opportunity. My friend, Shri Nilakhe from Akola, accompanied me, and we reached Teen Murti House before the given time and were ushered through the gate after verification.

It was a bright winter morning. Several groups were waiting to meet the prime minister who was mixing with the groups. He was an aristocratic man from an eminent family, yet spoke to people one-on-one and appreciated their opinions. Nevertheless, he was irascible with fools or timid people. How could one not be somewhat timid and overawed in such a presence? When Panditji met the group that had come from a village in Haryana, he placed a hand on the shoulder of the leader of the group, who was the sarpanch of the village, and asked him about the place to which he belonged. The awe of proximity to such a great leader perhaps overpowered the sarpanch who became extremely nervous and started trembling. Jawaharlalji lost his temper and remarked that he had asked a simple question and was not scolding him, but the sarpanch could not open his mouth! The prime minister asked the group to visit the new pilgrimage centres of India like Bhakra Nangal, Hirakud, Bhilai, etc. and also to see the show 'Holiday on Ice', which was being performed at the National Sports Club. While he was moving on to the next group, Shri Khanna called me. The golden moment of realizing my dream had come, but I was nervous and could not stand by his side for the photograph.

He angrily remarked that I wanted to have a photograph taken, but did not even know how a photograph was taken. 'Come nearer and face the sun,' he ordered. We complied. The camera lights flashed and the photograph was taken. Shri Khanna asked me to collect the photograph in the evening from the gate of Teen Murti House. That photograph is one of my most valuable treasures.

When I went to collect the photograph, Shri Khanna was not there, but a middle-aged lady named Vimla Singh, who had seen us that morning, was present. It was time for the prime minister to return home and the staff was getting ready to receive him. I enquired whether it would be possible to meet the prime minister for a few minutes. As she had seen us being photographed with him in the morning, she took us inside the residence after ascertaining that there was no other visitor. A beautiful golden retriever greeted us. Smt. Singh asked us to wait in the drawing room, where a life-sized portrait of Dr S. Radhakrishnan hung on the wall. What admiration Panditji must have had for that scholar! We were offered a cup of coffee, which we gratefully accepted as we awaited the prime minister's arrival. He entered the drawing room without a cap, looking tired. I saw his shining bald head for the first time. 'Who are you and where are you from?' he asked, enquiring further whether I had not received a copy of the photograph. I showed him the photograph and he smiled as he left the drawing room with Smt. Indira Gandhi, who was also present. What good luck! I met him twice.

## ASSOCIATION WITH BAR COUNCIL

The Maharashtra Bar Council is a statutory body under the Advocates Act, 1961. It comprises twenty elected members and the Advocate General is an ex-officio member. The council serves for a term of four years. The registered members of the council were almost invariably elected only from the members of the Mumbai and Nagpur High Court Bar Associations. There was a growing feeling that the council did not take up issues concerning mofussil Bars. Therefore, for the 1969 elections, the leaders of the Akola Bar met informally and decided to nominate a candidate for election from Akola. My name was unanimously chosen and accordingly the form for my candidature was submitted. Stalwarts like Ram Jethmalani, Ramrao Adik from Mumbai and V.R. Manohar from Nagpur were also candidates in this hotly contested election.

Akola Bar, substantially supported by the neighbouring Amravati Bar, took great interest in this election, and I was astounded to find, when the results were declared, that out of 103 votes from Akola I had secured 101 votes! This was unique and unparalleled! I was declared elected in the first round and was fourth in order of preference. The three above me were Shri Ramrao Adik, Maharashtra's great political leader, Shri V.R. Manohar, the eminent lawyer from Nagpur, and one Shri Mohite from the Pune Bar. I received innumerable messages and greetings from all over Maharashtra, particularly mofussil areas. My joy knew no bounds when I received the following telegram at Akola from Ram Jethmalani even while counting of the votes was in process: 'Congratulations Outstanding Success Proud of you. Jethmalani'.

The four-year tenure on the council and association with stalwarts from various Bars of Maharashtra was a great learning experience for me. Encouraged by the success of even a mofussil lawyer in the election, there were many candidates from provincial towns in the next election. Akola Bar decided to sponsor a candidate once again. There was unanimity about my name, but I insisted on a change so that others too could have the opportunity to serve on the council. Groups started forming and two names finally came to the forefront. Efforts by senior lawyers to bring about a settlement failed, which meant a division of votes. At the last moment, both groups agreed to withdraw their candidate if I contested. I filled in the nomination form and was elected, but not with the previous massive majority. This time even the votes from Akola Bar were divided. During my second term, I was unanimously elected as vice-president of the council. Thus ended my official position on the council, but never my association with it.

## PRESIDENT OF BGE SOCIETY: MY ALMA MATER

The Berar Education Society is a renowned educational institution of the Vidarbha region. It runs arts, commerce, science and law colleges in Akola and the nearby town of Karanja. The colleges had a record of producing brilliant students, securing high positions in the merit list of university examinations. Although I was once a student of its law college, I must confess I was not in the category of brilliant students!

A position on the managing committee of the society was much sought after, and the elections for this body were hotly contested. All of Akola's elite and those from the neighbouring areas were members of the society. Even outsiders took an interest in the elections. In 1975, a new body was to be constituted. There were sharply divided factions operating in the process and the dispute eventually reached the High Court where I represented one group professionally. Ultimately, the parties reached a settlement and by unanimous agreement finalized the names of the office bearers and members of the managing committee. I was chosen as the president, and Shri Satyanarayanji Goenka, a social worker and a scintillating Hindi orator, as the secretary. Although I was pleased and honoured at being unanimously chosen to this position, it was very embarrassing since I was counsel to one group. This event was a matter of great publicity.

The tenure of our committee was successful and we were fortunate to have not only a united team on the committee but also the full cooperation of the staff. Periodic differences were amicably resolved, thanks to the cooperation of the members. We were usually able to build a consensus on issues. For example, even before our tenure began, construction had started on a huge library building, which was being funded by a grant bestowed by the University Grants Commission (UGC). On its completion, the building had to be inaugurated. Several names were suggested for this purpose, which included dignitaries such as the governor, the chief minister of the state and the Chief Justice of Bombay High Court. I suggested the name of Hon'ble Justice Shri M. Hidayatullah, former Chief Justice of the Supreme Court of India, who had settled down in Mumbai after retirement. Two factors influenced my choice: he was a book lover, which was reflected in his judgments and writings, and he had received his primary education in Akola where his father had been posted as the Sub-Divisional magistrate (SDM). What better person could there be to inaugurate this library! I shared my thoughts with the secretary, other members of the managing committee and senior members of the Society, the majority of whom agreed. Justice M. Hidayatullah was duly invited to be the chief guest. At his august hands, the building was inaugurated in a function largely attended by the elite of the town and of neighbouring places.

Despite the usual inevitable groupism prevailing in educational institutions all over India, the faculty and administrative staff of this institution were usually cooperative, and barring a few unpleasant incidents such as the initiation of disciplinary proceedings against some members of the staff including the principal, we had a successful innings. At the far end of our term, a challenge arose when the administrative staff gave to the state government, as well as to the Society, a notice of strike. Their long-standing grievance was justified as their demand for payment of arrears of their salary as per the new scale had gone unheeded and they had finally lost patience. The strike was to commence a week or two before the university examinations. I called the leaders and tried to persuade them to postpone the strike, at least until the examinations were over, in the interest of the institution to which they belonged. The leaders expressed their helplessness, as it was a unanimous decision of the general body. I called a meeting of all the staff members and made a fervent appeal for postponement, appealing to them to uphold the reputation of the prestigious institution with which they were permanently associated. I reminded them that the members of the managing body and the students were only there temporarily. I promised them our best efforts to expedite the implementation of the decision of the government. Concluding, I asked, 'So what is your response to our appeal only for the postponement of the strike?' I vividly recollect the scene. There was a low murmur in the hall initially, but after some time, they indicated acceptance of our appeal. We were so relieved! I thanked the staff for their fine gesture despite the justice of their demands. Fortunately, the government released the payment shortly after this incident.

Berar Education Society has prospered and grown over the years. When it celebrated its platinum jubilee under the chairmanship of the state minister for education on 6–7 February 2010, I had the honour of being invited as the chief guest—perhaps in my dual capacity as a past student as well as president. It was a grand function attended by a huge gathering of dignitaries, academicians and past students from several parts of India. A souvenir was published by the society in which I contributed an article under the caption 'My Alma Mater, Some Reminiscences'. It was a memorable event, which gave me the added pleasure of meeting my old friends and acquaintances in Akola.

## TWO DAYS WITH JUSTICE M. HIDAYATULLAH

When I met Justice Hidayatullah at his Malabar Hill flat in Mumbai to invite him to inaugurate the UGC library building, the first question he asked me was, 'Why a retired person?' My answer, that it was for two reasons—the first being his known love for books and the second, his association with Akola—seemed to please him. He smiled and showed me a bundle of typed papers that were lying on the table. These were his memoirs, in which he had referred to his school days in Akola. He recounted how he had escaped death by snakebite while going to his Urdu primary school. Both references (reproduced below) are to be found in his autobiography, *My Own Boswell* in Chapter III 'I go to school':

At Akola an incident occurred which I cannot help mentioning. We used to go to school on foot through open fields surrounding our bungalow. Akola has black cotton soil and weeds of a particular kind (called Tarota), grow to knee height with yellow flowers attracting myriads of yellow butterflies matching the colour so faithfully as to look like the flowers themselves. We used to avoid going through the tarotas but did this when we were late and in a hurry.

One day we cut across the fields and I was very nearly bitten by a cobra. Fortunately, I did not step on him but I can still see in my imagination his hood spread out and the wicked eyes. I was wearing, what in India are called 'shorts', which are trousers up to knee. If the cobra had chosen to strike, there was nothing to save me, however, he did not, and uncoiling himself slithered away. Going to school was out of the question for me. I was trembling with fear and remained dizzy for an hour or two afterwards.

Priests, both Muslim and Hindu, were consulted and we received diverse counsel—a case of *quot homines, tot sententiae* [as many opinions as there were men]! The Muslim priest said some prayers over me and recommended giving alms to the poor and sending food to the mosque for a week for the congregation, as thanksgiving. The Hindu priests put mustard

oil in a flat pan and asked me to see the reflection of my face in
it. They suggested sending a cobra image in gold to the temple
devoted to the worship of the Nag (Cobra). The Hindu Head
Priest consulted his books and said that as the 'Nag Maharaj'
had not chosen to strike, this foretold a great destiny for me.
The episode, however, was productive immediately of one good
result. We were allowed to use the family tonga (one horse
carriage) to go to school!

Justice Hidayatullah kindly accepted the invitation and we agreed
on a convenient date for the function. As I left his flat after a long
and interesting conversation, he told me that he would like to stay
in Akola for an extra day, as he wanted to have a look around
the town and revive his childhood memories. I was delighted by
his desire to stay in Akola for a longer time.

On the day of the function, he reached Akola by the Mumbai–
Howrah Mail in the early morning and was met at the station
by members of the managing committee of the BGE Society,
principals of the four colleges and office bearers of the Akola
Bar Association. When the coolie put his suitcase in the car,
Justice Hidayatullah took out ₹50 and handed it to him. We
tried to prevent him, but he did not listen, remarking that in
addition to pension, he was earning sufficiently even in Mumbai
from legal opinions and arbitrations! He was felicitated at the
Akola Bar Association, following which he visited his old Urdu
school and the Boat Club, where he showed us the spot where
he had encountered the snake. At the Urdu school he located
the classroom where he had sat, recollected the name of one of
his teachers and enquired whether any of his legal heirs were in
Akola. It was found that the teacher's grandson, a tongawala, was
living in the town. Shri Hidayatullah insisted on meeting him,
called him to Circuit House, fondly talked about his grandfather
and gifted him some amount.

The next day was comparatively free for chat and interaction.

Justice Hidayatullah was a good storyteller with a unique style of narration, brimful with satire and subtle wit. One story he told related to a friendship from his Nagpur days with another renowned judge, Justice Vivian Bose, for whom he had great admiration. Both were fond of performing amateur magic shows at Bar functions in Nagpur. One such performance entailed the opening of the magic box without manually untying the rope. Justice Bose entered the wooden box and lay down inside. Then the box was tied with a rope. The magic lay in untying the rope without touching it or the box. The magician this time was Justice Hidayatullah. His magic failed, despite repeated efforts. After some time Justice Bose started knocking as he was feeling suffocated. The theatre was full, and as per Justice Hidayatullah's witty narration, he had a dilemma before him. Should he save a dear friend or to save his reputation as a magician? The choice was really difficult, but he decided to save the life of a friend at the cost of permanent loss of his reputation as a magician! As a result, he never tried to show off his magic prowess thereafter.

While speaking about the Supreme Court, Shri Hidayatullah narrated his experience while sitting on a division bench with Justice J.C. Shah, a learned and quick judge from Mumbai. Justice Hidayatullah was against the practice of a thorough reading of the brief by judges at home, making up their mind and consequently disposing of the matter without hearing the lawyer. Justice Shah, on the other hand, always read the files thoroughly and denied lawyers time to argue. Despite his best efforts, Justice Hidayatullah could not persuade Justice Shah to change his ways and so, as the senior judge, he would deliberately feign ignorance about the matters showing that he had not even touched the brief. He would question whether the matter was a civil or a criminal one; would ask about the Act involved in the matter, etc. As he said, he was being deliberately mischievous, but Justice Shah could do nothing about his pranks!

Perhaps Justice Shah broached the subject with the Chief Justice because on one Sunday, the Chief Justice invited both of them for breakfast and after some time started talking about the awkwardness of display of open differences between two judges on the bench. Justice Hidayatullah responded that the Chief Justice himself was responsible for this. When the Chief Justice asked how, Shri Hidayatullah replied that the Chief Justice should apply his mind while constituting the benches. How could a cart move properly if a bullock and a racehorse were paired to pull it? To a query by the Chief Justice as to who was the bullock, Justice Hidayatullah replied that the Chief Justice knew the answer. He as well as the Chief Justice had a hearty laugh. Justice Shah just smiled. The net advantages were that they had a good breakfast in the Chief Justice's house and the Chief Justice never again committed the mistake of forming a bench with the two of them. Shri Hidayatullah wittily ended the anecdote by remarking, 'What a relief to both of us and to the administration of justice!'

Another story he narrated was about the habit some judges of the Bombay High Court had of repeatedly writing the names of the lawyers in a judgment while noting down their submissions. Once, one Mumbai lawyer was arguing an appeal against a judgment of the Bombay High Court, which Justice Hidayatullah was not inclined to admit. At the end and as a last resort the lawyer said he had a grievance about the absence of hearing by the High Court—to which Justice Hidayatullah remarked that the lawyer was not justified in making that statement since his name appeared at least eleven times in the ten-page impugned judgment! There was laughter in the courtroom and before the lawyer could say anything further, Justice Hidayatullah called the next matter.

From his conversation one could gather that Justice Hidayatullah was very fond of Urdu, in which he was well-versed. He had asked me to learn Urdu and in fact had written a letter to me to that effect, which I have fondly preserved. I tried to learn Urdu but was not successful.

## PRESIDENT RDG WOMEN'S COLLEGE

A great social worker of Akola, the late Smt Radha Devi Goenka, although herself not very educated, had established an institution that imparted education to girls from montessori to matriculation levels. In course of time, she also established a women's graduate college. I had the privilege of being chosen as the founder president of that women's college, which is one of the leading women's institutions of the area. It has grown enormously. The college celebrated its silver jubilee recently under my chairmanship. Our senior, Justice Chandrasheker Dharmadhikari, a scintillating Hindi and Marathi orator and a Gandhian, was guest of honour. It was greatly satisfying to visit that fully-grown institution after decades and to interact with the students and the faculty. Smt Radha Devi, who was more than 100 years old, also attended the function albeit with great difficulty.

## YOUNGEST PRESIDENT OF THE ROTARY CLUB

I was associated with several organizations in Akola and had the privilege of being invited as speaker or chief guest at several social functions in the town and surrounding places. One such club was the rotary club, into which I was inducted by the rotary governor of district 315, Shri Hasham Premji, father of Shri Azim Premji, the founder of WIPRO. In a formal chat with rotarians, he once asked what percentage of past rotary presidents made up membership of the club. Somewhat puzzled by this, I asked him the relevance of the question. With some pause, he informed me that it was one of the loose tests to assess how active that particular club would be! He explained that the general experience was that the higher the percentages of past presidents, the lower the efficiency of the club. This explanation was most unexpected! I had thought that a higher number of past presidents would make for experienced and efficient functioning of the club. I was not convinced by Shri Premji's hypothesis though I do believe it may be true for some, but not all clubs, depending largely on the nature of the past and present presidents and members involved.

I was elected club president in 1968-69 and had the privilege of being the youngest president of that club. The governor of rotary district 315 (which included Mumbai city within its fold), had appointed me as the Governor's Group Representative for the Rotary Clubs for the towns of Akola, Amravati, Khamgaon, Bhusawal and Jalgaon. As president I once attended a weekly meeting of the Rotary Club, Delhi, held at Hotel Imperial on Janpath Road. On that day, Union Minister Dr Chenna Reddy, Minister for Iron and Steel, the Chief Guest, was to deliver a talk on the iron and steel policy of the Government of India. I recollect that the secretary of the club, Shri Kapoor, introduced the chief guest in the following terms: 'MBBS by qualification, sugar grower by occupation and union minister for iron and steel, ladies and gentleman, I present to you, our guest speaker Hon'ble Dr Chenna Reddy'.

This anecdote relates to a discussion with Hon'ble Shri Justice Madhav Reddy who was Chief Justice of the Bombay High Court. Bombay High Court has three benches—Nagpur, Aurangabad and Panjim (in Goa). The Chief Justice fixes the place of postings of judges. There is a practice of rotating judges from one bench to the other for about two months. They are called visiting judges. Once during my rotation posting for two months in Mumbai, we were discussing the lack of qualifications for the posts to which our political leaders are appointed when I narrated the credentials of Dr Chenna Reddy. On hearing me, the Chief Justice started laughing heartily. I asked if he knew Dr Chenna Reddy and was thoroughly embarrassed when he said that Dr Reddy was, in fact, his brother-in-law! He nonetheless agreed that both Shri Kapoor and I were right.

My professional commitments were such that I found it difficult to make up the mandatory seventy-five per cent attendance required by Rotary and so tendered my resignation from the club although my family's association with the Rotary movement continues till this day.

## MY VISIT TO (THEN) USSR

From the time I was quite young, the United Soviet Socialist Republic (USSR) fascinated me. Its massive size, stretching from the Baltic and Black seas to the Pacific Ocean, which even the sun required about eleven hours to traverse; the 1917 revolution that Lenin had led against exploitation and orthodoxy; the unparalleled change in the mindset of the people, wrought in a single generation, all captured my imagination. I was a member of the Indo–Soviet Friendship Society and visited the USSR as part of its delegation in October 1971. Our itinerary included visits to the cities of St. Petersburg (Leningrad), Moscow, Tashkent and Samarkand.

St. Petersburg was a grand and beautiful city constructed as the new capital of the Russian Empire by Emperor Peter the Great. The city, located in the north-western part of the then USSR, was built on the banks of the Neva River, which flows into the Gulf of Finland. The city was renamed Leningrad in honour of Vladimar Ilyich Ulyanov, better known as Lenin, founder of the Russian Communist Party, leader of the Bolshevik Revolution and the first head of the Soviet State, who led the country from 1917 to 1924.

In Leningrad, we visited the fortress where Maxim Gorky was imprisoned. We also had a glimpse of the personality of Peter the Great with whom modern Russian history begins. A giant of a man in size and ability, he was nearly seven feet tall and was a shipbuilder, sailor, astronomer, bookmaker and strangely enough, even a dentist. One of his hobbies was to extract teeth! The city also gave us glimpses of Russian orthodoxy as seen, for example, in the segregation of marriage halls—there were some in which a second marriage could not be celebrated. The statues in Leningrad, as in other cities of the erstwhile USSR, are also worthy of comment. While there were many statues of Lenin, other political leaders were noticeably absent although those of artists and poets like Pushkin and symbols of national wealth—such as coal (called black gold), cotton (called white gold), wool (called soft gold) and tea (called green gold)—were seen in many places.

Most touching was the visit to the Piskariovskoye cemetery on the outskirts of Leningrad, the final resting place of nearly five lakh civil and military martyrs who lost their lives defending the city during World War II when the besieged city withstood German and Finnish forces for about 900 days from September 1941 to January 1944 after Nazi Germany invaded the Soviet Union. The population of Leningrad was mobilized to build anti-tank fortifications in support of the city by lakhs of army defenders. The city was surrounded and supply lines cut off by the enemy. The blockades and the siege claimed lakhs of civilian lives, as citizens died of starvation, diseases and the German artillery attacks. We saw hundreds of houses that still bore the marks of the artillery attacks. In January 1944, the enemy was driven out and the siege ended. The government awarded the Order of Lenin to the city and bestowed the title 'Hero city' as a tribute to its resilience in weathering one of the most gruelling sieges in world history. As we walked through the beautiful cemetery full of rose plants, Tanya our Russian guide, a smart and knowledgeable native of Leningrad, was emotional as she told us there was not a single family in the city that had not lost at least one member during that terrible time. Her own family was no exception. The cemetery housed a small museum in which several articles, photographs, letters, etc. spoke poignantly of the years of strife and struggle. How hopeless the people of Leningrad must have been in the face of the invading force's confidence and yet they determinedly kept their city safe. An exhibit we saw was an invitation card from a German commander for the celebration of the anticipated German victory in the hotel Astoria! The myriad emotions of that struggle were simply expressed in the bronze statue of a Russian mother that bore the inscription 'None of you is forgotten; nothing is forgotten'. It is worth mentioning that the statue bore no details or honorifics of the leader who unveiled the statue, a feature which, as an Indian, I expect to see on every statue, building, road, bridge, etc.! A telling statement of the social values that prevailed in the USSR at that time.

From Leningrad we went to Moscow, which continues as the capital of present-day Russia and lies in the valley of Moskva River, a tributary of the Volga. Moscow's heart is the fortified enclosure of the Kremlin (central fortress) in which government establishments are located. Along the wall of the Kremlin lies the Red Square, the ceremonial centre of the capital. Alongside the wall is the famous Lenin mausoleum where the embalmed body of Lenin dressed in a three-piece suit and necktie and looking as fresh as if he were alive lies in a glass box. We were very excited to see the mausoleum. Years later, when I had the opportunity to see the mausoleum of chairman Mao Tse-tung in Beijing, I unwittingly remarked on the superiority of the embalming of Lenin.

A great treat during our Moscow visit was witnessing a performance of the famous ballet 'Swan Lake' at the Bolshoi (Great) theatre, the central citadel of culture in Moscow and one of the most magnificent theatres in the world. Surprisingly, while returning to the hotel after the performance, we saw two or three persons begging for alms! This was unexpected in socialist USSR!

We saw a huge sports stadium in Moscow with arrangements for all sorts of games except cricket. When we asked about that, Tanya told us that developing countries like the USSR could not afford a luxurious and time-consuming game like cricket and in fact they wondered how a developing country like India could afford it.

It was apparent that the USSR gave priority to science and technology and hence had many achievements in that sphere. Its accuracy at forecasting weather, for instance, was impressive. We were keen to have a glimpse of the heavy snowfall the region was known for and asked our guide whether there was any chance of our witnessing it. She checked the weather forecast and informed us that there would be snowfall the following night at about 1.00 a.m. We were astounded at the accuracy when within minutes of the given time our wakeful group was mesmerised by the sight of falling snow! A lesson for India where forecasts are often dodgy.

Two newspapers were published in USSR, the main being *Pravda* (or Truce), three crore copies of which were printed and published from ten cities. The peculiar feature of the newspaper was that the front page was reserved for news and photographs relating to the production of crops, minerals or industrial products and for the people responsible for such contributions to the nation. Political news was relegated to the inner pages. We found news of the outbreak of the Indo-Pakistan war in a small column on page 15 or page 16 of the newspaper.

Religion was taboo in the Soviet Union and Karl Marx's famous phrase, 'religion is the opium of the people' was widely propagated. Hence, there was no rush of visitors at either churches or mosques, although religious feelings had not totally disappeared, especially amongst the older generation. Our local guides in Moscow and Samarkand admitted that their grandparents visited religious places and practised some rituals even at home. Although Christmas was not an official holiday, it was widely observed and we saw pictures of a Santa Claus-like figure who was described as 'Grandfather Frost'. The youth, however, had changed considerably, and appeared devoid of religion.

The State owned all housing and allotted flats based on the number of family members and the needs of the occupant and not on their status. The largest flats were four-bedded. It was therefore common for a manager and lower-level employee to live in the same apartment building.

Moscow had many huge modern hotels and we ourselves were staying in one of them, the Hotel Ukraine, a twenty-nine-storied facility with no room service! This huge hotel was managed by a woman—which was almost a rule across the Soviet Union.

Shoes were amongst the most costly consumer goods in USSR and I was advised to carry a few extra pairs to barter for goods that were cheaper there. I had taken two pairs of leather shoes for that purpose, but did not even dare to mention the possibility to anyone and so the shoes came back to India with me, after enjoying a tour of the USSR! In opposition to the cost of shoes was the cost of bread. Bread, whether bought in the restaurant or the market, was extremely cheap. Jam, a luxury item, on the other hand was very costly and the price of butter fell between the two.

Some Indian friends and embassy staff had told us that there was always a shortage of consumer goods in the markets of Moscow. Indian plantains and Wills Gold Flake cigarettes were very popular and we once saw a huge line in front of a departmental general store where those, and other consumer products, were available after a long time.

Despite the cold and despite the scarcity of products, the popularity of ice cream in all seasons was unparalleled. A popular anecdote doing the rounds at the time was that when Sir Winston

Churchill visited Moscow during the World War and saw a line of people shivering out in a blizzard in front of an ice cream shop, he remarked, 'Ah! These people never will be conquered!'

Medicines were cheap. Treatments in the hospitals, including operations, were free. The Soviets not only believed in the dictum that prevention of disease was better than cure, but also strictly acted upon it. Our delegation had an occasion to experience that when Shri Pujari, a co-traveller, developed diarrhoea after consuming some Indian fried snacks, which most of us had carried from home—having been forewarned about the absence of spicy food in Russia. Since we were to fly to Tashkent the next morning, we reported the indisposition to the hotel manager for medical assistance. Within half an hour two doctors arrived in an ambulance and took Shri Pujari to a hospital on the outskirts of Moscow city where he was put in a room in the isolation ward. No amount of pleading with the doctors had any effect. Neither was anyone allowed to meet him, nor was he allowed to keep his travel schedule. We were informed that he would be discharged only after five days and so the delegation had to visit Tashkent and Samarkand without Shri Pujari. Fortunately the day of his discharge coincided with our return to Moscow. When we went to the hospital to bring him back, we were denied entry but could see him through the glass wall of the air-conditioned room. On seeing us, he became emotional and had tears in his eyes because of the long and unjustified isolation in which he had been kept.

Naturally enough, Jawaharlal Nehru was the most popular and well-known Indian leader in USSR since he had played a great role, even pre-Independence, in building a bridge between the two countries. Another famous Indian in Russia was the late film actor and producer Raj Kapoor. Often in marketplaces people would approach us and say, 'Indis, Nehru, Raj Kapoor'. Raj Kapoor's famous film *Awara* and the song 'Mera juta hai Japani' (my shoe is Japanese) were very popular in USSR. Alexander, our guide in Moscow, told us that the film and song were so popular that Moscow had inspired many Muscovites to learn Hindi! As a result there was not only a Hindi school, but also a Tagore Club. When we visited the school we were surprised to find a portrait of Balraj Sahni, the famous film actor, and even more surprised to hear the schoolboys sing 'Saare jahaan se accha Hindustan hamara,' in Hindi. We also visited a Marathi school in Moscow where, despite our delegation being mainly Marathi, the headmaster confounded us by enquiring whether the scholar Datto Waman Poddar had finished his book on Shivaji Maharaj, of which none of us had any knowledge..

From Moscow we went to Tashkent, capital of Uzbekistan and the largest city in Central Asia. It was the centre of trade on ancient caravan routes to Europe and the Orient. Presently it is the main economic and cultural centre of Central Asia and also a centre for higher education and research, with several theatres, museums, parks and stadiums. We were therefore a bit surprised that our first sight on leaving the airport was of mule-drawn carriages.

The visit to Tashkent was very significant for us since it was in that city that our popular and dynamic prime minister Lal Bahadur Shastri had breathed his last. He entered into a ceasefire agreement on 10 January 1966, more than two weeks after the 1965 war between Pakistan and India. The agreement, mediated by Soviet Premier A. Kosygin, was quite controversial in India and is believed to have caused his death. The place where Lal Bahadur Shastri had breathed his last was not included in our itinerary, but at our insistence, we were permitted to visit it on our way back to the airport. It was a cottage-type construction inside a big grape garden. When we entered the gate, we noticed that the cottage was being cleaned.

Samarkand—one of the oldest cities of Central Asia—was our next stop. Once captured by Alexander the Great, it later became an important cultural and economic city of Central Asia as the capital of Timurlane's empire, though thereafter it declined and remained uninhabited for nearly half a century. It resumed importance only after becoming the provincial capital of the Russian empire, though only for a brief period. The old city has some of the finest monuments I have seen. We visited the big mosque, Timur's mausoleum and an impressive public square on the wide road situated on the old Indo-China trade route, named 'Lala Chowk' reportedly after some big Delhi merchant who had lived there.

We were booked to return to India on Air India flight: London–Paris–Moscow–Mumbai. We reached the Moscow airport some minutes before midnight, when our visa was to expire, and thereafter had a lengthy wait as our flight from Paris was scheduled for 3.00 a.m. We sat in the waiting room as the coffee shops only opened about two hours before the arrival of an aircraft. As we chatted with Tanya prior to departure, she lauded the achievements of the Soviets, such as the emphasis on equality, emancipation of women and above all the country's place as a world power. When we questioned her about the problems, such as the intermittent shortage of consumer goods and the restrictions in entry to certain public places, she defended it with the explanation that just as a sapling requires a tree guard to allow it to grow, USSR too needed some guard for protection and unhampered growth. She acknowledged the shortage of consumer goods but emphasized that the first priority was for USSR to grow strong and then bother about comforts and in that effort ensured that there was never a shortage of military or industrial products. She also added that no one had died of hunger in USSR nor did it suffer the ill-effects of the rampant inequality that prevailed in capitalist countries. Personally, I was in agreement with what she had to say. Before leaving, I presented her with a black metal necklace and Swastika pendant. She removed the pendant from the chain, returned it to me and kept the chain saying 'thank you'. I asked her why she had returned the pendant and she reluctantly told me it was because of the swastika's similarity to the hated Nazi symbol. She reminded me of what we had seen in Leningrad. Her eyes became moist as she told me that one of the victims of that siege had been her own brother, and the pendant refreshed the pain of his loss. Those were very touching moments.

As the coffee shops opened at their scheduled time, we had the luxury of coffee and queued to board the aircraft. Thus ended our memorable visit to USSR and, for me, my first foreign tour, which had also been my dream.

## SOVIET LEGAL SYSTEM: SOME PECULIAR FEATURES

Akola Municipal Council invited me to deliver a talk at the council hall on 29 October 1971, following my return from the USSR. I spoke on the 'Soviet Legal System: Some Peculiar Features'. Although the system must have undergone many changes by now, some features of that old system are worth adopting in the Indian legal system even today. For those interested, here is the text of the speech:

1.  What must be the legal system in a socialist country like USSR? This was the first question before me as I boarded the Air India plane as a member of the Indo-Soviet Cultural Society delegation. I only had a vague impression of the legal system there, and hence eagerly looked forward to expanding my knowledge and meeting Soviet brothers of my profession and other persons connected with the administration of law. A meeting was arranged by the Friendship Society at Tashkent with the judges and lawyers of the Uzbek Republic. We had also visited the Moscow Bar Association and had a session with the Presidium i.e., the working committee of the Bar

Association, which had a membership of over 950 practising lawyers. As is well known, the judges of the lowest rank of the judiciary i.e., the city peoples' courts, were elected by the citizens of the area over which the court had jurisdiction. Judges were elected for five years and every citizen who had attained the age of twenty-one years was entitled to vote in the election. The election took place by direct and secret ballot and any person who had attained the age of twenty-five years could be a candidate for the post. The candidate did not need to be either a lawyer or trained in law. There were, in fact, occasions when persons belonging to other vocations were elected to the post and on such occasions, they received training in law for a few months, after which the elected judges were expected to preside over the courts. The law required assessors to sit along with the judge during the trial. Assessors were elected in a general meeting of the Industrial and Official Workers and Peasants for a two-year period during which each assessor could sit in the court for about two weeks only. Assessors were elected and had equal status and powers as the judge. Two assessors sat with the judge and the judgement was pronounced according to a simple majority. The dissenting judgment though not published, was recorded. Hence, the two assessors could overrule a judge. Judges were supposed to report to the public about their performance every year and voters had the power to call back a judge if they were dissatisfied with that judge's performance.

2. The USSR comprised fifteen republics and the penal code, procedure code and some other laws varied in each republic, although some laws were common and the general system of administration of law was standardized across republics. Each republic had a Supreme Court, the judges of which were elected by the Supreme Soviet of each republic. We were informed that the monthly pay of the judge of the city

people's court was 200 roubles, whereas the pay of the judge of the Supreme Court of the republic was 250 roubles. This minor difference in pay between the person at the lowest and the highest rank of a profession was a peculiar feature not only of the legal system but also of other branches of life in the USSR. The Supreme Court had supervisory jurisdiction over all courts in the republic. The first appeal was to the District Court and the limitation for filing the appeal a mere seven days. Once the appeal was filed, there was an automatic stay of the impugned order and no grounds needed to be mentioned in the appeal memo. All that was required to move the higher court was the prayer that the judgment by the lower court was not in accordance with the law.

3. There was also a Supreme Court of the USSR and the chairman of the Supreme Court of each republic was an ex-officio member of the Supreme Court. The remaining judges were elected by the Supreme Soviet of the USSR. The sitting could take place even with two-third of the members of each bench. A unique feature of the Supreme Court of the USSR was its plenary sessions, which were held every three months. Participation of the Procurator General of the USSR was compulsory. The object of the plenary session was to assure uniformity of judicial practice. The Procurator Generals of every republic were invited to participate in the plenary sessions, and the propriety and legality of judgments of the Supreme Court of the republics or of the Supreme Court of the Union were freely discussed between judges, procurators and invitees.

4. The role of the prosecutor, called procurator in the USSR, was extremely significant in the Soviet legal system. Being the only officer of the court to have an identifying dress code made the procurator stand out in any court. The significance of their role was also seen in the fact that the procurator

served a seven-year term with a view to keep uniformity in law, had the right to intervene in any criminal or civil matters, including private disputes that were not connected with the State; had the power to stay the operation of the judgment passed by the court; could lodge a protest to the higher court against any judgment; and was duty-bound to bring any judgment he considered contrary to law to the notice of the judges in a plenary session. It was mandatory for all complaints to reach the procurator within twenty-four hours and he could move the court for review if convinced that any final or interim order passed by the court was not correct. However, the procurator's point of view was not binding on the court.

5. Soviet law was divided into three branches i.e., criminal, civil and military. The striking feature of criminal law was that if the judge was satisfied that the conduct of the accused in the interim between commission of the offence and the trial had improved, the judge had the power to release the accused as in these circumstances the accused was no longer a nuisance to society. The vice-president of the Moscow Bar Association told us that hooliganism was a common offence in the USSR. In addition, the city judge of Tashkent told us that the Uzbek Republic had no death penalty for first murder, though other republics did deliver the sentence through a firing squad. Undertrials were kept in jail while convicts were sent to labour camps, usually located in Siberia. Another forgiving feature of the Soviet system was that a first offender accused who admitted guilt could be released on the request of the collective working people by passing conditional judgment. This system was called public warranty and the judgment was conditional on the good behaviour of the accused in society. The penal code in USSR had been amended three times between 1922 and 1960.

6. The maximum court fee for any civil dispute was a meagre thirty roubles. Yet, there were very few cases pertaining to civil law and hence judges did not sit daily in the courts. Approximately forty per cent of all civil disputes related to divorce, although the divorce rate in USSR was much lower than in the USA. USSR law aimed to protect a marriage and family. Polygamy was prohibited. There were institutions called 'Palaces of Weddings' where only first marriages could be performed. Second marriages did not have social sanction and divorce could not be easily obtained, although it was possible on certain grounds such as not having children for a period of five years after the marriage. Disputes about custody and guardianship of children were also frequently seen in the civil courts. The concept of illegitimacy was foreign to the USSR, though I am not sure whether that was a reflection of their morals or their laws. The Civil Law allowed freedom of bequest and any person could deprive his legal heirs of inheritance, with the exception of minors and invalids who could not be deprived. Right to be maintained in old age, sickness and disability was one of the fundamental rights guaranteed under the Constitution of the USSR. The language of the court was the language of any of the republics of USSR as a result of which interpreters were permanent features in the working of the courts. When I asked a lawyer in Tashkent whether there were inter-republic disputes in the USSR, she appeared to be surprised at the thought.

7. Every factory had a representative body of the workers and the management called the Labour Disputes Commission. In case of a dispute between worker and management, the commission would adjudicate and if either party was aggrieved by the decision, it could move the people's court. Disputes between public bodies such as state farms and cooperative farms, enterprises and establishments were tried by the State

Arbitration Board, the members of which were appointed by the Union Supreme Soviet. There were also comrades' courts, which tried matters relating to minor labour indiscipline, failure to send children to school, maltreatment of parents, misbehaviour in public and other such matters. A comrades' court could sit at the spot and had the power to convict a person on the grounds of public nuisance. It was an open court in which any member of the public could be present and was entitled to ask questions and address the court on the substance of the case.

8.  The Bar was also different from the Bars in democratic countries. Every lawyer worked under a legal aid bureau, which was usually set up in every city and district. About forty-six per cent of the members of the Bar in USSR were women. The election of the presidium of every Bar association took place once in two years by secret ballot, and contrary to the cases of other vocations and professions, the legal profession was not State-controlled, though there were some restrictions and regulations governing it. Every legal aid bureau had a list of lawyers. Litigants who approached the bureau for representation would be allotted a lawyer, usually according to turn—although requests for a particular lawyer were given due consideration. Each Bar association fixed the limit of the fee, which was reserved for a common pool in a general meeting and which was subject to a maximum of thirty per cent fees. The Moscow Bar Association had fixed nineteen per cent as the limit for the common pool, of which five per cent was reserved for disabled and old members of the Bar. The balance was utilized for the library and maintenance of the Bar association. Income tax was payable monthly and was deducted directly by the legal aid bureau. Fees too were fixed by the legal aid bureau and there was no scope for bargaining. The fee for a criminal trial was generally twenty-five roubles,

though it could go up to fifty roubles for complicated cases if the head of the legal aid bureau permitted and the presidium of the Bar association recommended the increase. Additional fees at five to seven roubles per day could be charged for a trial exceeding three days. So, the spectrum of fees for a civil matter ranged between thirty to sixty roubles.

It would thus be seen that the Soviet legal system was quite unique and had several peculiar and good features.

## FRIENDS OF THE SOVIET UNION

The Soviet Union was a largely unknown territory for the average Indian until 1941 when Hitler attacked, though there was general sympathy and support based on the perception that the USSR stood staunchly against imperialism. The Soviet victory in World War II was greeted with great satisfaction in India, which also observed 2 July 1941 as an 'All-India day of Solidarity with Soviet Union', under the leadership of Rabindranath Tagore and Dr Bhupen Dutta (elder brother of Swami Vivekananda). The seed of friendship between India and the USSR was not sown by Prime Minister Nehru but by freedom fighter Nehru who, along with Smt. Sarojini Naidu, had formed an organization called 'Friends of Soviet Union' (FSU) in 1941. No wonder 1941 was often called 'the year of India's discovery of USSR'!

On 15 November 1981, I was invited to preside over the inauguration of a huge FSU regional convention at Nagpur. The convention was attended by its national president, Shri Nurul Hassan, and by Union Minister for Planning Shri Shankarrao Chavan, Member of Parliament (MP) Shri Vithalrao Gadgil, the famous Gandhian Smt. Nirmala Deshpande, along with a delegation from USSR comprising Shri Geroge Effiminco, Minister of Higher Studies Ukraine; Dr Shirko, Director of

Institute of Oriental Studies, Moscow; and Shri A.G. Kashrine, Counsel General of Soviet Union in India. I could not control the temptation of narrating my personal experience of USSR based on my 1971 tour. I therefore spoke of the drastic change in society that moved from extreme orthodoxy to a socialist mindset within a single generation—an accomplishment unparalleled in world history.

In fact, as one Russian author put it, 'no one can love or understand Russian people who do not love orthodoxy.' Chief of British Imperial Staff had expected Hitler's armies to go through the Soviet Union 'like a hot knife through butter'. However, the knife was neither sharp nor hot, nor did it cut through the butter. The heroic fight that the people of the Soviet Union fought against all odds, in particular in Leningrad, influenced the course of world history.

## 'GLASNOST' AND 'PERESTROIKA'

I was invited to participate in a seminar on 'Recent Legal Reforms in Russia' organized by the All India Peace Council and Solidarity Organisation, the Nagpur branch of the World Peace Council, on 25 June 1989.

Mikhail Gorbachev's rise in or about 1985 caused a sea change in USSR. His efforts to democratize the country's political system and decentralize its economy led to the downfall of communism and the break-up of the Soviet Union. He brought about technological modernization to increase workers' productivity. The policies of 'glasnost' (openness) and 'perestroika' (restructuring) that he introduced ended the Soviet Union's post-war domination of Eastern Europe and were significant in his being awarded the Noble Prize for Peace. I had not witnessed the changed USSR, but out of great interest in that country had read some literature about how Glasnost and Perestroika were practised in Russia after 1985. When I visited Russia the legend was that Stalin, with a view to impress upon his supporters his style of functioning, sent for a chicken, plucked the feathers down to its naked flesh and released the bird. Instead of running away from Stalin, the fear-crazed chicken clung to his feet. Stalin threw a handful of grain for the chicken to eat and the chicken thereafter followed him everywhere. Stalin said, 'This is the way to rule the people.'

There are reasons to believe that after the introduction of Gorbachevism, the above legend, which Soviets once used to compliment Stalin's charismatic toughness and wisdom, was retold to demonstrate his inhumanity and infamy.

The Soviet Union remained a world power for many years both before and after 1985. However, to my mind its uniqueness lay in the place women occupied in society. An old Russian proverb says, 'A woman's road lies from stove to threshold'. Women were not even allowed to weave golden thread because of the superstition that the thread would become black by a woman's touch. In the USSR we had seen iron platforms on to which unfaithful women used to be thrown from the top of a tower by way of punishment. Soon after the October Revolution, Soviet women acquired, and continued to acquire, a unique place in society, which even today women have not achieved in many other societies.

Critics of USSR would say, 'Soviet Russia will collapse, if it does collapse, of boredom.' The so-called boredom ended with glasnost and perestroika.

# III

# JUDGE, BOMBAY HIGH COURT

### OFFER OF JUDGESHIP OF BOMBAY HIGH COURT

In the beginning of 1979, during the tenure of Chief Justice B.N. Deshmukh, my name was proposed for judgeship of Bombay High Court. Justice Deshmukh had been on the Nagpur Bench of the Bombay High Court for about two to three years before 1979. The other long-serving judge on the Nagpur Bench was Justice V.G. Wagle. I appeared before them several times. In 1979, a full bench comprising Chief Justice Deshmukh and Justices Gadgil and Jamdar was constituted to hear a reference in the criminal matter of legality of a search warrant under Section 22 (B) of the Forward Contracts Regulation Act, 1952. I was the lead counsel in the matter and had represented the accused right from the trial court in Akola. The points involved were: (i) the validity of a warrant issued for search and seizure without complying with the provisions of Section 22 (B) of the Act; and (ii) the limitations that applied to the use of the property seized in violation of Section 22 (B) as evidence in trial. The exhaustive judgment of the full bench authored by Chief Justice Deshmukh is *State of Maharashtra Vs. Jayantilal Poptlal Chandrani, 1979 Criminal Law Journal 1216*. During tea break on the second day of hearing, the additional registrar informed me that Justice Deshmukh wished to see me at Circuit House, where he was staying that evening.

The meeting started with a pleasant exchange. Justice Deshmukh asked me about my family and background before telling me that a policy decision to consider even mofussil lawyers for judgeship of the Bombay High Court was under contemplation, and that it had the concurrence of the Chief Justice of India, Justice Y.V. Chandrachud. He said he had observed my professionalism and reliability on the many occasions I had appeared before him and there was a consensus amongst senior judges in Nagpur regarding my suitability for judgeship. He had therefore decided to invite me to join the bench! So saying, he put the consent form before me for signature. Imagine my surprise! What a dignified manner of conveying the honour, a courtesy that I am told is becoming rarer and rarer.

I thanked him sincerely and requested some time to consider and consult my family and well-wishers, since uprooting from Akola was not an easy decision to take. Chief Justice Deshmukh graciously granted the request but asked me to decide quickly. He affectionately said that he was also my well-wisher and would like to proffer some unsolicited advice. I was both embarrassed and touched by his attitude. He pointed out that I had reached the top rung of practice in Akola, was reasonably well-placed in life and had earned a good reputation. However, I could never reach a high level of recognition as a lawyer in the small business community of Akola. He added that the new position would improve my status in society in general and the community in particular. Moreover, I would have the privilege of being the first mofussil lawyer to be so elevated. The salary and perks too were sufficient to lead a normal middle-class life. When I brought up the subject of my son Anoop, who was soon to become a lawyer and join my office, he said the decision for him to be my junior was wrong because he would never grow while working in my office. He reminded me of the proverb, 'No small tree can grow under a big tree'. He added that as a judge I would have the satisfaction of being able to do what I thought was right, which is difficult as a lawyer. Additionally it is a public duty, which as per convention, a lawyer does not decline to perform when called upon to do so. Justice Deshmukh asked me to consider all these aspects and take my decision, but within a time frame of two weeks.

I thanked him and, while getting up, foolishly asked him whether I had a chance of becoming a Chief Justice. He replied that only God knew that but on that expectation, I should not accept the offer. He hastened to add that he himself had been a mofussil lawyer from district Ahmednagar who had joined the judiciary as a district judge with no expectation of reaching this level, but by the grace of God was now the Chief Justice.

I went to Akola as soon as I was free of my duties and broached the subject first with my wife Kamla and then with Anoop. Both opposed the idea of leaving Akola and were reluctant to unsettle our recently settled life. Narendra and Sanjay, my other two sons who were college students at the time, were excited by the proposal. So were my elder brother, father-in-law and many close friends, but opinions were divided. I became doubtful and confused since there were balancing factors for and against. My friend and well-wisher, Shri Narayandas Khandelwal, had told me that all vital decisions of life are only fifty per cent correct when they are taken and only the subsequent events and circumstances (over which a man has no control) decide their correctness. So, whenever he was divided on a major decision, he flipped a coin and decided on a heads or tails basis. I used that method for the first time, but I cannot say that it was the last time. I ultimately decided to give consent and informed the Chief Justice accordingly. He was very happy and asked me to come to Mumbai by the first available train.

I went to Mumbai, met Chief Justice Deshmukh at his official residence in Malabar Hill where he affectionately received me, took my signature on the consent form and told me not to ask any more questions. As I was leaving, he told me that the appointment may not take more than a month or two, and I should start preparing to leave Akola. My appointment was announced, along with two others, sometime in the first week of April 1979. Chief Justice Deshmukh was so kind and considerate that he fixed the oath ceremony in Mumbai on my birthday, 26 April, just three or four days before the commencement of the summer vacation. We were administered the oath of office in the chamber of senior-most judge, Justice D.P. Madon, without any fanfare. One of the reasons for the hurry to administer the oath before vacation was to enable recovery of arrears of fees, if any, from clients during the vacation. Thus, for the first time, a mofussil lawyer—who was not a member of any high court Bar association—was appointed as a judge of the Bombay High Court. Was it not a matter of 'time and chance' that at the time a policy decision was taken about the appointment of mofussil lawyers, the then Chief Justice was Justice B.N. Deshmukh, before whom I had been fortunate to appear several times when he was in Nagpur?

Several of my friends, acquaintances, old clients and office-bearers of various social organizations came to the railway platform to give me a send-off as I boarded the Howrah–Mumbai Express from Akola to Mumbai to take my oath as a judge. I was overwhelmed by the love and affection each one of them showered on me. The Bar association of Akola and other neighbouring places, Rotary Club and other organizations arranged functions to felicitate the first High Court Judge from our town. Press reported the proceedings of some of the send-offs. I received several messages of congratulations on the phone, through letters and telegrams.

I returned to Akola immediately after a day's sitting in Mumbai, since the preparations for Anoop's marriage to Surekha, daughter of Shri Kashinathji Toshniwal, which was to take place in Nasik on 1 June 1979, had to be made. After the wedding, a reception was held in Maheshwari Bhawan, Akola, a day prior to our departure for Nagpur where I was to resume my duty as a judge. I had tried to include in the guest list as many persons as was possible since this was both my son's wedding reception and my farewell party to the town. Despite my exhaustive guest list, several friends were inadvertently excluded but showed their warmth and magnanimity by nonetheless attending the function although they did not hesitate to tease me for my oversight. Delighted as I was at their presence, their number was large and the stock of food was fast depleting. My friends and relatives who were in charge of the function quickly made arrangements for sweets and snacks from the market and so averted an embarrassing situation.

As I made my journey to Nagpur, which was to be my headquarters, the Bar association of the neighbouring district Amravati felicitated me.

## ASSUMPTION OF OFFICE OF JUDGE

Based on my experience as a lawyer, I had resolved that as a judge I would not inflict capital punishment and would not dismiss a matter at the first hearing in which a junior lawyer appeared for the first time. I scrupulously followed these resolutions.

The court resumed functioning after the summer vacation in the first week of June. As per the roster, I was to hear constitutional matters with senior judge, Justice B.C. Gadgil, before whom I had been a regular practitioner in the Akola District Court. Within a few days, an occasion arose for me to differ with the senior judge on a point that involved my second resolve. One young lawyer appeared before us and it was clear that he had no case. I could see that he was extremely nervous and guessed that it was probably his first appearance in court. I indicated to the senior judge that we should issue notice before admission, but not grant a stay.

Not knowing why I was saying so, Justice Gadgil was reluctant to issue that order as the matter lacked merit, the truth of which I did not doubt. I told him the reasons for my inclination and insisted we issue notice before admission, although I did not tell him of my personal resolution at this time. Everyone was watching and the senior judge, disagreeing with my insistence, called the stenographer to dictate the order. I whispered my resolve in his ear. He was taken aback and as a senior tried to persuade me not to adopt this course as a practice, because it could be misused. Noticing my determination, he, in a fair manner, issued notice before admission without granting any stay and told me that he would discuss this matter with me in the recess to which I agreed. I thanked him for his goodness in yielding to the adamant stance of a junior judge. In the recess, we discussed this subject and agreed to disagree. Barring this solitary incident, there has never been an occasion for any difference of opinion between us.

After his retirement, Justice Gadgil settled down in his home city of Nashik. Our good relations continued unabated. When I joined the Bar after my retirement as Chief Justice of the Orissa High Court, he frequently sent me briefs and met me whenever he was in Delhi. I must record his open-mindedness and straightforwardness in admitting during that period that my point about which he had a difference of opinion with me was really right, since we also have a duty to encourage young practitioners wherever it is possible so as to build a strong and effective Bar.

On the family front, the shift to Nagpur in June 1979 had delayed Anoop's entry into the profession and so he and his wife stayed in the official bungalow in Civil Lines along with Kamla, our younger two sons and myself. But soon after, Anoop obtained Sanad from the Bar Council and he and his wife Surekha shifted to a rented flat not far from my official bungalow. Anoop and I had decided that this was the correct course of action, although it met with great resistance from Kamla. She gave me examples of some judges with whom their married progeny, practising law, continued to live. Although I could not agree to accommodate her desire, I understood the pangs of separation she felt, which only increased when Devansh, our first grandchild, was born.

## LONG AND TENSE JOURNEY FROM AD-HOC JUDGESHIP TO PERMANENCY

A High Court Judge is usually first appointed as ad-hoc judge and for each high court, the strength of the judges—ad-hoc as well as permanent—is officially determined from time to time. Most judges serve as ad-hoc judges for two years after which they are appointed as permanent judges, if there is a vacancy. My case appeared no different: I was appointed as ad-hoc Judge on 24 April 1979 for a period of two years and, since a vacancy for a permanent judge in the High Court existed, expected to be appointed as a permanent judge. However, on 30 March 1981 the Chief Justice of the Bombay High Court, Hon'ble Shri Justice V.S. Deshpande, forwarded to me and the other ad-hoc judges a copy of the union law minister's communication dated 18 March 1981 to chief ministers of states, with copies to the chief justices of various high courts. It pertained to the newly introduced policy regarding transfer of High Court Judges from one High Court to the other.

Under Article 222 of the Constitution of India, the posts of High Court Judges are transferable, but in practice this was rarely done. The Chief Justice had passed a telephonic message to me to sign the consent/undertaking asked for in a particular form quickly because the period of my appointment for two years was to expire within three weeks. I was also informed that signing that form was a condition precedent to confirmation in the post. I found some of the contents, the language used and threatening attitude displayed in the communication to be derogatory for the constitutional post that the High Court

Judges were invited to occupy. In fact, it was a direct threat to not consider the continuation of the appointment unless the form asked for (which was not at all necessary) was signed. I shared my reaction with the Hon'ble Chief Justice over the phone, who tried to convince me that it was a policy matter of the government that was being universally applied and therefore there should not be any hesitation to sign the undertaking without which (as communicated to him) the term of the judges would not be extended. I discussed the subject with my colleagues in Nagpur, but I found no one raising objections in the matter.

In consultation with my sons, I decided not only to refuse the consent sought in this manner but also to voice my protest against the communication dated 30 March 1981. I also doubted whether that communication had been sent with the concurrence of, or after consultation with the Chief Justice of India. I was sure if that had been the case, the approach would have been different. I subsequently made this enquiry of the Chief Justice and found my suspicion was justified—he had no idea of this arm-twisting letter.

## REFUSAL TO SIGN UNDERTAKING DEMANDED BY UNION MINISTER OF LAW AND JUSTICE FOR CONTINUATION AS JUDGE

I am reproducing below the full text of the relevant correspondence, including my refusal dated 3 April 1981 (A,B,C):

### A

30.03.1981

Chief Justice
High Court at Bombay

My Dear Justice Mohta

Enclosed please find a copy of the letter addressed by the Law Minister, Government of India, to the Chief Minister of

Maharashtra, and a copy to me. Kindly note and do the needful.

Encl.: One                                                    Yours
                                                      (V.S. Deshpande)

The Hon'ble
Shri Justice V.A. Mohta
High Court, Bombay,
Bench Nagpur

<u>**B**</u>

D.O. NO. 66/10/81-Jus

Minister of Law, Justice and Company Affairs India
New Delhi – 110 001

                                              Date: 18.03.1981

My Dear

It has repeatedly been suggested to Government over the
years by several bodies and forums including the States
Reorganisation Commission, the Law Commission and various
Bar Associations that to further national integration and to
combat narrow parochial tendencies bred by caste, kinship and
other local links and affiliations, one-third of the Judges of a
High Court should as far as possible be from outside the State
in which that High Court is situated. Somehow, no start could
be made in the past in this direction. The feeling is strong,
growing and justified that some effective steps should be taken
very early in this direction.

       In this context, I would request you to obtain from all the
Additional Judges working in the High Court of your State
their consent to be appointed as Permanent Judges in any other
High Court in the country. They could, in additional *(sic)*, be

requested to name three High Courts, in order of preference, to which they would prefer to be appointed as Permanent Judges; and obtain from persons who have already been or may in the future be proposed by you for initial appointment their consent to be appointed to any other High Court in the country along with a similar preference for three High Courts.

While obtaining the consent and the preference of the persons mentioned in paragraph 2., above, it may be made clear to them that the furnishing of the consent on the indication of a preference does not imply any commitment on the part of Government either in regard to their appointment or in regard to accommodation in accordance with the preferences given.

I would be grateful if action is initiated very early by you and the written consent and preference of all additional Judges as well as of persons recommended by you for initial appointment are sent to me within a fortnight of the receipt of this letter.

I am also sending a copy of this letter to the Chief Justice of your High Court.

With regards,

Yours sincerely,

Sd/.

(P. Shiv Shankar)

To,

Governor of Punjab
Chief Ministers (by name)
(except, North-Eastern States, Punjab and Haryana)

## C

JUSTICE V.A. MOHTA          48/1, Civil Lines,
Nagpur

Dated: 3$^{rd}$ April, 1981

Dear Chief,

I am in receipt of your letter dated 30 March, 1981 along with a copy of communication dated 18 March, 1981 addressed by the Union Law Minister to the Chief Ministers of States with copy to the Chief Justice.

It was a painful reading; not so much for the contents but more for the language used and the approach and attitude displayed. To say the least, it is not in consonance with the dignity of office of a High Court Judge and is suggestive of certain consequences.

Let me refer to the plain truth. I have been persuaded to accept Judgeship of Bombay High Court in the name of public duty. Despite initial hesitation, I have done so at the cost of monetary loss for which I am not sorry.

Having once accepted, I had no mind of re-thinking on the subject of continuation from my side. However, situation created by new developments in (sic) indefinite, one-sided and confusing. It is also not clear as to whether the dispatch is made after consultation with the Chief Justice of India.

I will be obliged, if I am enlightened on the subject.

Thanking you          Yours sincerely,
(V.A. MOHTA)

◆

## REPEATED UNUSUAL EXTENSIONS OF TERM AS AD-HOC JUDGE AND MIDNIGHT OATH AS PERMANENT JUDGE

We had discussed the possible consequences of not signing the consent form. It could result in going back to reside in the new bungalow in Akola and resuming practice there and at Nagpur as before. Chief Justice Deshpande had been very kind to me and out of love and affection had advised me not to isolate myself, especially when no one else had raised this objection. He even delayed sending my reply to New Delhi to give me time to reconsider. I remained undeterred, even though it meant walking a lonely path. I had expected a reply at least on the question of whether the communication was in concurrence with the Chief Justice of India.

Time was of the essence as my tenure as ad-hoc judge for two years was to expire on 23 April 1981. I was mentally prepared for the change, as I had not received any communication till 20 April 1981 when I received communication that my tenure as ad-hoc judge had been extended, albeit for only six months. A second extension, for the unusually short period of two weeks only, was granted just a week before expiry of the first extension. Surprisingly, the Chief Justice of the Bombay High Court received the order for my appointment as permanent judge just a day before the expiry of my term as judge. For that reason, the Chief Justice delegated his authority to administer the required oath to the senior judge at Nagpur, Justice B.C. Gadgil, and at midnight, the oath was administered in his chamber no. 1.

This was such an unusual and unprecedented occurrence that it made prominent news in the press. I must admit that my relief at the end of many months of uncertainty was palpable. A few days later, I received a phone call from the Supreme Court Judge, Hon'ble Justice V.D. Tulzapurkar, congratulating me for the appointment and also for being the only judge who had refused

to comply with the demand made in the union minister's letter
dated 18 March 1981.

## STUDENTS' RIGHTS TO INSPECTION, AND/OR REVALUATION OF ANSWER PAPERS AND, RE-EXAMINATION

After just a few sittings on the Nagpur Bench, I was posted to the
Mumbai Bench for two months in accordance with the rotation
system of moving judges from one bench to another. In addition to
the main bench at Mumbai, the Bombay High Court has benches
in Nagpur, Aurangabad and Goa. In Mumbai, I sat with senior
judge Justice V.S. Deshpande—a fine gentleman who retired as
the Chief Justice of the Bombay High Court. As per the roster,
writ petitions were assigned to our bench. A pertinent matter
that came before us related to students' right to inspection and/or
revaluation of the answer papers in the examinations conducted
under the Maharashtra Secondary and Higher Secondary Board
Regulations, 1977. Regulations 102 (2), 104 (1) & (3) framed under
the Maharashtra Secondary Board Education Act, 1965, only
permitted evaluation of answer books, which process according
to the board did not include either inspection of the answer papers
or their revaluation. Eminent lawyers appeared for the petitioner
students as well as respondent board. In one group of petitions
was claimed only the right of inspection as a part of the process
of evaluation. In the other group, further right of revaluation of
answer papers was also claimed.

The board took the stand that these prohibitions were valid in
law and were, in any case, a matter of policy of the executive, which
could not be interfered with by the courts, irrespective of the
magnitude of the apparent error/errors and its consequences on
the career of students. The principle objection raised on behalf of
the board was that the burden of giving the right of inspection and
revaluation would be unbearable and impractical for the board.

There were prolonged hearings and the judgment was reserved.

We judges had several meetings to discuss these matters and were united in the decision to allow petitions that only claimed right of inspection of answer papers. Differences in thinking arose about the further right of revaluation on the demonstrable grounds of 'apparent errors'. The senior judge had reservations about that relief. I was of the view that the right of inspection of the answer papers must be realistic and had to be carried to its logical end of revaluation where errors in evaluation of the papers 'were apparent on the face of record'. Although the senior judge was convinced about the increasing necessity of having such a right, he gave me some prudent advice. According to him, the view I supported did not have any precedent and perhaps, therefore, would not be sustained by the Supreme Court. My thinking was that we should not consider that possibility if we were convinced about the apparent injustice perpetrated because of denial of such a valuable right affecting the career of the young generation. The reasons why I felt so strongly about that right were as follows:

i.   Right of revaluation is an integral and inevitable part of right of inspection, specially relating to objective questions.

ii.  Under Regulation 102(2) the board has the power to amend the result if it is affected by error or another matter of any nature.

iii. No human being is infallible and an examiner is a human being.

iv.  There is no wrong without a remedy in law.

v.   The concept of 'apparent error' can apply to objective type of questions, where the answer can be either wholly correct or wholly wrong.

vi.  The result of examination makes/mars the future of the young generation.

vii. Examination is not merely going through a ritual, its essence lies in fair appraisal.

viii. Valuation of an answer paper is a public duty, and the failure to perform, or mistake in performing it, is an actionable civil wrong.

Realizing my strong views on the matter, the senior judge asked me to prepare a draft judgement which I prepared and sent him a copy. After some days we had a meeting in his official residence 'Sarang' in Mumbai. In his usual appreciative attitude towards young lawyers as well as junior judges, he praised the draft but made a last effort to discourage me from insisting on such a view mainly because of his gut feeling that it would not be sustained in the Supreme Court. Although I did not view this as an issue of prestige, I was unwilling to accept the situation of helplessness. He showed me the draft of his note, which he told me he would add to the judgment. The concurring judgment with his note upholding the right of revaluation was delivered just after delivery of the judgment of upholding the right of inspection. The case was *Miss Avadhani Meena Ramchandra Vs. Maharashtra State Board of Secondary and Higher Secondary Education, Pune, AIR 1981 Bombay 126.*

These judgments received immense publicity in the national press. *Free Press Journal* in Mumbai, *Nagpur Times* and *Lokmat* (Marathi) wrote commending editorials. It gave me great satisfaction to have done my duty and taken a stand in a matter that I considered just. I must, however, mention that as apprehended by the senior judge, the Supreme Court did set aside both judgements denying the right of inspection as well as right of revaluation to the student. The national daily *Loksatta* wrote an editorial on 21 July 1984, criticizing it under the headline 'Astonishing verdict of Supreme Court'. Of course, the correctness of any judgment cannot be judged by the comments of the press or public opinion, but it is heartening to see that the present trend of judicial and administrative approaches is more inclined in favour of the rights of students.

It may be mentioned that, though late, the Central Board of Secondary Education (CBSE) has now statutorily recognized the right by permitting revaluation of answer papers.

## MAINTAINABILITY OF WRIT PETITION TO CHALLENGE RESULT OF UNIVERSITY EXAMINATION ON DEMONSTRABLE GROUNDS OF MALAFIDES OF THE EXAMINER AND FOR HOLDING FRESH EXAMINATION

After a few years, I had occasion to deal with another unusual case pertaining to a student's right of: (i) quashing the result of the practical examination in physics in the Nagpur University examination on the ground of demonstrable malafides of the examiners; and (ii) re-examination.

This was the case: *Ku. Jyoti Lonkar Vs. Board of Secondary and Higher Secondary Certificate Examination, Nagpur Division, Nagpur, AIR 1988 Bom 176.* The judgment was considered so significant that its gist was published on the day of my retirement as Chief Justice of Orissa High Court after sixteen years of my judicial career, in the daily *The Hitavada*—a popular central Indian daily—on 1 May 1995, under the headline 'Court comes to student's aid' with the following note:

> (This piece is dedicated to Justice V.A. Mohta, who has ended his judicial career after sixteen years long judge-ship [sic] on 25 April 1995 at Cuttack in Odisha, when he retired as Chief Justice of the High Court there)" Delivering judgment in the case *Ku. Jyoti Lonkar Vs. Maharashtra Board of Secondary and Higher Secondary Certificate Examination, Nagpur,* on 25 June 1987 with Justice W.M. Sambre as his colleague Judge, Justice

Mohta, has decided an unusual matter, wherein an examinee had sought quashing of the result of her examination on account of motivated unfair assessment of her performance in a practical examination made by her teacher.

The factual backdrop of the case is that the petitioner, Miss Jyoti Lonkar was a regular student of Bharat Junior College of Science, Hinganghat in Wardha district in Standard XII in the academic session 1985–86. Her teacher K.D. Singh was the solitary lecturer in Physics in the college and invariably used to be appointed as an internal examiner for the XII Standard practical examination in that subject conducted by the respondent-Board.

Jyoti was a brilliant student. She wished to join the Medical College and for that marks in Physics, Chemistry and Biology are of vital importance. Singh was her Physics teacher and was conducting a private coaching class. Along with many students she had also joined Singh's coaching class, but as he was concentrating more on teaching Mathematics, she stopped attending the classes. Annoyed over this, Singh had directly warned Jyoti sometime between October–December 1985, saying that he would see as to how she was able to join the Medical College. After receipt of complaint from her father, even the Principal of the College was rebuffed by Singh.

**Irregularity:** On 22 February 1986, practical examination in Physics was held. Jyoti did very well and expected to score 20 out of 20 marks, as she had done in Chemistry and Biology. As it was not over the same day, the examination was continued the next day. Though obliged under the Instruction no 5 for conduct of the Practical Examinations, to seal the answer papers and hand over the same on that very day to the examination-in-charge (the Principal), the answer papers were neither sealed nor handed over. The next day, at about noon, at the house of Singh, he and the external examiner Dhage permitted some of the students of his [Singh's] coaching class to correct their answer papers. In their answer papers marks were allotted thereafter.

On this irregularity, being reported to the Principal by the petitioner-student, he reprimanded both Singh and Dhage for violating the Rules and Instructions issued by the Board. Jyoti's father lodged complaint with the Board on 24 February 1986 and requested for inquiry. He was asked to approach the court of law.

Through a communication on 2 July 1986, Singh demanded from her ₹700 towards her coaching for two years 'free of cost'. The record of Singh was bad. In 1981 he had insisted that the external examiner must allot full marks in practical examination to the students of his coaching class. As he had not obliged Singh, there was quarrel between the two. After inquiry, the Board had debarred Singh from acting as examiner for a period of four years, by way of punishment. Though Singh denied allegations against him, it was brought to the notice of the Court through an affidavit by one Jagdish Jhakotia, that Singh used to conduct private coaching classes at his residence after charging fee for the same. Jhakotia himself had joined the class from August 1985 to January 1986. Singh also used to assure full marks to the students of his coaching class.

**Duty to act freely:** In the background of the fact that while in Physics theory, Jyoti obtained 67 marks—more than anyone, in practical she was allotted only 7 out of 20 marks, that is second from the bottom—the Court observed that an examiner cannot be treated above law. It may be debatable as to whether he has a duty to act judicially in each of his activities, but it is not debatable that he has a duty to act fairly. It is not only implicit in the very nature of the functions of an examiner, but is incorporated in the very regulations under which the examinations are being conducted.

The Regulations 82, 102 and 104 deal directly or indirectly with the subject. Regulation 102(2) provides for amendment of result of the examination, if it is affected by: (i) error; (ii) malpractice; (iii) fraud; (iv) improper conduct; or, (v) other matter of whatsoever nature. The last wordings used in this Regulation indicate that the list is merely illustrative and not exhaustive. Even exercise of discretionary power is vitiated if it is actuated by motives other than those for which power is granted. Bad faith vitiates the discretion. The concept of bad faith eludes definition. Amongst unending examples can be malice, dishonesty, vengeance, manipulation, fraud etc. A power is exercised maliciously if its repository is motivated by personal animosity towards those who are directly affected by its exercise.

Looking to the serious nature of allegations against Singh, the Court points out that in case those are found correct, it is plain that result of Physics practical examination is vitiated. Though it is correct to contend that burden of proof heavily lies on the petitioner and normal remedy in such matters is it (sic) approach a civil court. The real point is: is it a case where the petitioner should be non-suited in the writ petition on the ground of existence of alternate remedy. On well-settled principles in such matters civil suit is not an alternate efficacious remedy.

At the same time, the Court is clear in its mind that the general story put up by Jyoti about Singh having hostile animus against her and result of her Physics practical examination having been adversely affected by the said animus cannot be dismissed as a myth. Though more direct evidence of malpractice is desirable, it is impossible to obtain it. In the circumstances, the finding of the Court is that Singh was conducting private coaching class for consideration and he deliberately awarded less marks to Jyoti.

It appears that the external examiner played passive role in the examination. He seemed to have left the matter to the best judgment of the internal examiner Singh. Even such passive attitude on the part of the eternal examiner cannot be justified. After recording the finding that the Physics practical examination of the petitioner was vitiated by bad faith the Court quashed the result of her examination and directed the Board (to) hold practical examination in the subject for her, afresh.

**Dark side:** Stressing upon the importance of the judgment, Justice Mohta had pointed out quite eloquently that this petitioner brings into focus a darker side of our examination system. Such examples breed contempt for the teacher in the tender mind, which is absolutely bad for the health of the society. Students cannot be blamed for the attitude. If they work hard continuously, many times at the cost of the other pleasures and leisure to which they are legitimately entitled in the early age, and are deliberately deprived of the legitimate fruits, they are either frustrated or they enter into unhealthy competition in manipulations. It is of essence, therefore, that those guilty examiners should not be let off, if and when their objectionable activities see the light. No examination system can be fully foolproof. But that is no reason to overlook the increasing unhealthy tendencies and commercialisation of the educational system. Holding private tuition classes by examiners is one subtle mode of commercialisation. Many times what goes on is nothing less than extortion. The Board has done well in prohibiting the same by Clause 76 of Regulations, but, in the practical world (it) is different. What is required is taking stern action against the erring examiners whenever irregularities by them are brought to the notice of the Board. The Court left the decisions regarding nature of 'appropriate action' suggested by it to the Board.

By way of punishment to the Physics Lecturer Singh, the

Court directed him to bear the costs incurred by the petitioner, college Principal and the Board in the case.

To complete the story about my consistent views about young students' valuable rights pertaining to their career, it must be mentioned that this judgment was promptly and properly complied with. In the impartial re-examination Ku. Jyoti Lonkar secured 99 per cent marks, as reported by the Nagpur University.

## MIDNIGHT JUSTICE IN WHITE PYJAMAS

As a judge, I had two midnight experiences—one related to taking oath as a permanent judge in Nagpur, and the other relating to a hearing of a writ petition as a vacation judge in Mumbai in the summer of 1982. I was and continue to be extremely fond of theatre—mainly Marathi and Gujarati. On returning to my official residence in the vacation judge's bungalow in Mumbai after watching a Marathi play one midnight, my peon told me that some firebrand lady advocate along with a few other lawyers had visited the bungalow at 10.00 p.m. and had frantically enquired about the possible time of my returning home. He told me that they were waiting on the street outside the compound. Within minutes, the team came inside and I noticed that the firebrand lady was none other than the young and promising advocate, Indira Jaising, who held the office of Additional Solicitor General for India from 2009 to 2012. She wanted an urgent matter about the demolition of hutments of thousands of workers to be taken up then and there since the matter could not wait till the next day—thousands of hutments were to be demolished and dwellers forcibly evicted by the Bombay Municipal Corporation[4] in the early morning. I granted an interim stay order after hearing the

---

[4]Now known as the Brihanmumbai Municipal Corporation or the Municipal Corporation of Greater Mumbai.

parties. The account of what transpired at that odd time was reported in the next day's edition of the *Daily* dated 17 May 1982 under the headline 'Justice at midnight in White Pyjamas' (article included in Appendices)

The petition was placed for further orders in court the next day, during the hearing of which the Municipal Commissioner Shri D.M. Sukhtankar fairly stated that the programme of the demolition of the hutments at D'Mello Road, Mumbai, would be kept in abeyance.

When Smt. Indira Jaising was awarded the Padma Shree in 2005, she and other eminent members of the Bar were felicitated by the Supreme Court Bar Association on their achievement. She referred to this episode in that function of bench and Bar in my presence. I was touched by that fond public reference, when all I had done was to perform what was clearly my duty as a judge under the circumstances.

## PRACTICE OF WORKING HALF-DAY ON SATURDAY, BUT COUNTING IT AS A FULL WORKING DAY

The Bombay High Court had a practice of judges sitting for half a day on Saturdays but counting the same as a full working day. This was a subject of discussion amongst lawyers at the Bar and also some judges even before I joined the bench in 1979. After becoming a judge, I discussed this subject with my colleagues but, very few considered it a serious matter. I thought of raising it at the usual full court meeting of judges on 2 May 1982. What transpired for nine years on that subject is an interesting story, which is best read in my last letter dated 9 December 1991 to the then Chief Justice:

My Dear Chief,

1. This pertains to the practice of Court working only for a

half day on working Saturday. By my letter dated 31 March, 1982 I had drawn the attention of the then Hon'ble Chief Justice to this matter, since I thought that the practice, to say the least, is improper. The subject was included in the agenda of the Chamber Meeting of all Judges dated 2 May 1982. By majority judgment it was decided not to disturb the practice.

2. By letter dated 11 October 1984, I had requested for reconsideration of the decision. The item was once again placed on the agenda of the Chamber Meeting dated 15 December 1984. This time it was decided that Saturdays should be full working days. In the Chamber Meeting of the following year the decision taken in the Chamber Meeting dated 15 December 1984 was reconsidered and by majority of seventeen against eleven it was decided to restore the old practice. I extract the copy of the said decision:

   a. It is decided that the calendar of the High Court should be so prepared that as far as possible there is no working Saturday and in any event there should not be more than five working Saturdays. By a majority of seventeen against eleven it was decided that on working Saturdays the Court hours would be from 11.00 a.m. to 2.00 p.m., in view of the difficulties expressed by the members of the Bar as pointed out by the various Bar Associations and the remarks made by them.

   b. Justice Mohta has expressed the view that working for half a day on working Saturdays which is counted as a full working day is not permissible. This view is recorded, as Justice Mohta insisted that his view should be recorded. Some other views were also expressed to the contrary. However, the same have not been recorded here.

   c. The decision to work for half a day on working Saturdays

to be implemented from 9 June 1986.

3. I strongly feel that the subject needs reconsideration. We cannot count half working day as full working day, in counting 210 working days.

4. Indeed existing conditions warrant that we voluntarily decide to increase the working hours as well as the working days.

May I request you to include this subject in the agenda of our ensuing Chamber Meeting.

Yours
(V.A. Mohta)

◆

Ultimately this practice was discontinued, but the point to be noted is how sometimes, even at the highest level, there is reluctance to admit the wrong and continue the same by making it a prestige point. I knew and even now know how hard judges work even at their residences. Avoidance of work was certainly not the reason for vacillating resolutions.

## A LOQUACIOUS JUDGE

I have always been a talkative person. Judicial functioning was no exception to that basic trait. Once, when I developed a throat pain while functioning as a judge in Nagpur, my son Dr Narendra took me to the ENT specialist who diagnosed the problem as laryngitis from which, according to the doctor, generally teachers and lawyers suffer since their job involves ceaseless talk. The specialist light-heartedly asked me how a judge, whose job is to listen, could suffer from such trouble? My son sarcastically told him that he would soon know the reason why. This led all sitting in the consultation room to have a hearty laugh.

Even on the bench I would talk and freely discuss issues with lawyers. Once in Mumbai, after a long day's hearing, a lawyer asked for an adjournment on the ground that there was trouble with his tongue. I not only granted that request but thanked the lawyer for seeking adjournment as my ears had also started aching! The courtroom resounded with laughter as the day closed on an amusing note that the press picked up and considered worthy of reporting in the next day's paper!

My brother judges would frequently tease me for my talkativeness. I recall that once while sitting with Justice R.A. Jahgirdar—one of the finest human beings I have come across—he impetuously seized a sheet of paper, wrote something and passed it on to me. It read,

'Vallabhdas, why silence today? R.A.J'

I could not control my laughter, keeping the lawyers sitting in the courtroom guessing about the contents of the note.

## MEMORABLE MEETING IN LONDON WITH RT. HON. LORD DENNING, MASTER OF THE ROLLS

In the summer of 1981, Kamla and I took a tour of England and Europe. I was very keen to meet Lord Denning, a well known forward-looking judge, whose short and pithy judgements were admired across the entire legal world. The Indian High Commission had arranged the interview. It was just after court hours at the high court. We entered his chambers to find him sipping a cup of hot water and were delighted when he asked whether I had received his message requesting me to accompany him to the Lawyer's Day programme being held at Lincolns' Inn, which was near the high court. Although we had not received the message since we had left our host Dr Kabra's house early for a day of sightseeing, we took this heaven-sent opportunity to spend some more time with him. This pleased Lord Denning and as we chatted, he enquired about my age and standing as a judge and also fondly remembered his visit to Nagpur some years prior, which had been organized by the well-known old and reputed publisher of law journals and books—All India Reporter Pvt. Ltd., Nagpur.

After some formal talk, I came to the question I was keen to ask him: 'How to write judgments like yours?' He countered my question by asking whether I knew that the House of Lords generally set aside his judgments. He sarcastically added that as an exception, one of his judgements had been recently confirmed but when he had rechecked the same, he discovered that it was incorrect. He then asked me what I liked about his judgments. I told him it was 'the short sentences, simple language and the style'. He replied that the habit was born out of practice, developed due to his belief in the need to do so, and he further told me that to achieve that result to his satisfaction he used to rewrite them several times. He further remarked that judges in India seemed to try to make their decisions as long as possible. As the interview was coming to a close, he asked me whether I would undertake the practice required for writing short judgments. What an embarrassing question! My truthful reply was that although I would love to do so, the solution was impractical considering the pressure of work. I added that sometimes judges did not get time even to correct typing mistakes. Although Lord Denning was aware of the heavy workload in India, the magnitude eluded him. In the course of the conversation he remarked that even in England the workload situation was becoming increasingly difficult and that in the previous year there had been a record number of about a hundred new cases in the court. When I told him that it would be equivalent to the number of new filings every week in one high court in India, Justice Denning was stunned and remarked, 'How can the system work?' setting the cup of hot water he was drinking on the table.

Apart from his extreme felicity in all aspects of the judicial process, another outstanding feature of this great man was his courtesy. Initially, when he invited us to the function on the lawns of Lincolns' Inn, Lord Denning gave us a note written on his letterhead for the gatekeeper to allow us entry. He planned to join us at the venue following a short detour to his home, which was very close to where we were. We were touched by his kindness in not only enabling our meeting with many members of the Bar and enjoying a live performance of a band but most of all, by his kind consideration in informing Kamla that he had specially arranged orange juice for her. Moreover, when we reached the gate of the venue, we found him standing nearby carrying his stick and in the same dress as earlier. I was surprised, but he said that on second thoughts he had abandoned the plan of going home and instead had come directly to the venue so as to be able to meet us at the gate, thereby avoiding any possible inconvenience to us at the function.

During the inevitable photo sessions that are part of such functions, I was very keen to have the privilege of being photographed with Lord Denning, but hesitated to monopolize him for the photograph. Perhaps anticipating my predicament, he himself called the photographer and asked for a photograph with us. The final evidence of his courtesy was seen when we received that photograph at our Nagpur address, soon after we reached there.

Lord Denning was my ideal, though I could never reach the high level of his command over English, scintillating style and striking simplicity. However, I always did try to follow Ernest Hemingway's advice that the old simple words are the best; Shakespeare's fiat that 'brevity is the soul of wit'; and Sir Bertrand Russell's advice that 'short story form is the best way to convey an idea'.

During our visit to London, the Indian High Commissioner

Dr Sayeed Mahmood invited us for tea to India House and broached the subject of the Union Law Ministry's policy about taking consent in writing from judges with relation to transfers. According to him, situations prevailing in some high courts demanded selective transfers, but when I talked about the objectionable contents of the letter, he kept silence. He asked me whether I had signed the form or not. When I told him about what I had written, he just smiled.

## CRIMINAL ACTION AGAINST ACHARYA VINOBA BHAVE

A public interest litigation (PIL) was filed against (1) Acharya Shri Vinoba Bhave, (2) the District Superintendent of Police of Wardha and (3) the State of Maharashtra, in the Nagpur Bench of the Bombay High Court. Shri Bhave had undertaken a fast unto death at Paunar (District Wardha) on the ground that his purpose of life was over. After some days his health deteriorated and there was a public outcry for State action to save his life, even if it entailed his being arrested for undertaking a fast unto death, since his action was tantamount to an attempt to commit suicide, punishable under Section 309 of the IPC. At that time, senior judge Justice S.P. Bharucha was a visiting judge from Mumbai to Nagpur and he and I together constituted a division bench for hearing writ petitions. As soon as I entered the chamber of the senior judge to take my seat on the dais, he opened discussion on this matter on which he wanted me to take the lead as this was a sensitive case from the Vidarbha area, with which I was more familiar. I suggested that we should not interfere in the writ jurisdiction in the matter, with which he agreed. The courtroom was full when the matter came up. One member of the Bar handed over a piece of paper to the court clerk on which was written, 'Vinobhaji has passed away a few minutes ago'. Learned counsel for the petitioner did not dispute the event, but he was not inclined to withdraw the petition on the grounds that the public interest was involved and the point should be adjudicated on merits. Without giving much scope for any arguments, the following order was passed: 'The subsequent event has rendered the petition infructuous.'

## SENIOR JUDGE AT NAGPUR BENCH

In course of time, I became the senior-most judge of the Nagpur Bench. I had the privilege of inaugurating courts at several places in eight districts of the Vidarbha area, over which the Nagpur Bench had territorial jurisdiction. These included the following—Shegaon, district Buldana; Tehlara, district Akola; district Gadchiroli; Pulgoan, district Wardha; Pusad, district Yevatmal; Sakoli and Gondia, district Bhandara; and Yevatmal. At Pulgoan, the court was inaugurated at a function chaired by Congress leader and former lieutenant governor of Himachal Pradesh, Smt Prabha Rao. The district judge of Wardha, Shri S.H .Nirkhi, read out a letter making a fond reference about me from the retired district judge, Shri Jamshed E. Sanjana, who was my senior colleague in Akola Bar.

On the demise of eminent judges such as Hon'ble Justices M. Hidayatullah and J.C. Shah, full court references were made in which I had paid tributes to those great judges. Press had reported those references. In connection with the reference relating to Justice Shah I had received a touching letter from senior advocate of Akola, Shri V.M. Rohankhedkar who had inducted me to the Rotary Club, Akola, even when I was a student in the LLB final class in Akola. It read as under:

16 January 1991

My Dear Vallabh Das,

Greetings, Good wishes and 'Hari Om'. I very much appreciate your speech the other day at the Full Court Reference [on]

Paying Tributes today [to] J.C. Shah—One of the distinguished Chief Justices of India.

I feel it is a tribute to a sandalwood tree—by a younger sandalwood tree.

Yours
Dada Rohan

◆

In 1987, the Bombay High Court celebrated its 125th anniversary at Mumbai as well as at all benches. I had the privilege of presiding over a full court reference in Nagpur on 14 August, the news item about which was reported in the daily *The Hitavada* dated 15 August 1987 with the headline 'A Judge asks for Judgment'.

## CHIEF JUSTICE P.D. DESAI: CONCILIATION COURTS

From the year 1991, the Bombay High Court had one of the finest and ablest Chief Justices, Justice P.D. Desai. Justice Desai's judicial career started from the Gujarat High Court as puisne[5] judge. He served as Chief Justice of Himachal Pradesh and later as Chief Justice of the Calcutta High Court before being transferred as Chief Justice of the Bombay High Court to tide over the situation arising from the unfortunate circumstances relating to the four sitting judges of the high court. Justice Desai was a strict disciplinarian, a dauntless and self-respecting person, renowned for his knowledge of civil law. Hidden in the iron frame was a heart full of love and compassion. He had established conciliation courts in the hilly areas of Himachal Pradesh, which were extremely successful and popular. Even common people in the area fondly remembered him and expressed indebtedness to

---

[5]Hon'ble Judges other than the Chief Justice of the high court.

him for the service rendered in simplifying and improving the judicial process in the state.

Justice Desai broached the subject of establishing conciliation courts in Maharashtra beginning from Nagpur area during his visit to the city. On 25 November 1994, conciliation courts were inaugurated in the District Court premises, Nagpur. They were also opened in various places like Wardha, Amravati and Akola. During our tour of those districts, I recollect asking him as to which lawyer had impressed him most during his stints in Gujarat, Himachal Pradesh, Kolkata and Mumbai. He named senior advocate Shri Dipankar Gupta of the Calcutta High Court. Since I rejoined the Supreme Court Bar in 1995, I have had the good fortune of knowing Shri Dipankar Gupta who was, at that time, occupying the position of Solicitor General for India. One day, when in the company of friends in Delhi, I could not check the temptation of conveying Justice Desai's opinion to him.

Justice Desai was held in high esteem by all. He was succeeded by another able and fine Chief Justice, Shri Justice M.K. Mukherjee, who was elevated to the Supreme Court in 1994 where I had the privilege of appearing before him when I resumed my legal practice after retirement from the judiciary in April 1995. The Supreme Court Bar was and continues to be unanimous that he was one of the best judges for criminal jurisdiction. On the eve of Justice Mukherjee's departure from Mumbai, a small get-together was arranged at the residence of a brother judge, Shri Justice Ashok Agarwal. Justice Mukherjee was a very social and friendly person who would freely mix and talk with judges. During the course of the meeting he asked me which of the chief justices I had worked with I considered best. In his witty style he prefaced the question with the warning, 'No cheating'. My instantaneous reply was 'P.D. Desai'. When I batted the question back to him, his spontaneous response was 'same'. What a magnanimous and open heart! We soon realized that

Justice P.D. Desai was also Chief Justice of the Calcutta High Court to which Justice M.K. Mukherjee belonged.

It is apparent that Chief Justice P.D. Desai had left his mark during his tenure as Chief Justice of the Calcutta High Court as an independent self-respecting judge and a strict administrator. In the matter of recommendations for appointment of judges of the Calcutta High Court, he selected individuals strictly on merit and in this he refused to be influenced by government recommendations and/or objections. During his tenure he had forwarded two names of eminent lawyers: (i) Smt. Ruma Pal; and (ii) Shri Tarun Chatterjee, who were later on elevated to the Supreme Court and who made their mark in the Supreme Court. In the warrant of their appointment, he found to his great surprise one more name of a person whom he had not recommended. His self-respect and concept of independence of the judiciary came in the way when he was expected to administer the oath to an individual whose name he had not recommended. But in the interest of the prestige of the judicial system, he found a respectable way out—he took leave on the day of the oath-taking ceremony and delegated his authority to administer the oath to the senior-most judge of the high court. To complete this story it may be mentioned that even the third judge was elevated as a Supreme Court Judge, and in course of time became Chief Justice of India.

A striking example of Justice Desai's strict administration was the stoppage of the long-standing practice of lawyers abstaining from work at court on the demise of a member of the Bar. The Calcutta High Court had a large number of Bar members and court work used to be frequently brought to a halt. The Calcutta High Court Bar threatened to go on strike but Justice Desai did not yield. The Bar went on strike, which continued for a pretty long period. During the period there were protests and demonstrations against Justice Desai, but he did not yield even at the cost of losing his popularity. Since he did not yield, ultimately some consensual formula was worked out to offer condolences to the departed souls—lawyers, judges and national leaders. Consequently the wastage of working hours ended.

I have fond personal and professional memories of the late Chief Justice P.D. Desai. He had great faith in me and always trusted me in all the matters relating to the Nagpur Bench, at which I was the senior judge. He used to consult me even in other matters. While in Ahmedabad, on our way to Dwarka (Gujarat) for a visit after my retirement from the judiciary, Justice Desai invited Kamla and me for lunch at his residence. On the menu was Gujarati dal, of which I have always been fond of. As Smt Desai had passed away, Justice Desai's adopted daughter was in charge of the household and she started pressing me to have another serving of dal, which I had already consumed to my heart's content. In the end, she softly whispered in my ear that Justice Desai had himself prepared the dal knowing that I was fond of it. I was astounded by both his kindness and his knowledge of my preference. Kamla told me that Smt. Desai knew about it and from there must have flowed Justice Desai's knowledge. This simple and affectionate gesture truly marked the warmth of his soul, which was usually masked by his outwardly dry and strict personality.

He was repeatedly offered Supreme Court Judgeship by one of India's finest chief justices—Chief Justice M.N. Venkatachaliah—which he declined for the reason that he had once been superseded. Examples of his great qualities—such as grace, magnanimity and self-respect—are becoming increasingly rare.

## EFFECTIVENESS OF LEGAL AID SCHEME, ETC.; UNUSUAL SETTLEMENT OF MARRIAGE DISPUTE BY ACTUAL DELIVERY OF GOAT

I was appointed as one of the members of the Committee for Implementing Legal Aid Scheme (CILAS), which was headed by the Chief Justice of India. I have always believed and continue to believe that Indian conditions demand settlement of disputes through lok adalats, mediation and conciliation, the last being the best mode. Hon'ble Shri Justice A.M. Ahmadi, who was greatly interested in this movement, inaugurated the first High Court Lok Adalat conducted at the Nagpur Bench. Lok adalats were held at several mofussil places in the Vidarbha region, and they were all grand successes. My experience has been that in the rural areas, lok adalats comprising local people are more successful than those comprising only lawyers. I vividly recollect lok adalats in a newly-formed court in Telhara district, Akola, where more than a dozen adalats were formed. Maximum settlements were reached in adalats comprising local people. An outstanding example that deserves mention is the lok adalat at taluqa Chikhli. It related to a matrimonial dispute between a young husband and wife from a remote rural area. The divorce was held up on the wife's demand that she be given some property for her maintenance. The husband was agreeable in principle, but he indicated that he had no property. The dialogue between the husband and wife was somewhat like this:

**Husband:** I don't mind, but I have no property whatsoever.

**Wife:** False.

**Husband:** Name the property

**Wife:** Female goat.

**Husband:** The goat died after you left the house.

At this point, a member of the lok adalat who belonged to the husband's village exclaimed that the husband's version was not correct, and that the goat was alive. The husband's silence indicated the truth of the lok adalat member's statement and he had no another alternative other than to agree to the divorce and put his thumb mark on the settlement deed. The girl's mother was thoughtful and practical and said her daughter would not sign the settlement until the goat was actually delivered into her possession. There was a stalemate. Everyone was helpless. I sat watching the proceedings along with the district judge. The mother's apprehension was not unfounded. Even if the settlement was signed, there was no guarantee of its execution. There could be a defence—true or false—about the death or disappearance of the female goat. The village was about ten to twelve kilometres from Chikhli. I made a suggestion to the district judge that we arrange for a jeep to take both parties to the village along with the member of the lok adalat who had exposed the husband's lie, and a court officer, and bring the female goat to the venue of the lok adalat after the lunch break. The husband tried to avoid doing this, but had no choice and so the girl's mother, her husband, the local lok adalat member and a court clerk went to the village and brought the female goat to the venue. The settlement was signed and the consent decree was also executed by delivery of a living goat.

## ROLE OF PRESS IN PUBLIC LIFE: MEETING WITH MARATHI POET 'KUSUMAGRAJ'

I am not a proponent of the belief that a judge should maintain complete aloofness from social life to ensure proper functioning. Of course social life can't be too frequent and/or non-selective. In fact, that should be so even when one is not a judge. Nevertheless, for obvious reasons a judge must be more careful and choosy about the social functions and/or activities attended. I kept that discipline in my mind. One such function was the Foundation Day celebration of the Nagpur Union of Working Journalists at which I was invited to deliver the presidential address. The subject was the 'Role of press in fighting erosion of public life'. Addressing this well-attended symposium were the elite of Nagpur—Shri Jal P. Gimi, vice chancellor of Nagpur University; Shri D.B. Ghumre, chief editor of the local daily, *Tarun Bharat*; Shri K.H. Deshpande, eminent senior lawyer from the high court bar; Shri Gev Awari, Member of Legislative Assembly (MLA). The subject maintains relevance even today.

The point I made during my address was that while exposing scandals in public life is a part of service to the community, the need of the hour is not only to expose the dark side of public life but also to highlight its brighter side, which is increasingly missing in the press. A striking though common example of this bias is a news item I recall reading in Mumbai—a policeman risked his life to catch a smuggler, rejecting the offer of a large bribe. This heroic act found mention on the last page of one daily newspaper, in a small column of about 2/3 inches while the front page of that newspaper was devoted to a murder committed by a rich industrialist.

By contrast, the Marathi daily *Deshdoot*, published from Nasik, honours ordinary persons who render exemplary service to society, borne of intuition and a sense of duty, with no expectation of any recognition or reward. A selection committee comprising well-known persons of the area, and who do not have any connection with *Deshdoot*, identifies the unknown heroes. This excellent idea was the brainchild of the famous and respected Marathi poet and Jnanpith awardee Shri Tatya Saheb Shirodkar, popularly known as Kusumagraj. As the chief guest at the annual function on 15 September 1988, I spoke on the 'Role of press and courts in the society'. This well-attended function at which I had the golden opportunity of meeting Kusumagraj ended past midnight.

In the wee hours of the morning, while I was still asleep in the circuit house, the chief editor, Shri Suresh Avdhoot, and some social workers woke me up. I was surprised to see this gathering, carrying a big bouquet at such an odd time but soon discovered the reason. Late at night, Press Trust of India (PTI) had flashed the news that poet Kusumagraj had been selected for the Jnanpith award in Marathi literature and the gathering desired that before Kusumagraj awoke and heard of the award through some other source, he should be woken up and felicitated at my hands. I was overjoyed on receiving the news and also having the God-sent privilege of being the first to break this news to him and offer a bouquet. We rushed to his bungalow where he was woken up to receive us. The news was conveyed and bouquet handed over, but his simplicity was such that he received the information and our heartfelt felicitation with his natural serenity. He just smiled and said, 'aabhar', which means 'thank you'. The honour of greeting him on that momentous occasion was and continues to be one of the most pleasant and satisfying moments of my life. In connection with the award function I had received a touching letter dated 4 October 1988 from Shri Deokishan Sarda—founder of *Deshdoot*.

## BUZO

Buzo, our Alsatian dog, was an integral member of our household in Nagpur. 'Alsatian' and 'German Shepherd', are names for the same breed. The former is linked to a place called Alsace in France, and German Shepherd, of course, is linked to Germany. 'German Shepherd' was widely used in America, where the breed was quite popular. However, during World War II, the British were reluctant to call their dogs 'German' and hence they preferred the name 'Alsatian'. After the War was over, the name was changed back to German Shepherd. Whether you call it Alsatian or German Shepherd, this breed of dog is an intelligent, loving and loyal companion.

Buzo entered our bungalow as a pup. As is the inherent nature of the breed, he was extremely sentimental and jealous.

So, when our grandchildren were born, Buzo felt neglected and became quite disturbed. He would show his indifference toward all of us, though when the children grew and started playing with him, he abandoned his melancholy and reverted to his loving nature. He was a beautiful and majestic creature and quite popular in the Civil Lines area of Nagpur where we lived at the time. On the rare occasions when I took Buzo with me for a walk, the children on the street identified me not as a judge but as the owner of Buzo. Everyone in our family, especially Kamla, was greatly attached to him. Around 1992, when I was transferred from Nagpur to Mumbai, my two sons who were still living with us in Nagpur had to vacate the bungalow and shift to rented premises where the accommodation of Buzo was difficult. Kamla and I took him to Mumbai. Buzo's health started going down, and he was suspected of suffering from diabetes. We never knew that even a dog could suffer from that most common human disease. In Mumbai there is a famous hospital for animals and birds where after examination and on medical advice he was admitted. He was also allotted a bed. Despite all possible treatments and care, his condition worsened and became pitiable. I personally contacted the head of the hospital, who advised me to put him to rest, since there was no chance of his revival. That harsh decision became inevitable. It was heartbreaking. We all remember him often even now, but I could never keep a dog after that, though even in Akola we had two smart country dogs.

At present, my two sons in Nagpur have dogs. Narendra's hospital has a labrador, Tuffy, and Sanjay has a beagle, Coffee. His daughter Pooja is not only a great dog lover but has extensive knowledge about animals, birds and nature. She treats Coffee almost like her sister.

## CHANGE OF HEADQUARTERS FROM NAGPUR TO MUMBAI: WARM SEND-OFF BY BAR

As I mentioned, we shifted from Nagpur to Mumbai in 1992. This was a result of Chief Justice P.D. Desai's keenness to make Mumbai my headquarters as soon as possible. The Nagpur High Court Bar Association gave me a very affectionate send-off on 15 December 1992, the account of which was widely reported in the press.

There is always an element of exaggeration in send-off speeches for which discount has to be given, but I was touched not only by some of the sentiments expressed in them by the prominent senior as well as upcoming junior members of the Bar but also by the record attendance at the function and the warmth of the send-off. The description of my being 'a born judge' would fall in the discounted category, but I was happy and satisfied to know that the Bar felt that its members received equal treatment in my court and that I was not influenced by the personalities or seniority of members of the Bar. Well-known senior lawyers are entitled to get and do get respect, but that is a different matter.

Juniors need encouragement in the larger public interest, including the administration of justice. Juniors are the future of the Bar, which every person connected with the justice delivery system is obliged not only to build, but also to enhance the prestige and effectiveness. Many able lawyers lag in their careers for lack of opportunities to display their abilities at the right time. This is truer of those who do not belong to established families of lawyers. I do believe that it is every judge's duty not to forget that at one point of time he also belonged to the category of struggling juniors. The feeling or the thought in the mind of some judges that encouraging juniors amounts to favouritism is short-sighted and wrong. Of course, a courtroom cannot be converted into a classroom for teaching law, but the issue revolves around the attitude that is publicly displayed and not the order passed. In any case, I had a principle that I followed without exception: any young lawyer appearing before my court for the first time would not lose the case at that stage at my hands. I confess that I was quite liberal in issuing notice before admission in such cases and was strict about the interim order. I have already referred to the first incident that took place in my first sitting as junior judge on the division bench in Nagpur.

I must mention that some of the High Court judges from Nagpur have been legends. I was a pigmy compared to those illustrious predecessors with whom I could not even dream of claiming equality. Nevertheless, I did and do claim equality with them in a desire to do justice.

## HUMOUR: ITS VARIETY AND IMPORTANCE IN LIFE

Humour is not funny. It is serious. It is a social lubricant. In fact, it is what may separate man from other creatures. In life, problems always exceed solutions. However, as famous author Mark Twain has said, 'against the assault of laughter, nothing can stand'. Mahatma Gandhi wrote 'If I had no sense of humour, I would long ago have committed suicide.'

'Laughter is the best medicine' is a popular column in one of the world's most widely circulated magazines, the *Readers Digest*. I have read that laughter has a curative potential even in sickness. In the USA there are institutions specializing in offering humour packages to help people get more 'smileage' out of their life even during sickness, since humour falls in the range of positive emotions, which have a substantial role to play in recovery. Humour is reported to be a good supplement to Vitamin C because it interrupts panic of sickness, though it is not a substitute for medical attention. Research shows that there is a link between a sense of humour and longevity. Realizing the importance of humour in human efficiency, some entrepreneurs have resorted to humour therapy to extract higher efficiency from human resources at all levels.

It is aptly said 'humour is the shortest distance between two people'. However, it has broadly two varieties, nourishing and toxic. The former variety brings people closer and invites them to engage in positive repartee, while the latter variety divides people by expressing contempt and ridicule. The higher form of humour is to laugh at your own self and the lower form is to laugh at others. Its worst form is to laugh at the miseries and misfortunes of others. Woe betides the mortal who misuses this virtue; two thousand years ago when Draupadi tossed her taunt to the hapless Duryodhan, the mother of all wars was born! History knows it very well as Mahabharat. Non-aggressive self-defence is also a variety of non-toxic humour, even though it may not necessarily be nourishing. George Bernard Shaw sent Winston Churchill two tickets to the first night of his new play with a note, 'Bring a friend if you have one.' Churchill wrote back, 'Cannot possibly attend first night, will attend second if there is one.'

*Churchill: The Power of Words*, which comprises extracts from Churchill's speeches, articles and books (Ed. Martin Gilbert; DeCapo Press, Boston, MA; 2012), gives many examples of the great man's wit and humour. Churchill never failed to use his sense of humour whether during World Wars I and II, or even at the time of his death. Once, in 1916, when commanding a battalion as lieutenant colonel, he called all officers of his battalion together and gave the following advice in the midst of clash of arms on the field:

i.   Don't be careless about yourselves—on the other hand not too careful.

ii.  Keep a special pair of boots to sleep in and only get them muddy in a real emergency.

iii. Use alcohol in moderation, but don't have a great parade of bottles in your dugouts.

iv. Live well but do not flaunt it.

v. Laugh a little, and teach your men to laugh—get good humour under fire—war is a game that is played with a smile.

vi. If you can't smile, grin.

vii. If you can't grin, keep out of the way till you can.

While administering the last rites the priest asked Churchill, as per ritual, whether he was ready to meet his Maker. Churchill's reply was, 'I am ready to meet my Maker. Whether my Maker is *prepared* for the great ordeal of *meeting me* is another matter.'

Although our jobs and roles in life have to be taken seriously, it is necessary to take ourselves lightly. This is most important in workplaces that, in the case of lawyers and judges, include courtrooms. Taking oneself lightly gives permission to be imperfect, which relieves inevitable stress, resulting in better and smoother performance of jobs and inter-personal relationships.

A sense of humour can diffuse even explosive situations. I read a story about an international conference relating to the Cuban missile crisis sometime in the early 1960s, where tension between delegates of different and opposing nations rose to a level where discussions were about to break, when a delegate with a sense of humour suggested the suspension of the discussion for some time and narration by delegates of their favourite stories. A Russian delegate told a story of a question and answer television session where a question was asked about the difference between capitalism and communism. The answer was that in capitalism 'man exploits man' and in communism it was just the other way round. This light touch broke the tension and the conference went on smoothly, though as expected, without a clear result.

It appears that even a dry and cruel person like Mao Tse-tung had a sense of humour. A delegation from the USSR had gone to China to meet Mao with a view to improving the souring relationship between two major communist world powers. At the end of the meeting Mao gave a curt reply to the effect that in view of the attitude displayed by the Soviet Premier Nikita Khrushchev, relations between the two countries could not improve for a hundred years. The leader of the Soviet delegation was a pleasant and persuasive negotiator, who impressed Mao. When he suggested that differences be forgotten in the interest of communism, which both countries espoused, Mao replied with a rare smile, 'Comrade, you are so sweet and persuasive that for your sake and because of your persuasion I will reduce the period by ten years.'

The positive power of humour is however best articulated in Mahatma Gandhi's response to the secret behind his self-control despite innumerable pressures, which was reported in the *Harijan* as being a 'sense of humour'.

Raising a toast, especially amongst friends, can be memorable if sprinkled with humour. At one time raising a toast was an art, which is now being forgotten. See the following classic examples, '*Champagne* to real friends and real *pain* to *sham* friends'; or, 'May we have more and more friends and need them less and less'.

Some examples of the sense of humour of famous people and their attitude towards humour deserve mention.

Chief Justice P.B. Gajendragadkar was appointed vice-chancellor of Bombay University[6] on the day after his retirement from the Supreme Court. Dr P.V. Cherian, then governor of Maharashtra and chancellor of the university, presided over the public function to honour his appointment, which was held in Bharatiya Vidya Bhawan, Mumbai. It was addressed, interalia, by Kulapati Shri K.M. Munshi. I was fortunate to be present in Mumbai that day

---

[6]Now known as the University of Mumbai.

and hence attended the function. Dr Cherian in his presidential speech remarked that it was a great honour for the university to have Chief Justice Gajendragadkar as its vice-chancellor, but he (Dr Cherian) had two objections to the appointment. One was the length of the name, Prahladacharya Balacharya Gajendragadkar, which would increase the budget for printing, and the second was the practical difficulty of not only being required to keep the appointment secret till the last minute before his retirement, but also of making the appointment on the very next day. He begged the Chief Justice's pardon for the inevitable lapse in fully complying with the condition. Kulapati K. Munshi referred to his recent appearance before the Constitution Bench of the Supreme Court (which comprised five judges), presided over by Chief Justice Gajendragadkar. As soon as he rose to address the court, questions were hurled at him by the judges one after the other, without giving him time to even answer. He finally told the judges, 'I feel like Draupadi before the five Pandavas; I would handle all of you, but please one at a time.' Chief Justice Gajendragadkar's reply was to the effect that he was happy to note that even at that old age, Kulapati Munshi had not lost the youthful spirit for which he was known.

The late Khuswant Singh too had a tremendous sense of humour mixed with frankness. I had the privilege of attending a function in his honour at FICCI auditorium in New Delhi where he was conferred the title 'Honest man of the year'. A purse of some lakhs of rupees was also given. The function was presided over by the then Union Minister Shri Jaswant Singh and was graced by the presence of several dignitaries including Shri Chandrababu Naidu, the then chief minister of Andhra Pradesh. Khuswant Singh's speech, full of humour, was somewhat like this:

> The award is for being an honest man of the year and therefore it is necessary for me to be honest today. It is the general

practice of donating the money received on such occasions for some public cause. I am not going to do that because the amount is too big to be parted with. On this occasion I must also disclose that I have one dirty habit and that is of picking up ball pens from the folders that are given to the delegates and guests at public functions. I have acquired the skill of doing that successfully without letting the persons sitting on either sides know about my theft. Today before coming to the dais I was sitting in the front row between Chandrababu Naidu and Jaswant Singh. They can check their folders. They will find the ball pens missing.

And he took out those two ball point pens from his pocket and showed them to the huge gathering. The audience burst into laughter.

Kaka Hathrasi was a famous Hindi poet known for his humorous verse. Among his several classic narrations, one related to his being a completely unworldly man who did not know how to bargain in the market. Once, while going to Varanasi for a conference, he asked his wife whether she wanted anything from there. His wife, 'Kaki', asked him to bring her a Banarasi sari. Knowing his impracticality, the wife had warned him that he should not purchase a sari without bargaining and the best way to bargain was to reduce the price to one-half of what the shopkeeper quoted and never to deviate from that broad formula. Kaka went to a famous sari shop and selected a sari. The bargain started as under.

**Kaka:** 'What's the price?'

**Shopkeeper:** ₹4000.

**Kaka:** I will pay ₹2000.

**Shop keeper:** All right make it ₹3000.

**Kaka:** I will pay ₹1500.

**Shop keeper:** All right pay ₹2000 you offered in the beginning.

**Kaka:** I will pay ₹1000.

**Shop keeper:** What is this Kaka, you are such a famous person. Take one sari as a gift from me. Suspecting foul play, Kaka replied, 'In that case you will have to give two'!

Kaka Hathrasi's mission had been to make people laugh. So sincere was this mission that he wanted to make people laugh even when he died. He had expressed a desire during his last illness that his dead body be carried for cremation on camel back. This desire was fulfilled by the relatives, albeit reluctantly, just to honour his wish. What an unusual attitude.

Sadly the humour and repartee that courtrooms were once famous for are fast disappearing. In my view that is one reason why there is an increasing trend of avoidable conflicts in courtrooms. I strongly believed not only in keeping the atmosphere in the courtroom free of avoidable tension to the extent possible, but also in keeping it lively. The ever-increasing and unending burden and pressure of dockets in the courts today leave little time for a human or humorous touch that, nonetheless, abound in and about court.

Some judges on the bench talk too much and some do not even open their mouths. There is a story that well demonstrates these extremes. A young boy expressed a desire to see the proceedings of a courtroom. His grandfather took the boy to a courtroom being presided over by a division bench. It was a rare accident that both the judges belonged to the category of silent listeners. For a long time the boy witnessed no movements from either judge as they just listened to the submissions of the lawyers. After some time a fly sat on the nose of one of the judges, upon which the Hon'ble Judge moved his hand. The young boy exclaimed loudly, 'Grandpa, one of them is alive!'

In another instance, one young lawyer asked for an adjournment before a judge. The judge asked the reason. The young man was hesitant to give the reason. The judge refused to grant the adjournment unless he was satisfied about the correctness of the reason. That shy young man hesitantly gave the reason. 'My lord, my wife is likely to conceive.' The judge looked at him and remarked, 'Young man, what you want to say is "deliver". But, no matter, adjournment is granted since in any event, your presence will be necessary.'

Some world-famous judges seriously believed in the necessity of humour in court, along with good administration. The great American judge, Earl Warren, belonged to this class. His good humour, good will and good sense did much to unify the court in spirit. If anyone wanted to quickly locate him at a gathering, he had only to look for a group of people and could almost be sure of Justice Warren being in the middle of it.

Even a dry person like Justice M.C. Setalvad disclosed his sense of humour in his memoirs. He had occasion to go to Rajkot to the court of judicial commissioner, who sat on the chair on a platform with two black dogs sitting within two feet of him on either side. Shri Setalvad writes that he was uneasy while arguing and does not remember what happened to that case.

Judges sitting with a pet dog by their side is not uncommon in judicial history. The banter between an Irish judge, who belonged to that category, and the famous barrister John Philpot Curran is well known. The judge missed no occasion to humiliate Curran, who perhaps was his competitor at the Bar. While Curran was arguing a point in full swing, the judge showed his indifference to the arguments by starting a dialogue with his dog. Curran stopped his argument and when the judge asked him to continue, he retorted by expressing regrets saying, 'I am sorry, My Lord, I thought your lordships were in consultation.' Curran usually came off the victor in these verbal duels. Once, while forcibly pressing a point of law, the judge remarked that if that was the law, he would have to burn his law books. Curran's reply was, 'why burn; better read them.'

Lawyers and judges with a sense of humour have been remembered longer than their more famous and successful contemporaries. An oft-quoted example has been that of Theobald Mathew, the longest serving director of public prosecutions, who had authorized the prosecution of D.H. Lawrence's controversial book *Lady Chatterley's Lover* on the ground of obscenity. Sir Patrick Hastings, a famous British barrister, politician and an Attorney General, wrote a touching tribute to Mathew:

> If from the many figures that I know so well there is one who stands out among them all, it was one who was known to few people outside his own profession, but loved by everyone in it; a man with a mind that saw humour in everything, and a heart that held sympathy for everyone. I can see him now, strolling through his beloved Temple, where he loved to saunter, perhaps arm-in-arm with a distinguished judge, commiserating with him upon the stupidity of the Junior Bar, or sympathising with a member of the self-same Bar upon the stupidity of Judges. No one was too highly placed to be safe from criticism, no one was too lowly for his friendship and encouragement; many a pompous Silk has been chastened and subdued by his caustic comments; many a quivering Junior has been uplifted by his kindly smile. He knew when sorrow was so real that it could be shared in silence; when troubles were so imaginary that they could best be laughed away. Perhaps Theo Mathew did not achieve the great success of others I could name, but then he did not want success; he was a glorious companion and will be remembered long after many of his more famous contemporaries are forgotten. To me he will remain forever as a living picture of all I have loved best at the Bar.

## ENQUIRY INTO ACCIDENT OF INDIAN AIRLINES AIRCRAFT AT AURANGABAD

Indian Airlines Boeing 737 VT-ECQ was flying a scheduled Delhi–Udaipur–Aurangabad–Mumbai flight when it met with an accident at Aurangabad airport during take-off. Fifty-five lives were lost and the aircraft was destroyed in the ensuing fire. The Government of India requested the then Chief Justice of the Bombay High Court to select and spare a judge of the Bombay High Court for the purpose of conducting an enquiry into the accident. Chief Justice Mukherjee took my consent and recommended my name. I was appointed to hold a Court of Enquiry with two assessors, Shri S.N. Gupta, Deputy Director Air Safety, Air India, Mumbai, and Captain V.B. Mahesh, Deputy Director (O.P.S) (Retired) Air India, Mumbai. The enquiry was an open one and was conducted in the historical Courtroom No. 1 of the Bombay High Court in which Lokmanya Tilak's famous trial for treason, which resulted in his being sentenced to imprisonment, had taken place.

After considering several reports, factual as well as technical, and oral evidence of witnesses, the Court of Enquiry submitted a report, dated 25 December 1993, making as many as twenty-five recommendations to the Government of India. It was a matter of great satisfaction for me and the assessors that not only were we able to submit the report within the prescribed time but were also able to refund more than half of the amount initially allocated for the expenses to conduct the enquiry. The Government of India accepted the report and its recommendations.

There is nothing so great about finishing an enquiry within time or refunding more than half of the amount allocated, but I mention this since I know it is a common belief that no report of any court, commission or enquiry has been submitted within the prescribed time. Recently, I came across a write-up under the caption 'No enquiry report in time' published in a famous monthly, giving some examples of delayed reports and emphasizing that the phenomenon is without exception. It is a tragedy of our public life that the media is becoming increasingly negative. I am sure there must have been several reports that were published in time, though their number may be less than those delayed. One of the exceptions to the negative reporting can be discerned, interalia, from the following paragraph in *The Indian Express* newspaper dated 28 August 1994 about this enquiry:

> The highlight of the inquiry was that the centre has accepted all twenty-five recommendations made by Mohta. It was completed before the scheduled date and the Commission spent ₹5 lakh against the Centre's budgetary provision of ₹12 lakh.

I was extremely happy about the public reactions to our report. One of them was by my then brother High Court Judge in Mumbai, Hon'ble Justice S.H. Kapadia (who retired as Chief Justice of India).

The report begins with the following introduction in Part I:

> This accident was unbelievable. Boeing 737 aircraft in its take-off phase hit a lorry laden with cotton bales moving on a perpendicular public road at a distance of 410 ft. from Aurangabad 09 runway end in the hot noon of 26 April 1993.
>
> The utter disbelief of a common man can be illustrated from the following spontaneous counter questions that the lorry owner asked the lorry driver when the latter telephonically reported the accident to him, 'Were you flying?'

During the course of the enquiry, it was found that the altitude and speed traces were not available on the flight data recorder file of the aircraft, as a result of which its profile during take-off from Aurangabad with values of speed, height, time, etc. could not be estimated. This estimation was possible only through simulation of aircraft performance with various deviations of loads and rotation techniques in a simulator that had the capacity to provide an accurate output. In this case, a simulator fitted with the engine type on the old aircraft (JT8D-9A) was required, which was available only with Boeing Company in Seattle, USA, the manufacturers of the aircraft. A study of the 'human factor' in the accident was also involved, for which expert advice from the Ames Research Centre of the National Aeronautics and Space Administration (NASA) Moffet Field, San Francisco, had to be obtained, as suggested on behalf of the Government of India. Assessors assisted us in the formulation of certain broad questions for these studies.

The Government of India arranged visits to Boeing Company in Seattle and the Ames Research Centre in San Francisco in mid-August, 1993 which proved to be a great learning experience for me. After analysing various aspects of the matter, including the results of simulation exercises and expert opinions, we reached the following conclusions:

C. 1 FINDINGS:

1. There was no defect either in the aircraft or in the engine performance.
2. There was no sabotage by explosives or otherwise.
3. The aircraft was overloaded. Its extent was about 1 ton. However, this over-loading as such did not contribute in degrading the performance of the aircraft.
4. There was P1's error in initiating delayed rotation[7] and in following wrong rotation techniques.
5. Weather condition did not affect the aircraft's performance.
6. Aurangabad airport and its surroundings were not

---

[7]'Rotation' is the term used to indicate the point at which the pilot (P1) 'pulls' the aircraft's nose up—this is done as soon as the aircraft attains a certain critical speed—and the aircraft proceeds to lift off the ground.

properly maintained. The NAA failed to perform its duty of regulating mobile traffic on the Beed road during aircraft's operation. The NAA also failed in not showing the unregulated traffic in the Obstacle Charts and also not issuing NOTAM about stoppage of practice of regulating traffic.

7. Aurangabad airport requires improvements. Those improvements include (i) extending the runway length preferably by additional 3000' (ii) making permanent arrangement for out [sic] regulating the traffic on the Beed road, and (iii) providing modern facilities at the airport considering Aurangabad's importance as an international tourist centre and developing industrial town.

8. By and large adequate post-accident actions were taken by the NAA and others.

C.2 CAUSE OF ACCIDENT:

Causes of the accident were (i) Pilot's error in initiating late rotation and following wrong rotation technique, and (ii) failure of the NAA to regulate the mobile traffic on the Beed road during the flight hours.

Before concluding the narration about this enquiry, I must mention a blunder that I unwittingly committed. After some discussions with about five different groups at Ames Research Centre dealing with specific factors of human behaviour in the flight with the aid of selected results of simulator exercises at Seattle, I asked one of their group leaders, a research psychologist, as to what according to her could be the possible reason for the accident. After a pause her hesitant reply was, 'For that, we all will be eagerly awaiting your report.'

What a dignified answer!

## CHAIRMANSHIP OF SELECTION COMMITTEE FOR POST OF VICE-CHANCELLOR OF NAGPUR UNIVERSITY

The Academic Council of the University of Nagpur had nominated me as its representative in the selection committee for appointment of the vice-chancellor under Section 10(1) of the Nagpur University Act. I headed the Committee, which included two reputed academicians from Maharashtra. The Act is aimed at making the university independent of governmental influence. The independent committee recommends names of three or four candidates to the chancellor (who is also the governor of Maharashtra) based on interviews and examination of their records. It is then the chancellor's prerogative to make the final selection.

After the exhaustive process of inviting applications through public notices, studying their works and record, and taking oral interviews, our selection committee unanimously recommended the names of four academicians. This exercise consumed a lot of energy and time. What transpired thereafter will be clear from the following correspondence between me and the Hon'ble Chancellor.

CONFIDENTIAL                                    Date: 27.10.1993

Dear Chancellor,

The Selection Committee, in its third meeting held on 26.10.1993 at Mumbai, has unanimously selected following four persons for appointment as Vice-Chancellor of the Nagpur University under Section 10(1) of the Nagpur University Act, 1974.

Shri Bedge G.R.
Shri Bhave S.V.
Shri Dr Choubey B.S.
Shri Dr Suryawanshi S.A.

Enclosed herewith is a copy of the Minutes of that meeting and Bio-datas [sic] of the above persons.

With warm regards,

Sincerely Yours,

Sd/-

(V.A. MOHTA)

Encl.: As above

To,

His Excellency Shri P.C. Alexander,

Governor of Maharashtra,

Raj Bhavan, Malbar Hill,

Bombay-35

◆

The reply soon followed.

Confidential        CS/NU/AUC-1/93/C/(1467)/3276

Governor of Maharashtra Raj Bhavan

Malabar Hill

Bombay-400 035

P. C. Alexander                                    20.12.1993

Dear Justice Mohta,

Thank you very much for your letter of 27th October 1993 forwarding therewith the names recommended by the Selection Committee for the post of Vice-Chancellor, Nagpur University. I have interviewed them but for various reasons I am not able to approve any one of the persons recommended by the Committee. I would therefore request you to hold a meeting of the Selection Committee again and give me a fresh panel of names early. I know that I am giving you a little more trouble but I do hope you will understand.

With regards,

Yours sincerely,
Sd/-
(P. C. Alexander)

Shri Justice V. A. Mohta,
Judge,
High Court,
Bombay-400 032

◆

This letter was followed by a telephonic message from Raj Bhawan (not from Raj Pramukh) that the matter was urgent and hence a fresh selection should be made without loss of any time. I duly replied to the letter.

December 21, 1993

Dear Chancellor,

I have received your letter of 20th December, 1993 acknowledging my letter of 27th October, 1993 (forwarding therewith the names recommended by the Selection Committee for the post of Vice-Chancellor, Nagpur University) followed by a telephonic message from your office requesting for giving a fresh panel of names and that too early, as the matter was urgent.

I presume, there must have been very compelling reasons for calling a fresh panel of names. But for my personal reasons, it will not be possible for me to undertake this onerous exercise over again.

*Aidandas Mohta (Father of the author).*

*Hiradevi Mohta (Mother of the author).*

*Dana Bazaar House, where the author was born.*

*In deep discussion.*

*Inaugration ceremony of a library: With Justice C.S Dharmadhikari.*

*Jaisalmer Maheshwari Mahasabha: As Chief Guest along with
Maharaja of Jaisalmer.*

*Judges farewell to the author before his departure to Orissa as Chief Justice: With Justice S.H. Kapadia (Former Chief Justice of India), Justice B.P. Saraf, Justice A.P. Shah and others.*

*With Former Chief Justice C.S. Mookherjee.*

*With Lord Denning, former British Judge.*

*Swearing-in as the Chief Justice of Orissa High Court.*

*Unusual gathering of all sitting judges of Orissa High Court, on Holi, at the residence of the author, then serving as the Chief Justice.*

*A rare tribute: Author being felicitated, without there being any such convention, by the then Governor of Orissa, before his retirement as the Chief Justice.*

*Book release ceremony: Anoop Mohta, F.S. Nariman,*
*P. Chidambaram with author.*

*Book release ceremony: With S.C. Chitale (AIR),*
*Arun Jaitley and Justice Arijit Pasayat.*

*At the 1998 SAARC Conference, along with Ram Jethmalani.*

*On the Great Wall of China with wife, Kamala.*

*Celebrating 50 years of togetherness.*

*Celebrating 75th birthday.*

*Celebrating with his peers.*

*The happy couple.*

*The family in the 1990s.*

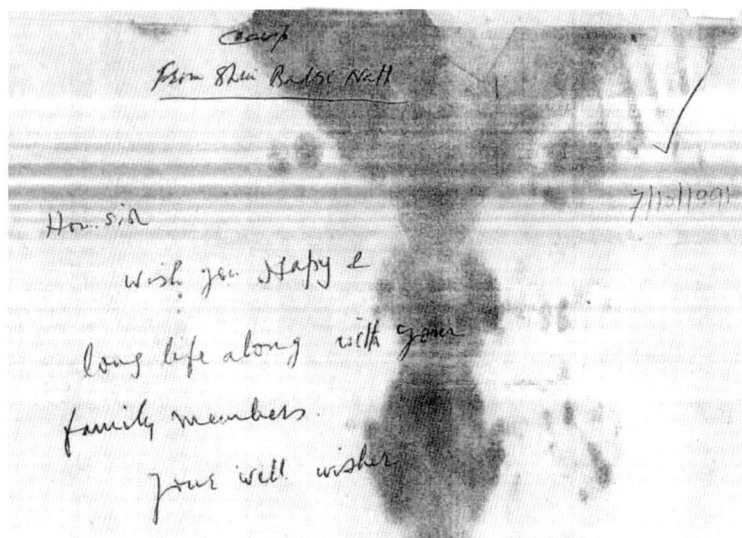

*Letter from an unknown well-wisher, 7.10.1991.*

ब्रजलाल बियाणी
अकोला. (विदर्भ)

फोन ५१६६
५१/५२ जावरा कम्पाउण्ड,
इन्दौर (मध्य-प्रदेश)
ता-३१-१०-६५

प्रिय वल्लभदास

सविनय वन्दे

मैं आपसे मिला । हमेशा के अनुसार कुछ बातें भी हुई और मेने मार्ह आइंदानजी और मेरे संबंधों को लेकर लेख लिखने की आपसे प्रार्थना की । मेरी प्रार्थना के अनुसार अनेक कामों और बाहर बाहर जाना होते हुए भी आपने समय निकालकर लेख लिखा, अत: मुफे खूब प्रसन्नता हुई ।

आपने जो लेख लिखा, उसका मैंने अवलोकन किया । लेख अति उत्तम हैं यह लिख दूं तो गैरवाजिब नहीं होगा । फिर एक दिन में आपने यह लिख दिया, वह तो अधिक सराहनीय हे ।

आप कहते थे कि आप लिख नहीं सकते । लेखन की आदत नहीं, अत: संकोच था पर आपके लेख को देखकर मैं यह कह सकता हूं कि आपमें लेखन कला की अज्ञात शक्ति है । कभी कभी हमारी शक्तियों का हमको पता नहीं रहता और वो शक्तियाँ बिना उपयोग के नष्ट हो जाती है । मे यह कहूं तो अनावश्यक नहीं है कि आप में शक्ति तो विषमान है उसका उपयोग और वृद्धि आपके हाथ में है । अत: लेखन कला का कुछ व्यासंग अवश्य करने की और ध्यान दें ।

मैरी स्थायी सूचना और आग्रह है कि आपको यथाशिघ्र नागपुर में जाकर काम आरंभ करना चाहिए, अवश्य ध्यान दें ।

आपके सब काम व्यवस्थित चलते होंगे । सब कुटुंबियों से मेरा यथायोग्य कहें । पत्र दें । प्रसन्न रहें ।

श्री —— रासजी

आपका नम्र
*[signature]*
(ब्रजलाल बियाणी)

---

*Letter dated 31.10.1965 from Shri Brajlal Biyani, whom the author credits for making him realize the potential of being a writer.*

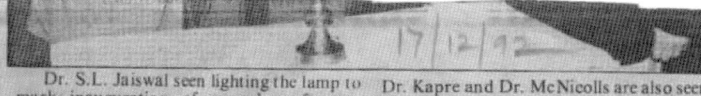

Dr. S.L. Jaiswal seen lighting the lamp to mark inauguration of annual conference. From left Dr. B.K. Sharma, Dr. S.R. Pande, Dr. Kapre and Dr. McNicolls are also seen in the picture.

## FROM THE COURTS

# HC Bar bids farewell to Justice Mohta

[Legal Correspondent]

NAGPUR, Dec. 16:-

Unlike similar other occasions in the past, which were too formal for one's comfort, on this occasion today (Wednesday), admiration and gratitude expressed were mutual, right from the hearts and genuine in nature. The occasion was a function organised by the High Court Bar Association here to bid farewell to Justice V.A. Mohta, who will now onwards be sitting at the High Court's principal seat at Bombay.

After complimenting the Nagpur Bar on it being equal to the best Bar anywhere else, Justice Mohta took this opportunity to remind the lawyers that it would be better if the Bar's unity was not used frequently for utilising the last working day before the week-ends (Friday) for abstaining from the court-work, as despite all the differences and controversies, 'the show must go on'.

Perhaps the biggest achievement of Justice Mohta during his more than 13 years long tenure in the city, is the instant personal rapport he is able to strike with anybody and everybody, whoever comes into contact with him. His good nature and his capacity to laugh at himself has generated immense

goodwill for him. He succeeded to keep court-room lively, in spite of drab and dull nature of legal proceedings. His firmness in handling so called high and mighty lawyers, unswayed by their reputation on paper, as is the case with our batting in South Africa, can be believed, only after seeing it. He has done so with extreme fineness and without offending them in the least.

In the absence of the President R.V. Patil, the two Vice Presidents Adv R.G. Deshpande and Adv. M.N. Ingle conducted the meeting. The judge was presented bouquet and a memento on behalf of the Bar.

## New H.C. roster from Jan. 4

[Legal Correspondent]

NAGPUR, Dec. 16:-

After winter vacations, from January 4 onwards, the division bench for writ matters, at the High Court here, will consist of Justice H.W. Dhabe and Justice Gulabrao Patil. This will be the first roster with Justice Dhabe as Senior Judge. For first appeals and letter patent appeals, the division bench will comprise Justice H.D. Patel and Justice M.B. Ghodeswar. Justice Ashok Desai and Justice B.U. Wahane will be incharge of division bench for criminal cases.

The single judge jurisdictions will be with

## Hike in medical

*Press Report about Bars Farewell at Nagpur, 17.12.1992.*
*(Newspaper: Hitavada).*

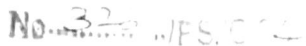

RAJ BHAVAN
MALABAR HILL,
BOMBAY 400 035

16 September 1994

P. C. ALEXANDER

Dear Shri Justice Mohta,

I was happy to know about your appointment as the Chief Justice of Orissa High Court. Kindly accept my heartiest congratulations and good wishes.

With kind regards,

Yours sincerely,

*Aroamund*

(P.C.Alexander)

Shri Justice V.A.Mohta
Judge, High Court Bombay
BOMBAY

JUSTICE V.S. SIRPURKAR

Dated:17.09.1994

Dear Bade Bhaiyya,

The news of your elevation as a Chief Justice of
Orissa High Court was a welcome and pleasant change in
the otherwise dreary and routine life of Nagpur. The
news was being awaited by all of us impatiently, with lot
of speculations going on as to the State which you would
eventually be heading. Please accept my bountiful of
congratulations.

Starting at a district place and reaching to the
dizzy heights of heading a State Judiciary is no small
feat; but you are known for the strength in your wings
to fly at the great heights. This long career of yours
has had many glittering facets, such as your sparkling
career as a lawyer, your whole-hearted contribution to the
public life of Akola, your brilliant participation and
constructive role played as a Member and Vice Chairman
of the Maharashtra Bar Council and finally your consummate
and long innings played at Nagpur for twelve years as a
Judge. You have undoubtedly set up a goal for we Junior
Judges. Your affable nature, deep insight in law and
ability to simplify the problems, legal or otherwise, are
awe inspiring. I am certain, this is not the last stop
in your illustrious career. I wish you well, and Kumkum and
other family members join me in these expressions. We all
pray   Almighty to give you more strength to reach to the
still higher goals in life.


Yours sincerely,

*Ballu*

(V.S.SIRPURKAR)

To
The Honourable Shri Justice V.A.Mohta
(Honouable the Chief Justice Designate),
High Court of Bombay,
BOMBAY.

"nirant" juhu tara road bombay 400049

14.9.1994

My dear Judge,

The news that has now been confirmed leaves me personally sad as it is unlikely that I will again have an opportunity to appear before a Judge before whom it was both a pleasure and a challenge to appear. A pleasure because you were always courteous and pleasant; a challenge because unless one was well-prepared it could be awkward, to say the least. All of us will be very sorry to lose an outstanding Judge and it is poor consolation to the Bombay Bar that the people and advocates in far-off Orissa will immeasurably gain!

May I end this with my congratulations, — best wishes for the future and, personally, thanks, for the kindness and courtesy you have always shown.

Yrs

Atul Setalvad

*Letter from Late Shri Atul Setalvad, Senior Advocate and son of Late Shri Motilal Setalvad, First Attorney General of Independent India.*

# Ashok H. Desai

B.Sc. (Econ.), LL.B., Barrister, Senior Advocate

8, Golf Links (1st Floor), Lodhi Road, New Delhi-110 003. Tel. : 462 0948

14, Ram Mahal, J. Tata Road, Bombay 400 020. Tel. : 222346 ● 2048181

September 19, 1994.

Dear Chief

    I am delighted to read about your transition to the Orissa High Court. I had hoped that you might be moving in this direction. But perhaps more of that later on.

    I am sure you are going to enjoy presiding over the High Court and the experience of living in Orissa. I fondly recall our association of more than 30 years ago in the Laxmi Bank case at Akola as also the pleasure of arguing before you lately in Bombay.

With warm regards,

Yours sincerely

Hon. Mr. Justice V. A. Mohta,
Chief Justice,
High Court of Orissa,
Cuttack.

*Letter from Shri Ashok Desai,*
*Senior Advocate and Former Attorney General of India.*

JUSTICE D.R.DHANUKA  22nd September 1994.

PERSONAL

Dear brother Mohta,

We are all rejoiced over your appointment
as the Chief Justice of the State of Orissa.
The President of India has honoured not merely
you but all of us by making a suitable appointment
to the highest judicial office in the State
Judiciary. We have known each other for several
decades. I wish and pray that you are further elevated
in the Apex Court.

If the future historians write history of
this High Court concerning the performance of
Judges during last two decades, your name is
bound to be included in such history as one of
the few best judges of our High Court during this
period.

I am given to understand that you shall be
in Bombay after 8th October 1994. Please be
kind enough to accept our invitation for a
dinner function at my residence.

With personal regards,

Yours sincerely,

( D.R. Dhanuka )

Hon'ble Mr. Justice
V. A. Mohta
High Court, Bombay.

# A Judge asks for ju[d]ger

**[Legal Correspondent]**

NAGPUR, Aug. 14: — While presiding over a full-Court reference to mark the 125th anniversary of the founding of the Bombay High Court, the senior Judge here, Mr. Justice V.A. Mohta proffered a test. It consisted of 4 questions. This was in answer to a question whether this High Court, with 'an illustrious past', has served its object.

In his Court-room, crowded with lawyers this morning, he posed these four questions:

Has the Court earned the confidence of the public?

Does he believe that, in this Court, 'Right is

Might'?

Whether in this Court substance is holier than procedure?

Short of answering the questions himself, the Judge only told the gathering that if the answer to all these questions is in affirmative, then the Court has served its object.

Striking a critical note, Justice Mohta asked, "which was real justice"? The judicial order passed by Justice Daver in 1908, sentencing Lokmanya Tilak to six years imprisonment and calling him a 'diseased and perverted mind', or the administrative decision of Justice Chagla of putting a tablet with few lines of Tilak on outer wall of the High Court, in 1956, to

mark the birth-a... manya, with a vie... ment for injustic... caused to the grea... he Judge observed... can say with pric... klings of failings... human weaknesse... brilliant record of ... maintained. Refer... the Court at Nag... praised the great ... existing between th... here. The help rece... the High Court sta... difficult task easy.

---

# 125 years of High Court

## (Contd. from Page 1)

Concluding reference, Justice Mohta expressed hope that this great High Court would continue to stand as a symbol of liberty and justice and would enjoy the confidence of the people, whom it seeks to serve.

Responding to the reference, the Government Pleader, Mr. M.P. Badar said that whatever is good, is required to be preserved, strengthened and perpetuated, while bad trends need to be eliminated. He emphasised that Justice provided here should be real, cheap, swift and effective.

Awareness of demands of social justice to serve public good is needed. Substance and not the form is material. In this context he quoted Marathi poet Keshav Sut.

**FOR EYE TESTING**

# KHANNA OPTICAL CO.

**BUTY CHAMBERS, SITABULDI, NAGPUR**

TIMING:

**10 To 12 & 4 To 7 P.M.**

*Press reporting dated 15.8.1987 in Hitavada*
*(Leading newspaper from Nagpur) of ongoings in Court.*

May 18th 1984

ROYAL COURTS OF JUSTICE
STRAND, LONDON, WC2A 2LL

Mr Justice Mohta

of the High Court

Nagpur

India.

v Li ...h

will be coming to the place here.

I will send him to the

entran

D-----

*Letter from Late Lord Denning, British Judge.*

improvement of our relations, a goal which we believe is earnestly desired by both our governments and peop...

attack.
It said the raid was "part of the continuing task of enforcing the total exclusion zone around the

...genuine military Governor of the Falklands described it as a "vulgar psychological action."
...message to Radio Continental of Buenos Aires, General

# Justice at midnight

**By Maneck Daver**

BOMBAY, May 16

JUSTICE never sleeps at night. If it does it can always be roused.

That was the experience of the pavement-dwellers of P. D'Mello Road who faced an imminent threat of eviction today morning. It was a midnight drama at the residence of Justice V. A. Mohta, the vacation judge of the Bombay High Court, that helped earn a reprieve for the pavement-dwellers.

At 9 p.m. on Saturday night, the residents on the footpath of P. D'Mello Road were informed about the planned eviction in the early hours of Sunday morning. The entire Municipal machinery was held in readiness to move at the

crack of dawn. But the Corporation did not reckon with the doggedness of the Lawyer's Collective, who has been constantly championing the cause of the pavement population.

The advocates immediately set legal wheels in motion and contacted Protonotary Khade, who referred them to Chamber Registrar Nagesh. From 10.15 p.m. to midnight, the Collective tried contacting the judge telephonically, but to no avail. At midnight, the advocates and the Registrar rushed to his residence, where the judge, cordially received them wearing a white shirt and pyjamas.

The Municipal counsel, D'Mello, was summoned, heard, and the judge passed a stay order at 1.30 in the morning.

The advocates then rushed to the

Police headquarters at Crawford Market to serve the operative part of the order, which was not yet typed, on the cops.

Thus, justice was meted out in white pyjamas.

The order which is a testament to the humanity of the judiciary, transcends "the controversy about the alleged breach of directions in the Supreme Court for the present", and considers the fact "that not merely legal issues but human problems concerning nearly 20,000 homeless persons is involved."

The petition will be placed for further orders on May 19, 1982.

Meanwhile, Municipal Commissioner D. M. Sukhtankar has stated that the demolition programme would be held in abeyance for some days.

*Press Report of 17.5.1992 about a midnight hearing conducted by the author in an urgent matter.*

# Justice thy name is

## Shri. VALLABHDASJI MOHTA

Your Honour,

This is not an appointment -
This is the place just meant for you !

Whenever you exercised justice
it was nothing but "just" -
Even the culpables accepted it.

Your Honour, you've always practised
nothing but "the truth"

Even judas never dared to come near you
though you justified your share of belonging
to the society at large,
by becoming inseparable part of it.

Justice was never only a duty, Your Honour-

But is has been more like a Religion for you

We all have reverence for you,

We wish you,
A long healthy eventful life
to give JUSTICE for the sake of it -
to all the needy -

May God justify all our feelings for you.

In your Honour - From Representatives of Your court of Fraternity,

- v.b. bhave
- s.a. pinto
- kamal shahu
- mahendrasingh chawhan
- vinod bharat
- amarji sobti

- prakash chawhan
- ravindra gandhi
- achal shahu
- brijkishore bhattad
- kishor biswas
- a.v.r. mudliar

- dilip parikh
- k.k. bagree
- vijay patel
- satish vyawahare
- madhukar thosre
- vikram vora

I realise that the Vice-Chancellor for Nagpur University has to be selected early. The only way for me to help this process is to tender my resignation which I hereby do clearing the way for early constitution of the new Selection Committee.

Kindly accept the same and oblige.

Thanking You,

With Warm Regards,

Sincerely yours,
    Sd/-
(V.A. Mohta)

To,
Excellency Shri P.C. Alexander,
Governor of Maharashtra,
Raj Bhavan, Malbar Hill,
Bombay-35

◆

After my communication dated 21 December 1993 was received, the Hon'ble Chancellor personally phoned me to request the withdrawal of my resignation, to which I courteously but firmly declined.

News of my resignation reached academic circles in Nagpur, as was evident from the write up that appeared in the Marathi daily *Tarun Bharat* on 2 January 1994 under the headline 'Selection of Vice-Chancellor'. The gist of the write up by a famous educationist, Shri M. G. Vaidya, was that what I had done was correct, and that the assumption that in the appointments of vice-chancellors there is no governmental interference is a myth. He also mentioned the historical record of interferences—with the only exception being that of the Chief Minister Shri Shankarrao Chavan. I had not the slightest doubt that the total rejection of the list must have been the result of some political interference. I have no idea what ultimately happened to that appointment since soon thereafter I left for Odisha to assume office as Chief Justice of the Orissa High Court.

## CHIEF JUSTICE M.N.VENKATACHALIAH: GREAT SCHOLAR, YET HUMANE

I had the good fortune of meeting Hon'ble Mr Justice M.N.Venkatachaliah, Chief Justice of India, in 1993 when he made a two-day visit to Nagpur to deliver the convocation address at Nagpur University. It was his first visit to Nagpur. In my capacity as the senior-most judge of the Nagpur Bench of the Bombay High Court, I had the privilege of spending quite some time with him. We, the members of the bench and also the members of the Bar, had heard so much about Justice Venkatachaliah both as a judge and a human being, that his visit generated a great deal of excitement. He was, and is until this day, rated as one of the most outstanding Chief Justices of the country. He was a great believer in the principle that uncertainties in court decisions shatter the confidence of the public in the judiciary, which theme is reflected in his lone and glorious dissent in the well-known case—*A.R. Antulay Vs. R.S. Nayak, (1988) 2SCC602.* These are his observations on the subject:

> It is true that the highest court in the land should not, by technicalities of procedure forge fetters on its own feet and disable itself in cases of serious miscarriages of justice. It is said that 'Life of law is not logic; it has been experience.' But it is equally true as Cardozo said: "But Holmes did not tell us that logic is to be ignored when experience is silent." Those who do not put the teachings of experience and the lessons of logic out of consideration would tell what inspires confidence

in the judiciary and what does not. Judicial vacillations fall into the latter category and undermine respect of the judiciary and judicial institutions, denuding thereby respect for law and the confidence in the even-handedness in the administration of justice by courts. It would be gross injustice, says an author, (W.G. Miller in his "*Data of Jurisprudence*", 1903, William Green & Sons) to decide alternate cases on opposite principles.

These all-time valid observations framed in his usual scintillating style had made a great impact on my mind regarding his personality. His judgments displayed his love for the ebb and flow of narrative.

In Nagpur, Justice Venkatachaliah addressed a gathering of lawyers and judges. Everyone was impressed by his genuineness and social values. His most touching speech was before the trainee judges of the Maharashtra judiciary in the Maharashtra Judicial Training Institute at Nagpur, of which I was then in charge. I have retained a copy of his speech. It is embarrassing for me to reproduce the whole of it although the following lines from his address will give readers a glimpse into his personality and his attitude towards the judicial system.

> I expect this institution to train judicial personnel to become not only good judges, but great human beings. If a man is not a respected human being—respected by the members of his family, by his friends, by his colleagues, and thought very highly of in a matter of his moral attainments, it is unlikely that he will become a good judge. Judicial qualities are entirely different from those that pass off today as attainments. A purely intellectual mind, a purely logical mind or a mind capable of legal certainties will not answer my definition and conception of a judicial personality.

Justice Venkatachaliah is a great human being and it is no wonder he was a great judge. He is a deeply religious person with a strong faith. I have been a beneficiary of his good will. Within a few months of his visit to Nagpur, I received a communication about my appointment as a member of the committee constituted to recommend the revision of pay scales and service conditions of High Court and Supreme Court Judges. Hon'ble Shri Justice Sagir Ahmed, the then Chief Justice of the Jammu and Kashmir High Court, who retired as a Supreme Court Judge, chaired it. The third member was Shri Justice U.L. Bhat, then Chief Justice of the Madhya Pradesh High Court.

The first meeting of the Justice Sagir Ahmed Committee was held at Delhi. I travelled to Delhi to attend, and during this visit the Chief Justice called me to his official residence and enquired about me and my family background. He recollected his visit to Nagpur and told me that he had heard a lot about my reputation there. He also appreciatively referred to the judgment that I had delivered in Mumbai some time earlier in the case of the world-famous jockey Pesi Shroff against Bombay Gymkhana Club, holding that the writ petition against the respondent club was not maintainable as it was not a 'State' within the meaning of Article 12 of the Constitution of India.

I was touched not only by his appreciative and encouraging words but also by his affection. He asked me whether I had ever met Senior Supreme Court Judge Shri Justice J.S. Verma. When I answered in the negative, he asked me to meet him on that very day. I made an appointment and went to the residence of Justice Verma in the afternoon. He also affectionately received me and asked me questions about my family and career. During a somewhat detailed conversation, he asked me questions about some judges from Mumbai and sternly told me that he expected honest and frank answers from me. I did not betray his expectations, though some questions were quite embarrassing for me to answer. Justice Verma told me that the Chief Justice and he both considered me to be a good judge with a reputation deserving of higher positions in the judiciary, minimum being Chief Justice of a high court. Later on the Chief Justice informed me that my appointment as Chief Justice of a High Court may not take a long time and I should be ready to shift from Mumbai.

Justice Venkatachaliah's love and encouragement continues even after my retirement from the judiciary in 1995. It is embarrassing for me to mention, but I am unable to check the temptation of doing so, that till date I am only the third judge from any high court to be appointed as chief justice. Chief Justice Venkatachaliah and Justice J.S. Verma were desirous of elevating me to the Supreme Court, but I understand fully and genuinely that there would have been no justification for supersession of any of my then senior judges in the Bombay High Court.

In this connection, the foresight of my youngest son Sanjay deserves mention. The rumour of my possible elevation to the Supreme Court had perhaps spread in Nagpur. On my visit to Nagpur he asked me whether there was any basis for the rumour. I replied in the negative. But his instant suggestion was that even if an offer were made I should not accept it. The reason he gave was that if I took up such an offer then after attaining sixty-five years of age I would be miserable because of the free time on my hands since as a retired Supreme Court Judge I would no longer be permitted to practice law in courts—the only thing that I could otherwise do in retired life. Perhaps he thought that I was not capable of doing anything else. He knew me and he was correct. Regardless, the offer for elevation to Supreme Court did not come and hence there was no occasion to make a choice.

My close friends and relatives ask me even today whether I would have declined the offer had it come. My answer has been that perhaps I would not have. The fact is that except for an open plot in Akola and a flat in the Samta Judges Co-operative Society in Mumbai I had no other property at the time of my retirement. My Akola bungalow Sankalp had been disposed of to raise funds for the flat in Samta in Mumbai. It was only post retirement, when I set up a legal practice from May 1995, that I was able to earn and accumulate some wealth. What luck! And I remember Sanjay's words.

Justice Venkatachaliah, after his retirement, reluctantly became chairman of National Human Rights Commission and subsequently was chairman of the National Commission to Review the Working of the Constitution, a well-deserved recognition of his great merit. The terms of reference required the commission to examine, in light of past experience, how best the Constitution could respond to changing needs to provide an effective system of governance leading to socio-economic development of India within the frame of parliamentary democracy and to recommend changes in the Constitution. The two-volume report that the committee submitted was the product of monumental research.

In 2004, India's second highest civilian honour, the Padma Vibhushan, was conferred on Justice Venkatachaliah by the President of India. Since 2013, he has served as chancellor of the Board of Trustees of Shri Sathya Sai Institute of Higher Learning at Puttaparthi. He engages himself in reading books and is regularly invited to lecture on a variety of social and legal subjects all over India and abroad. He is at present eighty-six years of age and is active in social service. The exemplary standard of public life that he maintains is seen in his refusal to accept the work of the Arbitration Tribunal after his retirement, although it is highly lucrative work. I know how desperate the parties were to refer their complicated disputes to his arbitration.

## REJECTION OF PROPOSAL OF CHAIRMANSHIP OF ENQUIRY COMMISSION ON COMMUNAL RIOTS IN MUMBAI

The demolition of the Babri Masjid led to the outbreak of communal riots in Mumbai. Many innocent lives and properties were lost. A commission was to be appointed to inquire into these riots. Chief Justice M.K. Mukherjee, in consultation with the senior-most judge, Smt Justice Sujata Manohar, chose me to head that commission. One morning Justice Sujata Manohar phoned and asked me to meet her at her residence, which was on the way from my Malabar Hills home to the high court. She communicated the decision to me. Chief Justice Mukherjee, who was in Kolkata at the time, also spoke to me on the phone. I was grateful for their confidence in me, but expressed my inability to accept the assignment. She asked me the reason, but I was embarrassed to disclose the reason because I had been instructed to keep my imminent appointment as Chief Justice a secret. There was urgency in the appointment of the Enquiry Commission and within two days thereafter, the appointment of Justice Shrikrishna was announced.

## FIXING RESPONSIBILITY; PUNISHMENT AGAINST STATE SECRETARY

I had to deal with proceedings under the Contempt of Court Act against high government officials on many occasions. A case that I vividly remember relates to the repeated disobedience of judicial orders by the state education secretary in the matter of taking a long-pending decision regarding recognition of a college. When, despite the last opportunity given to comply with the simple direction, the direction was ignored, the court ordered the presence of the secretary and, realizing he was not remorseful even at that late stage, we sentenced him to undergo imprisonment till the rising of the court and also to pay a personal fine of ₹1000. The incident was widely reported in the press and highly appreciated in academic circles. An editorial appeared in a Marathi daily dated 11 September 1993, titled 'Justice is Alive'.

## SOME IMPORTANT JUDGMENTS IN THE LATER PART OF MY TENURE IN MUMBAI

### Case Relating to the Bombay Sales Tax Act, 1959

In the early period of my tenure as a judge of the Bombay High Court at Nagpur, when I sat on a division bench as a junior judge, I had had a difference of opinion with the senior judge in a hotly contested case relating to the Bombay Sales Tax Act, 1959. The matter was referred to a third judge. The point related to an interpretation of an entry in the Schedule of the Act. The substance of the matter was whether commercial articles like handbags etc., manufactured out of cotton fabrics, could continue to fall in the category of 'cotton fabrics'. The Chief Justice of the Bombay High Court as a third judge agreed with my view that cotton fabrics lost their identity (of being a fabric of cotton) after conversion into commercial products and hence should not be classified as 'cotton fabrics'. The matter was of great importance and public interest and was reported in a Nagpur daily.

### Clause 13 (VI) of the Rent Control Order

The other case that attracted public attention related to the validity of a provisio to Clause 13 (VI) of the Rent Control Order, under which even if a negligible portion of a house is occupied by the landlord, his bona fide need for additional accommodation could not receive legal backing. I had struck down that provisio as being violative of Article 14 of the Constitution of India.

### Case Relating to Muslim Women (Protection of Rights on Divorce) Act, 1986

One controversial case related to the Muslim Women (Protection of Rights on Divorce) Act, 1986. A single judge had held that even matrimonial issues arising out of that special Act fell within the jurisdiction of the family court, established under the Family Courts Act. Overruling that view, the division bench, over which I presided, held that the 1986 Act was special and was a complete code with respect to rights of divorced Muslim women. Moreover, it was a later legislation than the Family Court Act and yet it had not conferred jurisdiction on the family courts.

## Legality of Bail for Drug Offenders

The last judgment I delivered before leaving the Bombay High Court pertained to the legality of giving bail to drug offenders because 'charges' and 'persons' were illegally linked in the charge sheet submitted by the police. There were differences of opinion between single judges of the Bombay High Court on the question, hence the matter was referred to a division bench over which I presided. We upheld the view that granting bail to drug offenders on that basis was wrong.

## Legal Status of Gwalior Royal Estate

Another case that deserves mention, not so much for the point of law involved but for its context, related to an old and controversial income tax reference on the legal status of the estate of His Highness Maharaja J.S.M. Scindia of Gwalior pertaining to the assessment years 1970–1971, which remained pending in the High Court for many years. Chief Justice P.D. Desai constituted a bench comprising Justice U.T. Shah, who was an ex-member of the Income Tax Tribunal, and myself for its early disposal. The income tax officer, commissioner and Income Tax Tribunal had concurrently held that the Gwalior estate was not impartible and was not governed by the rule of primogeniture since: (i) neither custom nor grant in the matter was established; (ii) the ruler had no unlimited sovereign powers; (iii) the estate was family property, originating in a jagir given to the family from which maintenance was given to the members of the family; and (iv) succession after 1956 was governed by the Hindu Succession Act, which was a complete code on the subject. We held it to be Hindu Undivided Family (HUF) property.

The decision depended upon the following interesting history of succession. The House of Scindias traces its lineage to the Rajput family of Shilledars under the Bahmani kings, one branch of which held patelship of a hamlet, Kannerkhera, near Satara in present-day Maharashtra. The founder of the Gwalior dynasty was Ranoji Scindia, who rose in the favour of the Peshwas along with Malhar Rao Holkar, the founder of the House of the Holkars of Indore. Ranoji Scindia was succeeded by Mahadji Scindia, who was succeeded by Daulat Rao Scindia. Daulat Rao's successor, Jayaji Rao Scindia, received several properties from the British government for the family's service during the 1857 Mutiny. His son Madhav Rao Scindia was followed by Jiwaji Rao Scindia, who signed the Instrument of Accession of his Gwalior State to the Indian Dominion. He used to file return of income in his individual capacity. Upon his death in 1961, his only son Madhav Rao Scindia II was recognized as a ruler in succession.

The Central Board of Direct Taxes had accepted the opinion of the Attorney General, Shri C.K. Daphtary, to the effect that the stand of the assessee was correct. The facts seemed to be quite clear and hence I was surprised at the reference. When I looked to Justice Shah for his reaction, he whispered that the reference was filed as per directions received from the Prime Minister's Office (PMO). He further told me that, as a member of the tribunal, he had had occasion to see the file containing the PMO's note. Out of curiosity, I directed the Income Tax Department to produce the whole record, which was readily complied with within a week's time. I perused the file and noticed the correctness of Justice Shah's impression.

We answered the questions in the affirmative and in favour of the assessee. The said judgment is *Commissioner of Income Tax Vs. Her Highness Maharani Vijaya Raje Scindia, 208 ITR 38.* Sitting on the income tax bench with a tax expert like Justice Shah was a great learning experience for me.

# IV

# Chief Justice, Orissa High Court

## APPOINTMENT AS CHIEF JUSTICE

My imminent appointment as Chief Justice of the Orissa High Court did not long remain a secret in official circles. During that period, an important case was being heard before the full bench constituted by then Chief Justice A.M. Bhattacharjee. The bench comprised the Chief Justice, Justice V.P. Tipnis and myself. After prolonged hearing, judgment was reserved. There was unanimity about the decision to be taken and, within a few days, I received a draft of the brilliant and learned judgment penned down by the Chief Justice. The draft judgment began with the following paragraph.

ORAL JUDGMENT (Per A.M. BHATTACHARJEE, C.J.)

When Tennyson became a Poet Laureate, Browning wrote that 'for a handful of silver, he left us, for sticking a blue ribbon in his coat'. One of us in this Bench is leaving us very soon for higher guerdon and though I do not say that he is doing so only for another handful of silver and for flying a Flag on his car, I would only say that we would be very sorry to miss him because this High Court would obviously become poorer by his departure. As we are told that the apprehended departure

> may take place any day, we have hurriedly sat together and have prepared our judgment in this case.

The learned Chief Justice's meaning was apparent. I was extremely embarrassed to be a party to the above paragraph. I contacted the Chief Justice, thanked him for the kind words and requested him to delete that paragraph. The Chief Justice invited me as well as Justice Tipnis to his residence where the subject was discussed. He indicated his reluctance to delete that portion as in his view there was nothing objectionable in it. Justice Tipnis agreed with him, but my embarrassment was such that I refused to sign and so he reluctantly deleted that portion.

President Shri S.D. Sharma signed the warrant of my appointment as Chief Justice of Odisha on 12 September 1994. I had received a personal phone call from his Excellency, the Governor of Odisha, Shri B. Satya Narayan Reddy, congratulating me on my appointment. The oath-taking ceremony in Cuttack was scheduled on 28 September 1994 and I planned to depart from Mumbai and reach Cuttack via Delhi accordingly. I was to reach Bhubaneswar on 26 September 1994, and as suggested by the Hon'ble Governor I intended to drive straight to Puri where I would stay overnight at the Raj Bhawan. Thereafter, following darshan of Lord Jagannath, I would proceed to Cuttack. My departure from Mumbai was scheduled for 24 September 1994. Congratulatory messages from several friends and well-wishers from Mumbai, Nagpur, Akola and other places started pouring in; the judges of the Bombay High Court gave me a warm send-off and a day before my departure for Odisha, the Bar association arranged a felicitation in which several senior lawyers—including then Advocate General of Maharashtra, Shri T.R. Andhyarujina—spoke generously about me. During the felicitation ceremony in the Bar association hall, my PA, Shri Tapadia, gave me a note that the Senior Supreme Court Judge Hon'ble Shri Justice Ahmadi wanted to talk to me urgently.

I contacted the Hon'ble Judge after the function was over and was surprised as well as shocked first to receive his snubbing for the delay in contacting him and then to be sternly told that I was being sent to Jammu and Kashmir in place of Odisha. Neither was any enquiry about my willingness made, nor was the time sought by me to think about the matter, given. I protested against that unusual and awkward proposal for which I had not given my consent. After ascertaining that there was no official change in the oath-taking ceremony at Cuttack, escorted by the registrar of the Bombay High Court as per convention, I proceeded to Bhubaneswar via Delhi, where I met Justices J.S. Verma and A.H. Ahmadi. I could not contact Chief Justice Venkatachalaiah since he was on his way to Bengaluru by train.

## OATH-TAKING CEREMONY

Unlike in Delhi or Mumbai, the oath-taking ceremony for a Chief Justice is a great ceremonial affair in Odisha. The general tradition is for the raj pramukh (governor) to administer the oath at the Raj Bhawan but in Odisha the oath is administered in the High Court itself. This well-attended function was, as per the tradition, graced by the chief minister, Biju Patnaik, his cabinet colleagues, all sitting and past judges, the members of the Bar and members of my family. At a tea party arranged in the High Court building, I interacted with the hon'ble governor, Shri Biju Patnaik and sitting and retired judges of the Orissa High Court.

## RESIDENCE OF CHIEF JUSTICE IN CUTTACK

The Chief Justice's bungalow was a massive building with nearly eight independent bedrooms facing a sprawling garden-cum-field spread over several acres on which were constructed cowsheds and doghouses. It boasted several fruit and flower trees and there was a large vegetable patch. I do not think the residence of any other High Court Chief Justice could match this bungalow in terms of size.

## FELICITATIONS AT NAGPUR AND AKOLA

Three or four weeks after I took oath, I went to Nagpur and Akola. The High Court Bar Association, Nagpur, and the Nagpur District Bar Association accorded me a warm welcome and felicitated me. I was also felicitated by several social organizations in Nagpur. At my hometown, Akola, I was felicitated by several organizations like the Vidarbha Chamber of Commerce, the Berar Education Society, Rotary Clubs, and above all, the Akola Bar Association. The felicitation function by my parent Bar association was most touching. Held in a specially erected marquee on the grounds of the district court, it lasted for four hours and was so vibrant that dinner could commence only after midnight! Several old and young friends made touching and fond references about my association with the Bar.

I rarely, if ever, visited Akola without spending many happy hours at the Bar association. I have always enjoyed being there. It is the only Bar association that I visited casually after joining the profession, and also after my retirement from the judiciary. My visits to all other Bar associations have only been on invitation to attend functions.

## CONFERENCE OF ALL INDIA FEDERATION OF TAX PRACTITIONERS

Being Chief Justice did not adversely influence my social life. I inaugurated a conference at Puri on 12 November 1994 in which Justice Shri Arijit Pasayat (the then judge of Orissa High Court who was later elevated as a judge of the Supreme Court), gave the keynote address. The guest speaker at the conference was Chairman, Central Board of Direct Taxes, Shri T.S. Srinivasan. Other speakers were Shri N. Mishra, Member, Income Tax Settlement Commission and Shri Sovesh Chandra Roy, Advocate General, Odisha. I had met Shri T.S. Srinivasan while sitting on the income tax bench in Nagpur, with Hon'ble Shri Justice S.P. Bharucha who later adorned the office of Chief Justice of India. Shri Srinivasan fondly referred to the speed with which our bench in Nagpur had disposed of the income tax references. I recollect him having made the unusual comparison of the speed of disposal of references by saying, 'it was like placing a burning matchstick near dry paper.'

## CONFERENCE OF SOCIETY FOR NUCLEAR MEDICINE, INDIA

I inaugurated this conference, held at Cuttack, on 14 December 1994. It was presided over by the Hon'ble Minister, Health and Family Welfare, Odisha. The guest of honour was the chairman of the Acharya Harihar Regional Centre for Cancer Research and Treatment Society, Cuttack. It was a grand function dealing with a specialized medical subject attended by well-known experts.

## ANNUAL CONFERENCE OF ALL-ODISHA LAWYERS ASSOCIATION

The All-Odisha Lawyers Association held an annual conference on 27 December 1994 at Phulbani, a district situated in the western hilly region of Odisha. The conference, largely attended by lawyers, lasted for two days. I was invited to inaugurate the conference. The journey by road to Phulbani was long and required an overnight halt midway. The convoy included not only police vehicles, but also two ambulances with medical and surgical facilities in charge of which were doctors who were specialists (MDs) and surgical specialists (MS). During the long and tedious journey, we inevitably needed to stop for tea or to answer the call of nature, but there were no resthouses or facilities on the road. As a result, the convoy would stop by the side of the road, which was awkward and embarrassing, given the watchful eyes of the qualified doctors and their team. It was unusual VIP protocol, but I was told that it was unavoidable in such areas of Odisha where there were no proper medical facilities to cope with emergencies.

## VISIT TO NETAJI'S BIRTHPLACE AND COLLEGIATE SCHOOL AT CUTTACK

National hero Netaji Subhash Chandra Bose was born, brought up and educated in Cuttack, where his father was a land-owning zamindar. I was very keen to visit Netaji's family house, where he was born on 23 January 1897. It is situated in Netaji Nagar, Cuttack, and is preserved as a national monument. Netaji's ninety-eighth Jayanti was celebrated not only at the place of his birth but also at Ravenshaw Collegiate School, Cuttack, where he was educated. I felt greatly honoured and privileged to have been able to visit those places and participate in the jayanti celebrations.

## ANNUAL CONFERENCE OF DISTRICT JUDGES IN ODISHA AND ESTABLISHMENT OF VIGILANCE CELL AND DISCIPLINARY ORGANIZATION

I had the opportunity of meeting members of the judiciary of the state at the annual conference of district judges that was held in the High Court building at Cuttack on 17-18 February 1995. It was a well-attended, successful conference, in which all sitting judges of the High Court participated. I delivered the inaugural address. We decided to set up a vigilance cell and disciplinary organization in the High Court and this decision was announced during the conference. This announcement and the reason why the cell was being constituted were referred to in the speech. The move was hailed by the dailies *Sun Times* and *Orissa Times*.

## KONARK DANCE AND MUSIC FESTIVAL

The annual Konark Dance and Music Festival is held against the backdrop of the Konark temple in Odisha. I was fortunate to be in Odisha on 19 February 1995 when the famous festival was to be held. World-famous Odissi dancer, Padmashree Smt Sanjukta Panigrahi, along with her Guru, Padmashree guru Pankaj Charan Das, had approached me for its inauguration. The Hon'ble Governor of Odisha, Shri B. Satya Narayan Reddy, also graced the occasion. It was an exhilarating experience. The function was televised internationally.

## INFORMAL AND UNUSUAL HOLI MILAN OF HIGH COURT JUDGES

Odisha has a rich cultural and religious heritage. It is a region replete with nature's bounty, both below and above mother earth. The state is equally endowed with a rich artistic and literary background. The traditional yet informal attitude and lifestyle of the people appealed to me greatly. Even High Court Judges were no exception to this. They met several times on social occasions and at each other's residences. The most outstanding example of informal and friendly behaviour, which I cannot forget, was the arrival of all High Court Judges at the Chief Justice's bungalow on bicycles on Holi day. Their faces and clothes were multicoloured and it was difficult to identify them at first sight. They included Justice G.B. Patnaik, Justice D.P. Mohapatra and Justice Arijit Pasayat, who in course of time respectively became Chief Justice of India and Supreme Court Judges. The scene was fantastic, full of warmth and camaraderie, which has kept it evergreen in my mind. I do not think this could have happened anywhere else.

## WITHHOLDING SALARY OF CHIEF SECRETARY OF THE STATE

Apart from some mining matters here and there, litigation before the constitution bench mainly consisted of writ petitions relating to payment of arrears of salaries of school teachers. In the beginning, my reaction was not to entertain writ petitions, since there were other remedies for recovery of arrears of salary. It did not take much time to realize that the number of petitioners was large and the arrears were only in thousands per person and that too from different areas of the state. Sadly, for that class of society, the stake was big and an alternative remedy was not efficacious. Unlike today, Odisha in those days was poor and the defence on behalf of the state was invariably the absence of funds. I adopted a policy of granting reasonable time to pay the arrears, sometimes also in instalments. I would also extend that period in genuine cases. Misusing this liberal approach, the delay in actual payment on behalf of the state became increasingly regular. In some cases, last chances were given and notices for contempt of court under the Contempt of Court Act were also issued, but without much effect.

In one group of cases, where there was repeated non-compliance even of the order giving last chance, I issued a notice demanding the personal presence of the chief secretary of the state. A last chance to clear the arrears was sought and was granted. When it was brought to our notice that arrears had still not been cleared despite the promise made, I passed an order restraining the state government from clearing the salary of the chief secretary until the arrears of salaries of the petitioners were cleared. On the given date the petitioners made a statement that they had received their dues. Noticing the compliance, we vacated the restraint order. I was informed that thereafter the instances of non-compliance of payment of teachers' salaries were not only reduced to a minimum, but indeed the process of payment of teachers' salaries was expedited. I was very happy to see this result.

## INTERACTIONS WITH GOVERNOR SHRI B. SATYA NARAYAN REDDY; CHIEF MINISTER SHRI BIJU PATNAIK; AND CHIEF MINISTER SHRI JANAKI BALLAV PATNAIK

Shri Biju Patnaik was the chief minister of the state at the time I assumed the office of Chief Justice of Odisha. I met him for the first time on the High Court premises where he had come to attend my oath-taking ceremony. He was a dynamic leader, who started the process of modernizing Odisha, a state that despite being extremely rich in minerals, forests, etc. had remained underdeveloped. My tenure in Odisha was approximately one year. After six months, a new chief minister took over. He was Shri Janki Ballav Patnaik—a learned person, an author of books and master of several languages including Sanskrit. It is a convention in all courts that since the Chief Justice has to deal with the administrative problems of the high court, there are meetings between him and the chief minister. As per practice, they are alternately held at their respective official residences. The chief minister pays the first courtesy visit to the new chief justice. Both these chief ministers were well known national leaders though their personalities were markedly different. They had visited my residence, but due to the brevity of my tenure, I could not pay a reciprocal visit to their residences.

The governor, Shri B. Satya Narayan Reddy, was a very friendly person with an informal attitude. He belonged to Andhra Pradesh and was an advocate by profession. It may be recalled that he was the governor of Uttar Pradesh when the unfortunate incident of the demolition of Babri Masjid at Ayodhya took place. I frequently received invitations to Raj Bhawan functions and, on one such occasion, had a memorable meeting with Shri Biju Patnaik in connection with a long-pending contentious issue of the promotion of a civil judge, in respect of which the decision made by the High Court was not being accepted by the chief minister. This matter had been discussed many times in the full court meetings of judges presided over by my learned predecessors, but no solution had been found. The governor was interested in sorting the problem out once and for all and had broached the subject with me. I examined there was no reason for varying the judges on the subject, who apprised me about the matter. I informed the governor that there was no reason for varying the decision, which had been considered threadbare more than once by the whole body of High Court Judges. The governor agreed, but wished to have a meeting with the chief minister and myself and suggested a dinner meeting at the Raj Bhawan. I said that the two senior-most judges who had been party to the previous decisions should also be invited to attend. Accordingly, a dinner meeting was arranged by the governor, which the chief secretary of the state and the registrar of the High Court were also asked to attend.

After some general discussions, the governor broached the subject and suggested that the long-standing problem should be sorted out finally. The chief minister's view was that he had examined the matter and he was convinced that it was an unjust decision. The chief minister asked for my opinion on the merits of the matter. I replied that my opinion was irrelevant since the decision had been taken and reviewed in full court meetings. I concluded by stating that in institutional functioning, what should matter is a collective decision and hence the decision was binding on me. I also added that he, as not only a chief minister of Odisha but also as national leader, would know that better than me. The chief minister looked at me for a while and then asked the chief secretary to bring the file and signed his approval. What a fair attitude by that strong man!

Another example of the chief minister's fair-mindedness that I experienced during that meeting is worthy of mention. In the general discussion, he also hinted at what he termed my 'unusual' order of withholding the salary of the chief secretary. I narrated the entire affair and then asked whether he still thought the order unusual. His stern reply was, 'Of course it was unusual, but justified.'

A few months later Shri J.B. Patnaik assumed the office of chief minister. Soon thereafter, he paid the usual courtesy call on me and we spoke on various subjects. His knowledge of the Indian ethos and command over several languages such as Sanskrit and Marathi impressed me. He could deliver discourses extempore in Sanskrit on the Ramayan or the Gita. He also explained the similarity between the Marathi and Oriya languages to me, and the historical background behind the same. I was to retire two or three months later and for various reasons could not return the courtesy call although we met on two occasions before my retirement.

## INAUGURATION OF NEW COURT AT KHURDA

I inaugurated the court of additional district and sessions judge at a new district, Khurda, on 6 April 1995. During the function, Justice Arijit Pasayat, then judge of the Orissa High Court, was the guest of honour. Several dignitaries were seated on the dais and I noticed the additional district and sessions judge (ADJ), who was to preside over that court, sitting in the audience and not on the dais with us. I have found such situations to be odd, but they are common, since the feeling in some quarters is that judges lower in rank to a High Court Judge are not supposed to share a dais with him/her. I encountered such a situation once even in Nagpur at the time of the inauguration of the Judicial Officers Training Institute. I called upon the organizers to immediately arrange for a chair for the ADJ on the dais because he was the head of the new institution and had to be presented in a dignified manner to the public.

## RECUSAL TO HEAR MATTERS

While presiding over a division bench dealing with writ petitions, an important matter concerning a mining lease was posted before our bench. It concerned the conflicting interests of several industrial houses including the Tatas, Jindals, Bhushans, etc. Several leading lights of the Supreme Court Bar such as Shri Shanti Bhushan, Shri P. Chidambaram, Shri Kapil Sibal and Shri G.L. Sanghi were appearing in the matter for different parties. It was a weighty matter that had been heard for more than two days when I received communication that my father-in-law had expired at Washim, his hometown in Maharashtra. The matter was adjourned to the next week at a date convenient to everyone. I was keen to return to Cuttack from Washim as soon as possible, and there was some resistance in the family to this, but I expressed the difficulty concerning the pending matter pertaining to mining leases. In the course of the discussion, I learnt from a close relation that he was a shareholder in one of the companies mentioned in that writ petition. During the return journey, I cogitated on the appropriateness of my hearing that matter. I did not know the extent of his shareholding, but I imagined it couldn't be large. After all, how many shares could a middle-class family from a semi-urban area buy?

The hearing had progressed considerably; the parties must have spent huge amounts to arrange the presence of bigwigs and two valuable working days of the court had also been spent. I returned to Cuttack on Sunday evening and the hearing was to resume on the next day. I was in two minds since there were balancing factors. My sixth sense told me to recuse myself. I shared my decision with the other judge when he came to my chamber prior to going to the courtroom. All lawyers, including the senior lawyers from Delhi, had assembled in the courtroom. I asked the court shireshtedar to call all the lawyers appearing in the case into the chamber. When they had assembled along with their respective teams, I told them of my dilemma and also my decision. All the lawyers led by Senior Advocate Shri Shanti Bhushan told me with one voice that there was no reason for me to recuse myself and that none of them had any objection to the matter being heard by our bench and they were prepared to sign the joint 'no objection' statement in case required. Indeed, they started the preparation of that note. I was also somewhat shaken by my decision, but did not budge. I expressed regret for the inconvenience caused to everyone, mainly the clients, and thanked all the lawyers for the confidence they had displayed.

I had faced such a situation earlier in my judicial career. I was presiding over a Bench dealing with writ petitions at the Nagpur bench of the Bombay High Court sometime in 1983. In Nagpur, there is a well-known Marathi daily *Tarun Bharat* printed and published by a limited company. During my early Akola days, I had purchased shares of that company then valued at ₹1,000. This must have been sometime in 1973-74. I had recused myself from hearing that matter, about which there is nothing much to write, but a few years ago, my attention was drawn back to the article by Shri L.T. Joshi, editor of *Tarun Bharat*, in its issue dated 30 September 2007 under the headline 'Judicial Recusal'. Those days the subject of judicial recusal had become a controversial topic before the Supreme Court because of an incident that had taken place about a mining matter in Odisha. That long article, after referring to a few previous instances on the subject, concluded with the following paragraph, the English translation of which is:

The judiciary is very important in our constitutional functioning and it has retained its importance. The ordinary man considers it to be the only resort for seeking justice. Hence, it is necessary that this institution is beyond suspicion. From that perspective, the concept of 'judicial accountability' has become necessary. That its necessity has arisen is unfortunate. The real remedy is that the judiciary itself imposes certain restrictions upon itself.

I will give one example. One matter concerning *Tarun Bharat* was placed before a division bench headed by Justice Vallabhdas Mohta. Hearing took place for some time. During the course of the hearing Justice Mohta remembered that while he was practicing in Akola he had purchased some shares of the company. As soon as this struck him, he expressed his disinclination to hear the matter. Even the lawyer for the opposite party expressed that neither he nor his clients (who were also present in the courtroom) had any objection to completing the hearing and showed willingness to put this in writing, but the Hon'ble Judge did not change his mind. The matter was transferred to another bench in which *Tarun Bharat* succeeded up to the stage of Supreme Court. But by this incident the impartiality of Justice Mohta was proved. Justice is not only to be done but must also appear to have been done. That is the true test of impartiality of judiciary.

On this subject what I feel is this—judges can honestly and conscientiously say and feel that they are not biased. Yet, the possibility of harbouring unconscious beliefs cannot be ruled out. In any case, a party can honestly harbour that feeling or apprehension. Why not prefer recusal?

## PARTICIPATION IN MAHARASHTRA STATE LAWYERS CONFERENCE IN AKOLA

The Hon'ble Chief Justice of India, Shri Justice A.H. Ahmadi, was to inaugurate the state lawyer's conference and the guest of honour was the Hon'ble Justice B.L. Hansaria, Supreme Court Judge, who had also been a distinguished Chief Justice of Odisha in the past. Though I was also invited as a guest of honour, there was no question of my being a guest at that conference since I was associated with the Maharashtra Bar Council as a member as well as vice-president, and the conference was being held in my hometown Akola. In reality, therefore, I belonged to the category of a host. Some judges of the Bombay High Court and senior advocates such as Rafique Dada also graced the event. Chief Justice Ahmadi and I were having lunch in a separate room during lunch recess. I was meeting Justice Ahmadi for the first time after assuming the office of the Chief Justice of the Orissa High Court. I have tried to reconstruct here the first part of the dialogue between us.

**Chief Justice Ahmadi:** How is Odisha?

**Me:** Fine.

**Chief Justice Ahmadi:** Odisha also says that the Chief Justice is fine. How is it that you have not visited me in Delhi during your visits, or even contacted me on the phone?

**Me:** I never came to Delhi after my last meeting with you on my way to Cuttack from Mumbai.

Perhaps the Chief Justice had some reservations about accepting the correctness of what I said, but it was a fact. I had not visited Delhi during that period. He then asked me about the number of existing vacancies for judges in the Orissa High Court and the vacancies likely to arise within six months. He also asked me why I had not thought of sending recommendations of names to be considered for the posts of the High Court Judges. My justification was the brevity of my tenure there and my lack of familiarity with the Orissa Bar. He expressed surprise at my attitude and told me that even chief justices with tenures of merely two to three weeks had been sending recommendations. He enquired whether I thought that there would be any problem in arriving at unanimity in finalizing the names. I emphatically assured him that this was not so and told him that the two senior-most judges had in fact broached the subject with me. The Chief Justice asked me to quickly send recommendations for the existing as well as future vacancies arising within six months. He also gave me some suggestions in the matter.

## RECOMMENDATION FOR FILLING IN VACANCIES IN THE ORISSA HIGH COURT

On reaching Cuttack, I called administrative judges Justice G.B. Patnaik and Justice D.P. Mohapatra and informed them of the Chief Justice's desire. They were both happy that I had agreed to send the recommendations. I told them to give me the names, which in normal course I would forward, since they knew the Bar better than I did. But they were unwilling to comply with this. So I instead suggested a formula whereby all three of us would prepare a list of nearly one and half times the number of the judges to be recommended and we should send the names of those who were common in the three lists, and decide upon the residual names. The administrative judges readily agreed to the suggestion and after four or five days we reassembled with our respective lists. In the three lists, there were only two names that were not common to all. After some deliberations, we unanimously recommended the names.

## PIGEONS AS MEMBERS OF THE STAFF OF THE POSTAL DEPARTMENT

Odisha is a vast land of forests, hills and rivers with no sufficient proper roads, bridges, etc. This is the reason why pigeons have historically been engaged as staff members of the state's postal department. The pigeons captured my imagination and I had a great desire to see the postal department and meet and witness the working of these non-human members of the staff.

Accordingly, Kamla, our grandson Devansh who was with us at the time, and I made a visit and witnessed how messages were dispatched/received to and from distant places. A special variety of pigeons were trained, which had the strength and stamina to fly for long periods of time even in adverse weather conditions. They carried messages written on paper tied to their feet. Records exist that show these pigeons were used to circulate a message about a public meeting to be addressed by Jawaharlal Nehru during the freedom struggle. Their performance of duty was demonstrated for us. It is amazing that they comply with the instructions pertaining to reaching a particular destination without any mistake. Clearly, intelligence is not the monopoly of human beings.

## GIVING DUE CREDIT: THE BEST GARDEN COMPETITION IN ODISHA

The annual garden competition was an eagerly awaited event in Cuttack at which the adjudicated best garden was awarded a prize at a public function. The High Court building as well as the chief justice's residence in Cuttack had massive, well-maintained gardens. Therefore, it was not surprising that one of these gardens was frequently adjudged as the best garden. Usually, a function was held in Cuttack to honour the keeper of the best garden and to give him the prize. I was invited to preside over the function. The garden of the High Court building was adjudged as the best and to my surprise and utter embarrassment, my name was announced to receive the prize! I called for the gardener, announced his name as the legitimate recipient of that prize and honour, and requested him to come to the dais, but the gardener started trembling with nervousness and did not dare to walk up to the dais. I then requested the registrar to bring him to the dais, on reaching which the gardener had tears in his eyes. I hope and trust that at least thereafter the prize was given to the gardeners and not to the owners of the garden.

## ODISHA: POOR, BACKWARD BUT RELIGIOUS STATE

Although extremely rich in mineral and forest wealth, Odisha lagged in development and was burdened by poverty in 1994-95. You can assess the economic condition of the state from the fact that there was only one income tax commissioner for the whole state. While visiting Berhampur court, Shri Mishra, the registrar, had remarked that it was a 'matabbar' (wealthy) area and drew my attention to the cycle rickshaw-pullers wearing banyans. It was a fact that generally rickshaw-pullers were found wearing only dhotis, with nothing on the upper part of the body.

Even in the cities of Odisha, a large number of people, not excluding judges, believed that black magic and superstition played a role in their lives, marriages, careers, etc. I have heard many unbelievable stories about how various types of black magic were used to advance the careers of people, even at the highest level.

Lord Jagannath is the beloved deity of people across all strata of society and the genuine love and devotion he evokes is truly remarkable. I have had the good fortune of visiting almost all Hindu shrines and religious places in India. The impression that I carried was that Lord Jagannath was a god of poor people— irrespective of their religious beliefs. The temple of Jagannath at Puri cannot be visited by a non-Hindu and this rule is so strictly followed that even the late Prime Minister Indira Gandhi was not allowed entry as she was married to a Parsi. Although such restrictions are not uncommon and are prevalent in other religions, I believe that religion cannot be a Bar for genuine devotion. The Jagannath temple is a living example of that. One

of the devotees of Lord Jagannath was a Muslim by the name of
Bhakta Salabega. He was not allowed entry into the temple, but
this did not affect his devotion. The story about Bhakta Salabega
goes as follows. He was the son of a Muslim subedar named
Lalbeg, and his Hindu wife. Salabega became a great devotee of
Lord Jagannath, who is considered to be an incarnation of Lord
Krishna. Salabega was miraculously cured of his wounds in battle
on account of chanting the holy name of Lord Jagannath. He
then went to Puri to have darshan of the Lord, but as he was a
non-Hindu, he was not allowed entry into the temple as per the
temple's tradition. He was so keen to have the Lord's darshan that
when he heard that the Lord's idol was to be carried in a Rath
Yatra he journeyed from Vrindavan to Puri, but became suddenly
ill on the way. He offered prayers to Lord Jagannath to wait for
him on the yatra till he arrived.

The cart of the Lord did not move until Salabega arrived.
The place where the cart remained stationary to give darshan
to the devotee was later eulogized by Salabega in his devotional
song. After his death his body was buried at that spot, and the
samadhi of this great devotee still stands on the main road of
the Rath Yatra in Puri in memory and honour of Salabega. The
cart of Lord Jagannath conventionally halts for a while near the
samadhi every year.

I am surprised this story is unknown outside of Odisha.
This unusual story of devotion unaffected by communal feelings
needed, and increasingly continues to need, wide publicity and
circulation in India in the public interest.

## OFFICIAL ORDER REGARDING MANDATORY REQUIREMENT FOR JUDICIAL OFFICERS TO WEAR A TIE

Some judicial officers from mofussil areas desired to meet me in
connection with their local problems. The meeting was scheduled

for 2.00 p.m. on a Sunday in mid-April. The temperature was soaring and an unforgiving sun blazed down. My previous meeting had been delayed and therefore the judges had to wait outside the air-conditioned room for some time. When they were ushered inside, they and their clothes were wet with sweat. I was surprised to find them dressed in suits and neckties despite the blazing heat. When I asked why they were wearing neckties, I received no response, but my PA informed me that some years previously a Chief Justice had issued a circular mandating the judges not to face the Chief Justice or a High Court Judge without a suit and tie! On the next working day, I broached this subject with the judges and with their consent issued an order withdrawing that circular.

## NON-USE OF RED INK

I have had several occasions to administrate private and public institutions including high courts but am pleased to say that I have not used red ink in the confidential record of any person; though in one or two cases, I did threaten to do so but with the sole purpose of deterring negative functioning. Remarks in red ink almost certainly cause permanent damage to the career of employees who generally belong to either the lower or middle cadre. I believe proper administration can be better achieved by using a human touch and fairness, mixed with some fear, rather than by permanently damaging someone's career.

## I GO TO SEE AN ORIYA PLAY

I was and continue to be fond of going to see plays in theatres. I had never seen an Oriya play in my life and had expressed a desire to see one. To my great pleasure and surprise, the judges of the High Court arranged a special Oriya play in a theatre, in which the audience comprised only the High Court Judges and a few members of the staff. What an unforgettable kind gesture!

## SEND-OFF BY CHIEF MINISTER

It is a long-standing convention in Odisha for the chief minister to give a send-off party for the Chief Justice on the eve of his departure from the state on his retirement. Hence, Chief Minister Shri J.B. Patnaik arranged a state dinner at the state guest house in Bhubaneswar. All the cabinet ministers, the secretary of the state and present and past High Court Judges attended the function. It was a touching send-off.

## UNPRECEDENTED SEND-OFF BY GOVERNOR

After a few days, the governor also arranged a send-off dinner. Other judges told me that it was the first time any governor had arranged such a function. It was a grand affair held on the massive lawns of Raj Bhawan on 21 April 1995. The limited gathering comprised the chief minister and the members of his cabinet, sitting High Court Judges, leading lights of the Odisha Bar and some administrative heads. It was a touching send-off followed by governor's speech, which went like this:

> Janaki Ballav Patnaikji, Chief Minister of Orissa; Shri Justice Mohta, Chief Justice of Orissa, distinguished guests and friends.
>
> We are gathered here this evening to express our deep regard for Shri Justice Mohta, Chief Justice of Orissa. He has earned respect from not only the legal profession, but also the affection and regard of all those who have been privileged to associate with him. In the short while that he has presided over the Orissa High Court, he has established very healthy conventions, which will ensure the harmonious and efficient

functioning of the judicial system. He has evoked the goodwill of all and built the confidence of the executive and the judiciary in each other.

When he lays down office in the next few days, we will lose the sagacity and wisdom of this eminent jurist. I can only hope that the traditions established by him will continue to inspire all of us. In Shri Justice Mohta, we found a sincere and staunch friend of Odisha, whose term of office as Chief Justice of Odisha will always be remembered for pragmatism and humane approach. I would like to convey to Shri Justice Mohta and his wife the abiding affection of the people of Odisha. I would also like to present both of them small tokens of our deep regard and affection for them.

## MEMORABLE LAST DAYS IN ODISHA AND POST-RETIREMENT VISITS

On my last working day as chief justice, only a few matters were scheduled for hearing. The last matter was heard for some time and at the end, a young lady advocate who was sitting in the court suddenly approached the dais and offered me a rose. It was a very embarrassing situation. I did not accept the flower but gratefully acknowledged the spirit of kindness and affection that the young lady wanted to demonstrate, telling her that such actions were not done in a courtroom.

The Odisha Judges Association had arranged a send-off for me on the High Court premises. Many from the subordinate judiciary and sitting judges of the High Court attended it. There were touching references to my tenure in the state. During my regime as Chief Justice in Odisha I had the good fortune of guidance from senior administrative judges in general, and Hon'ble Shri Justice G.B. Patnaik in particular. On the administrative side, I had Shri Hari Nayak, one of the finest and most reliable persons as my personal assistant. The senior administrative judges saw to it that the newly-built High Court guest houses at Cuttack and Jagannath Puri were inaugurated at my hands just before my departure from Odisha. I cannot forget several fine gestures of brother judges during my tenure and even after my retirement.

I had not had the good fortune of witnessing the grand festival of the Rath Yatra at Puri, which did not take place during my tenure there. Many judges invited me to revisit Odisha for that festival, which was to take place in July 1995, i.e. about three months after my retirement. Since we had a strong desire to attend that holy festival, Kamla and I went to Odisha and were not only warmly received at Bhubaneshwar airport as before, but were greatly and pleasantly surprised to note the presence of some of my erstwhile colleagues, who came there specifically to receive and accompany us to Puri.

I had the good fortune of experiencing the same love and regard in Odisha from the bench as well as the Bar even after a lapse of eighteen years, when I was invited to be a part of the inauguration ceremony of a new modern air-conditioned High Court building at the hands of then Chief Justice of India—Hon'ble Shri Justice Altamas Kabir—on 11 November 2012. The Orissa High Court Bar Association, through its president Shri Jayant Das, had arranged a get-together where I had the opportunity to experience the warmth and affection of the Bar members, seniors as well as juniors.

During the period of twenty years (from my retirement as Chief Justice in 1995 ), several members of the Orissa Bar have made it a point to meet me in the Supreme Court Bar or at my office—many times even without any legal work. I was and am touched by the love and affection showered on me by the Orissa Bench and Bar.

Who says treatment of a sitting judge and retired judge is never the same?

# V

## BACK TO PAVILION

### OFFERS OF CHAIRMANSHIP OF HUMAN RIGHTS COMMISSION ODISHA, COMPANY LAW BOARD AND LOKAYUKT KARNATAKA

As the time for my retirement approached, I started thinking about post-retirement life. I had a strong desire to resume practice in the Supreme Court, but there was no certainty about success at the Bar after a long gap of sixteen years. I consulted with several of my family and friends on this subject. Chief Minister J.B. Patnaik had broached the subject of establishing a Human Rights Commission in Odisha. He let me know that the consensus in the government was that it should be under my chairmanship. Justice R.N. Mishra, who was at that time the chairman of National Human Rights Commission (NHRC), had also broached the same subject with me, but I had no inclination to continue my stay in the state. About two weeks before my retirement, I paid a visit to Delhi for the purpose of searching for and finalizing the place for my residence and office. I paid a courtesy call to Hon'ble Justice B.L. Hansaria and Hon'ble Mrs Sujata Manohar. Both gave me the friendly advice that resuming legal practice in Delhi at my age and after such a long gap, especially when I had not been regularly practicing in the Supreme Court, was a risky proposition.

Justice Sujata Manohar suggested that I should consider accepting the post of chairman of the Company Law Board.

I landed in Delhi the day after my retirement and joined the Supreme Court Bar. Sometime thereafter Justice Rama Jois—former justice of the Karnataka High Court and Chief Justice of the Punjab and Haryana high courts—suggested I accept the post of lokayukta of Karnataka, the formation of which was being contemplated. Though I was touched by the feelings of my well-wishers, the idea of accepting any post lower than the one that I had occupied before did not appeal to me and I did not change my decision to resume practice.

## FIRST POST-RETIREMENT APPEARANCE IN SUPREME COURT

After bidding farewell to the co-justices, members of the staff, registry, members of the Bar, etc., who had assembled at the Chief Justice's house and at the airport at Bhubaneswar, I left Odisha without any loss of time. My son Anoop, who was then practicing law in Mumbai, had one Nagpur matter on the board of the Supreme Court a day after my arrival in Delhi. Resumption of my sanad to practice, which was kept under suspension during the judgeship, was necessary and for that my friend and erstwhile colleague Shri Justice V.P. Tipnis from Mumbai helped me. He procured my sanad from the Bar Council of Maharashtra. I received my sanad in the early morning of the day that I had the privilege of appearing before a bench of Hon'ble Justice R.M. Sahai and Justice S.B. Mazumdar in court no. 8. After finishing the argument, I met Mr Kapil Sibal outside the courtroom. He asked me whether it was embarrassing for me to address someone else as 'My Lord', when for a long period of sixteen years I was used to being addressed as such. I replied in the emphatic negative. The reply was genuine. My appearance on this first day was not as a senior advocate, which designation was granted to me by the Supreme Court after a month or so.

## SETTLING DOWN IN DELHI

When the Supreme Court reopened after summer vacation in July 1995, I started receiving briefs from Nagpur, Mumbai and Bhubaneshwar. Once I was designated as a senior advocate in the Supreme Court, which happened within a few months of my resuming practice, the number of briefs as well as the level of the fees started increasing. My practice grew slowly and steadily. Initially Kamla and I stayed in a big flat at Bathla House in Indraprastha Extension, East Delhi, as guests of the late Shri Justice B.P. Saraf of the Bombay High Court who had been my neighbour in a judges' complex in Malabar Hills, Mumbai. We stayed there for a few months and thereafter shifted to our residence-cum-office in a small, rented two-bedroom flat in a multistoried complex—'Poorvasha'—in Mayur Vihar, East Delhi. This was with the kind help of Shri P.N. Misra, senior advocate, who made this arrangement even during our absence from Delhi during the summer vacation and relieved us of the anxiety and difficulty of locating a property to rent in Delhi. It may be mentioned that it is very difficult for a new lawyer to get a property on lease in Delhi because of the general reluctance of landlords to rent out properties to lawyers. The property belonged to Shri P.N. Misra's sister and brother-in-law and the period of lease was two years.

During this period, I earned a good income despite the moderate fees that I charged, to the chagrin of some advocates on record, since it adversely affected even their level of fees. They suggested I charge higher fees. Of course those suggestions were 'welcome' and I readily and promptly accepted them and started implementing them slowly though not necessarily rigorously. The flat had to be vacated on the expiry of the two-year lease. Kamla and I wanted to have a house of our own in Delhi. Although at that time my savings were not sufficient to purchase a house, my new friend Shri U.R. Lalit, a senior advocate and one of the topmost criminal lawyers of the country, displayed remarkable generosity and trust towards me and volunteered to help me out even without my asking.

Shri Lalit was an ad-hoc judge of the Bombay High Court and extremely popular in Nagpur, where he was initially posted. I had the good fortune of appearing before him as a lawyer. During the Emergency, his term as ad-hoc judge was not extended and hence he had started practice in the Supreme Court. It was a loss to the bench, though a gain to the Bar. When he learnt that we were searching for a house, Shri Lalit suggested we look at a small independent house in Noida, near his massive bungalow. Considering our age, my sons did not permit us to opt for an independent house. The prices of flats were also quite high and we decided to raise money by selling an open plot that we owned in Akola. But, even that sale would not completely solve the problem of inadequacy of funds. We were therefore prepared to defer the idea for some time.

During our search for flats, Kamla immensely liked one flat, since its layout was similar to that of our former bungalow 'Sankalp' in Akola, which despite objections from her, I had had to sell to raise money to purchase a flat in a judges' society 'Samta' in Mumbai. Despite being a Bania's daughter and wife, she could not suppress her liking for the flat in the presence of its owner. As a result, he became adamant about the price quoted. She was reluctant to wait as her heart was set on that flat. One day when Shri Lalit enquired about the progress in the search, I disclosed the details. He asked what the likely shortage of funds was and I gave the approximate figure. He asked me to enter into the transaction immediately and give him fifteen days' time to give me the balance amount as a friendly loan for an indefinite period.

I was hesitant, but he snubbed my hesitation. I entered into the transaction with the flat owner, sold the plot at Akola, took the loan from Shri Lalit and purchased the said flat, in which I live until this day. Luckily, my practice prospered and I could repay the loan sooner than expected. I cannot forget the trust that Shri Lalit exhibited in me, even though he did not know me very well at the time.

Delhi's social life and attitude are somewhat odd. 'Address' matters most in the city. Many well-wishers have suggested that I should change my area of residence as well as office, but I have never felt like doing so. There is a sentimental attachment to that flat—both for its similarity to Sankalp and for Kamla's immense liking of that flat.

When I began practice in Akola and Tahasil, my mode of transport was a Hind cycle. After about two years or so I purchased an old Lambretta scooter. After about a year, I purchased an old Hilman car. I was completely ignorant about the mechanisms and accessories of the car. For some time I did not even know that the small rectangular mirror in front of the driver was meant for him to observe traffic behind the car and not just to see a face! I once took out that old Hilman car on a professional visit to a place named Akot, which was about forty kilometres from Akola. After crossing village Wagholi, the car just stopped. I thought there was no petrol and so asked a passer-by for help in procuring petrol. He opened the bonnet and noticed that there was sufficient petrol in the car, but there was no oil in the engine, as a result of which the engine had seized. He looked at me as if I was a fool, but did help in arranging a mechanic. The cost of this ignorance was heavy. The next car I bought was an old Fiat and the first new car was a Maruti 800 when I was in Nagpur. On my retirement in 1995, I purchased an old Fiat-NE from Nagpur, which I took to Delhi.

## BECOMING AN AUTHOR

*Arbitration and Conciliation*

My wife and I used to spend our long vacations with our three sons, two of whom—Dr Narendra and Sanjay—live in Nagpur, and Anoop, who lives in Mumbai. Sometime during the summer vacation of 1998, the managing director of All India Reporter Pvt. Ltd, Nagpur, an old and reputed publisher of law journals and books, approached me for authoring a book on the new Arbitration and Conciliation Act, 1996. I was taken aback by that unexpected proposal. I asked him why he had thought of selecting me as an author since, to his knowledge, I had never authored any book previously. His colleague Mr Fadnis, who was a librarian in the High Court Judges library at Nagpur during my posting there, had accompanied him. They both reminded me of various articles that I had written for newspapers and journals, including their own widely circulated monthly *All India Reporter.* I was quite diffident about my capacity to author a book. The offer was pressing and above all tempting. I took some time to give a final reply and after thinking over the proposal and gathering my courage, succumbed to the temptation of authoring a book.

Within a period of about eighteen months, I completed the manuscript by getting up at 3:30 a.m. or 4:00 a.m. almost every day. Since I was not computer-friendly, I prepared the draft by hand. It was a strenuous but interesting exercise. My eldest son Anoop—who was then practicing law at Mumbai—made a qualitative contribution to this book. Mr Fali S. Nariman, the leader of the Bar and an international authority on the subject of arbitration wrote the prefatory comments, which were dedicated to my father 'whose invisible hands always guided me at the crossroads'.

The book was released by Shri Arun Jaitley, then Union

Minister of Law, Justice and Company Affairs. The function was presided over by Hon'ble Shri Justice Arijit Pasayat, the then Chief Justice of the Delhi High Court, on 14 March 2001 at India Habitat Centre, New Delhi.

On the morning of that day, a piquant and embarrassing situation arose. The magazine *Tehelka* had levelled serious charges of corruption against then Union Minister Mr George Fernandes, due to which the Union Cabinet was to meet that very afternoon to consider the effect of the allegations upon the public. At about 10.00 a.m. I received a message from the publishers that Shri Jaitley's attendance was uncertain and could I therefore help in securing the presence of some other dignitary in place of Shri Jaitley. Securing the presence of a dignitary at such short notice and that too in a position of uncertainty was a difficult task since Shri Jaitley had informed the publisher that he would try his best to be present. My mind started the search.

I had the privilege of knowing Hon'ble Smt. Justice Sujata Manohar, Member, NHRC. I contacted her and acquainted her with the awkward situation that had arisen. She graciously accepted this eleventh hour invitation to stand in, should Shri Jaitley be unable to attend and assured me in a large-hearted manner that she would reach the venue half an hour before the scheduled time. I was touched by her gesture and courtesy.

At 6.30 p.m. the publishers informed me that Shri Jaitley would attend, though about fifteen minutes late. I conveyed the message to Smt. Justice Manohar, but she did not fail to grace the occasion as a general invitee. It was a memorable function largely attended by Supreme Court and Delhi High Court Judges, lawyers, the then Attorney General Shri Soli Sorabjee, and of course, Smt. Justice Manohar. The book was very well received and was reviewed or commented on by the Law Commission of India; the Right Hon'ble Lord Bingham of Cornhill, London, Senior Law Lord, House of Lords, London; the Right Hon'ble

Lord Michael Mustill, London; several present and past Chief Justices of India; Supreme Court Judges; and the Union Minister for Law. I was extremely happy to find that the Law Commission of India in its 176th Report had referred only to this Indian book and accepted the suggestions made therein not only about amendments in the law, but also the suggestion for a separate statute on the subject of 'state immunity'. The second edition of this book was published in 2008. It was co-authored by my son Anoop, who was by then a judge of the Bombay High Court. This edition was released at the hands of Hon'ble Shri P. Chidambaram, then Union Finance Minister. The function was presided over by Shri Fali S. Nariman. It was also very well attended by several sitting and retired judges of the Supreme Court, High Court and leading members of the Bar.

*Trade Marks, Passing of and Franchising*

In between the publication of the first and second editions of *Arbitration and Conciliation*, Justice Anoop Mohta and I co-authored another book, this time on the new Trade Marks Act, 1999, titled *Trade Marks, Passing of and Franchising*, in 2004. Hon'ble Shri Justice V.N. Khare, Chief Justice of India, wrote the foreword and Mr Soli Sorabjee, Attorney General for India, wrote the prefatory comments. I dedicated this book to my wife Kamla. The Indian Law Institute, New Delhi, adjudged this to be 'the best Indian book on the subject'. All India Reporter Pvt. Ltd published the second edition of this book. The foreword to this book was written by the Chief Justice of India, Hon'ble Shri Justice S.H. Kapadia, and prefatory comments by Shri Soli Sorabjee. These books gave me some recognition as an author and perhaps this led to the inclusion of my name in Marquis' *Who's Who in the World*, published each year from USA.

## INTERESTING CONVERSATION WITH LORD BINGHAM OF CORNHILL, HOUSE OF LORDS

The Supreme Court of India celebrated its golden jubilee in 2000. Shri Ram Jethmalani was the union minister for law and justice at this time. Several foreign delegates, including judges and lawyers, attended and participated in the celebrations. Right Hon'ble Lord Bingham of Cornhill, Member of the House of Lords, London, led the delegation from the United Kingdom. The law minister had arranged a dinner in honour of the delegation at his official residence. Shri Justice S.P. Bharucha (whom I had the privilege of knowing as a senior colleague in Mumbai and as a judge in the Supreme Court), introduced me during that function to Lord Bingham as a former Chief Justice of the Orissa high court, presently a senior advocate in the Supreme Court, and an author. Justice Bingham asked me what I found better—legal practice or judgeship. After some pause, my reply was 'fifty-fifty'. Justice Bingham remarked that I should not give a diplomatic answer, to which I replied that no one can be condemned unheard in Britain and so in India. On his smiling acceptance of my quip, I gave my reasons. The gist of these was that as a judge there is the satisfaction of being able to do what one thinks is right, but the income as well as social interactions are meagre. As a lawyer there is ample income and social interaction but not necessarily the satisfaction of doing what you think is right. The group gathered around us had grown by that time and before Lord Bingham could give his verdict, Justice Bharucha in his usual stern style remarked, 'I do not know all this; but I can tell you that this fellow has been almost the same—either as a judge or as a lawyer.' Justice Bingham, after hearing the intervener, Justice Bharucha, acquitted me honourably from the charge of diplomacy. Everyone burst into laughter.

## PARTICIPATION IN INTERNATIONAL CONFERENCES, SEMINARS, SYMPOSIA AND CONTRIBUTION OF ARTICLES TO NEWSPAPERS AND JOURNALS

Since my Akola days, I have been participating in conferences and seminars and contributing articles to legal/social journals, though with a small break during the period of judgeship. I restarted my participation and contribution when I resumed legal practice in Delhi. I had the privilege of being invited to speak and write on various legal subjects in national as well as international journals and seminars, conferences and symposiums arranged by various organizations, including high court Bar associations, judicial training institutes, Bar councils, law colleges, legal authorities, Confederation of Indian Bar, etc. One of my favourite topics has always been the law of arbitration and conciliation and the importance of Alternative Dispute Resolutions. I have delivered addresses at International Conferences in New Delhi and at South Asian Association for Regional Cooperation (SAARC) law conferences in Colombo (Sri Lanka), Karachi (Pakistan) and Paro (Bhutan). I am of the confirmed view that growing uncertainty in the higher courts' judgments is an obstacle to effective administration of rule of law. I have spoken on this subject in some forums and discussed this matter with some of the Hon'ble Judges and senior lawyers of the Supreme Court, most of whom seem to agree with this view. Two of my articles on the subject have been published, one in *The Indian Express* dated 13 July 1999 under the headline 'Tyranny of the frivolous' and the second in *Souvenir,* published by the Bar Council of Maharashtra in Nagpur, dated 12–13 July 2008 under the heading 'Uncertainty of law: A challenge to the judicial system & legal fraternity'.

I am of the view that the role of the legal profession in the administration of justice, especially with regard to the needy and downtrodden, needs to be enhanced. I was called upon to deliver a talk on that subject in an all-India seminar arranged by the Confederation of Indian Bar in New Delhi on 28 September 2013, which was presided over by Hon'ble Shri Justice H.L. Dattu, then judge of the Supreme Court of India.

## PHUKAN COMMISSION

After former defence minister George Fernandez's entanglement in the *Tehelka* sting operation, the Government of India, under the Commission of Enquiry, had appointed the Justice S.N. Phukan Commission to probe the allegations of corruption in the wake of the controversy generated by the *Tehelka* tapes of March 2001. The controversies led to the resignation of Shri George Fernandez. Justice Phukan, judge of Supreme Court of India, called me and requested me to assist him as a counsel of commission. While thanking him for the confidence reposed in me, I politely declined the assignment, inter alia, on the ground that a Bar under Article 220 of the Constitution could possibly arise against my appointment as a counsel before a commission, even one headed by a Supreme Court Judge. Article 220 prohibits a retired permanent judge of a High Court from practising before any authority in India, except the Supreme Court and the high courts—other than the High Court in which he was a permanent judge.

## SOME IMPORTANT AND INTERESTING CASES

I have appeared in several cases before the Supreme Court and high courts of various states such as Andhra Pradesh, Delhi, Karnataka, Madhya Pradesh, Kerala, Chennai and Rajasthan. Several judgments related to the cases in which I appeared have been reported in legal journals. Some important cases in which I had the satisfaction of contributing to the development of law are as follows.

*Raunaq International Ltd vs. I.V.R. Construction Ltd, 1999 (1) SCC 492*

This laid down exhaustive parameters about (a) dos and don'ts in public interest litigation; (b) elements of public interest; and (c) grant of stay on being satisfied that the allegations require serious examination. Most importantly it also held that where interim relief is to be granted, the person obtaining it must be made accountable and asked to reimburse the damages suffered by the respondent as a result of the interim order.

*State of Punjab Vs. Baldev Singh, 1999 (6) SCC 172*

A Constitution bench judgment of five judges, mandated to resolve diversion of opinions in the Supreme Court with regard to the ambit and scope of Section 50 of the Narcotic Drugs Psychotropic Substances Act, 1985. The basic conclusions were that: (a) it is imperative for the empowered or duly authorized officer to inform a person before search about his right under Section 50 (1) of being taken to the nearest gazetted officer or magistrate; and (b) non-compliance with that mandatory requirement may not vitiate the trial, but would render the recovery of the illicit article suspect and vitiate the conviction, where it is recorded only on the basis of the possession of the illicit article recovered in a search conducted in violation of Section 50.

*Shivajirao B. Patil Kawekar vs. Vilasrao D. Deshmukh, (2000) 1 SCC 398*

The short factual backdrop to the case is that the appellant Shivajirao Kawekar won an election in Latur (Maharashtra) constituency defeating the respondent Vilasrao Deshmukh (ex-chief minister of Maharashtra) by a large margin of over 30,000 votes.

The challenge to the validity of this election was upheld by the designated judge of the Bombay High Court on the grounds of commission of corrupt practices contemplated under Section 123 (3-A) and 123 (4) read with 100 (1) (d) (ii) of the RPA. This led to an appeal to the Supreme Court under Section 116 A of the RPA, in which I appeared for the appellant returned candidate.

A Supreme Court three-judge bench decision laid down the mandatory requirements to be stated in the pleadings in an election petition for challenging an election under the Representation of Peoples Act, 1951 (RPA). The Supreme Court accepted the contentions raised by me on behalf of the appellant, a returned candidate namely Shivajirao Kawekar, that the petition suffered from fatal infirmities of lack of several particulars and non-compliance with Rule 94 A read with Form 25 of Conduct of Election Rules 1951 framed under RPA, about form of affidavit to be filed with the petition.

The Supreme Court also accepted the contention that for proving the charge of 'corrupt practices' under Section 123 (4) of the RPA, it is necessary to state that not only the publication containing corrupt practices is with the consent of the returned candidate or his election agent or workers but also the said publication must disclose their names. It must give particulars about the dates and places where the publication has been distributed, along with the names of at least a few persons to whom they might have been delivered.

Moreover the bench ruled that there was absence of averments that: (i) the corrupt practices had been committed in the interest of the returned candidate; and (ii) consequent thereupon the result of election was materially affected as contemplated under Section 100 (1)(d)(ii).

The basis of the alleged corrupt practices were two newspaper articles by two different writers—one by Professor Mohan Kamble, editor of the daily *Jan Jagaran*, under the heading 'Mamulire', and another by Professor M.B. Pathan, editor of the *Weekly*, under the heading 'Lawa Lawi'.

The averments in the petition were not claimed to be based on the personal knowledge of the respondent, but were based on the information received by him, 'from the persons and newspapers mentioned in the said papers', which he 'believed to be true'. No name of any such person was mentioned nor did it contain: (i) a statement that the publications were made with the consent of the petitioner or his agent or worker; and (ii) that it materially affected the result of the election as contemplated under Section 100 (1) (d) (ii) of RPA.

The Supreme Court accepted the submissions on behalf of the appellant—that not only was the petition defective in law, but it was also unsubstantiated on facts. Inevitably, the appellant's election received the seal of validity from the Supreme Court.

*Girnar Traders Vs State of Maharashtra, 2004 (8) SCC 505, Division Bench decision; 2007(7) SCC 555 a three-Judge Bench decision; and 2011(3) SCC 1 a Constitution Bench decision*

The basic point in this matter was whether Section 11 (A) of the Land Acquisition Act, 1894 (LA Act)—prescribing a limitation for making award under Section 11 of the Act—would be applicable to land acquisitions under Chapter 7 of the Maharashtra Regional and Town planning Act, 1976 (MRTP Act). The first decision on the point was rendered in the case of *State of Maharashtra Vs. Sant Joginder Singh Kishan Singh, 1995 (Suup) 2 SCC 475* answering the said question in the negative.

M/s Girnar Traders, whom I represented, challenged the correctness of this view. After exhaustive hearing of both sides, the division bench was convinced that Sant Joginder Singh's case required reconsideration and hence it referred the matter for reconsideration by a larger bench comprising minimum three judges. A three-judge bench, by a majority, upheld the view propounded in the referring order but for various reasons— including differences of opinion on certain other aspects—referred the question to a larger bench of five judges. A Constitution bench of five judges heard this matter and ultimately upheld the view of Joginder Singh.

The undisputed factual background to this case was that the state government had the power to acquire the land for the same public purposes either under the LA Act or under the MRTP Act. If acquisition was under the LA Act, the limitation for making the award under Section 11 would apply, but if the acquisition was under the MRTP Act the said limitation would not apply. Thus, the state government had unrestricted power to pick and choose.

In the case of *Nagpur Improvement Trust Vs. Vithal Rao* involving interpretation of a similar provision in the Nagpur Improvement Trust Act (NIT Act) a larger bench of seven Supreme Court Judges had ruled that the existence of such power to pick and choose and give one owner treatment different from another equally situated was discriminatory and hence violated Article 14 of the Constitution. It was further reiterated that in law, classification could not be made on the basis of the authority acquiring the land. This larger Bench decision was binding upon the five-judge bench.

Strong reliance was therefore placed on that precedent at every stage of the prolonged hearing. In its eighty-four page judgment, the Supreme Court's five-judge bench decision in Girnar's case brushed aside the ratio of the seven-judge bench decision in NIT's case by a single line—reasoning that the seven-judge bench judgment had failed to examine the effect of the federal structure of the Constitution. With respect, it is difficult to locate either the logic or the propriety in this line of reasoning.

*Anand vs. Committee for Scrutiny & Verification of Tribe Claims, 2012 (1) SCC 113*

In this case, the Supreme Court for the first time accepted the repeatedly canvassed point that the 'affinity test'—which focuses on the ethnological connection with a Schedule Tribe (ST)—could not be regarded as a litmus test for establishing the link with a ST. Consequently, it could not be the sole criteria to reject the claim, the main criteria being the existence of pre-Constitution documents. This admission was made not only before the high courts, but also previously constituted benches of the Supreme Court.

*Unitech Limted and Another Vs. Union of India and Another (2016) 2 SCC 569.*

In this case, an interesting question of interpretation of the expression 'transfer' in Chapter XX-C, Section 269 UA (2) (D) & (F) and Section 269 UD of the Income Tax Act 1961 was involved. These provisions relate to the compulsory purchase of immovable property on behalf of the central government, where there is undervaluation of the property to evade taxes. Law presumes that undervaluation greater than fifteen percent below the fair market value is with a view to evade taxes.

(i) The expression 'transfer' as defined under Section 247 of the Income Tax Act is wide enough to include within its scope agreements or arrangements having the effect of transferring certain specified rights in the land, even though transfer does not amount to sale, lease or exchange as defined under the Transfer of Property Act. But mere possessory right on the land for the purpose of construction of building on the land without transfer of title in the underneath land is covered.

(ii) The Income Tax Authority in the instant case of collaboration agreement had held that the impugned transaction fell within the expression 'transfer' under the Act.

This adjudication and consequent compulsory purchase was

unnecessarily challenged by the assesse in the Bombay High Court on the grounds that (1) no transfer of property was involved in the agreement; (2) there was no undervaluation of the property in the transfer at all, which will be clear from the comparable sale transactions in the same locality. This is how the matter reached the Supreme Court before which inter alia the following contentions were raised:

1. Mere collaboration agreement of lease and transfer or rights in the building to be constructed in future is not covered under the Act, such transfer being only possessory in nature to enable construction of the building on the land;

2. There was failure to consider the relevance of comparable sale instances in the same locality and wrongly relying only on the sale transaction in a different far-off locality.

Challenges on both grounds were successful and the impugned orders were quashed by the Supreme Court by the above elaborate landmark judgment.

## WHEN A CASE CARRIES ON FOR THREE AND A HALF DECADES

Cases are won and/or lost not necessarily as expected, and sometimes, despite the best efforts of lawyers. There is nothing so great or unusual about this. Success always brings pleasure, but real satisfaction to a lawyer comes when he has done his best in performing his role. The degree of satisfaction is higher when the lawyer receives appreciation even from a client who has lost the case. This is becoming rarer and rarer these days. At the beginning of my practice in the Supreme Court, I received such rare appreciation in a letter from one Shri Harilal Asmar, Chairman, Malegaon Merchant Cooperative Bank Ltd, the following relevant portion of which deserves reproduction:

> With great effort and vehemence you have conducted my case
> for which I shall remain grateful to you. Even though the matter
> was entrusted to you at the 11th hour you had studied the case.
> Your persuasive arguments were quite impressive. I have lost
> the case but there couldn't be greater and better efforts.

During the hearing of a house rent control case of 1969 from
Akola in the Supreme Court by a bench presided over by Hon'ble
Shri Justice M.M. Punchi, he noticed in the record that the
cross-examination of the witnesses was by advocate V.A. Mohta.
The Hon'ble Judge remarked about the coincidence of the two
lawyers—the cross-examiner in the trial court and so also the
arguing counsel in the Supreme Court were both V.A. Mohta.
I had to clarify. There were not two Mohtas but only one. The
judges looked at each other in amazement. What a tragedy of
the system that the time lapse between the start and finish of the
case was three and a half decades.

## ARBITRATION AND MEDIATION

Under Article 220 of the Constitution of India, there is a restriction
on a retired permanent judge pleading or acting in any court
or before any authority in India, except the Supreme Court and
the high courts—other than the High Court in which he was a
permanent judge.

I have been appointed as sole arbitrator, or as chairman,
or member of an arbitration tribunal in innumerable cases on
consent of parties/institutions and/or by order of courts under
Section 11 of the Arbitration and Conciliation Act, 1996. Apart
from my practice, this activity has also kept me engaged. Some
important arbitrations that I have conducted relate to national and
international institutions including the likes of the Dawoodi Bohra

community (through its spiritual leader the Syedna), Reliance, Reckitt, Times of India and individuals such as India's Olympic gold-medallist Abhinav Bindra, among others.

The Arbitration Act and its working in India leave much to be desired. New arbitration laws all over the world are based on the United Nations Commission on International Trade Law (UNCITRAL) model law, which was basically meant for international commercial arbitration and not for ad-hoc and domestic arbitrations. This is what Lord Justice Mustill said in his keynote address at the Bahrain Congress for the International Council of Commercial Arbitration:

> If I had any adverse comment to make about the otherwise excellent discussions within UNCITRAL, it would be that most of those taking part were not so much dismissive of the importance of ad hoc arbitrations but unaware that they existed.

Two different regimes, one for international arbitration and the other for domestic arbitration, are a necessity, especially in countries like India. In Singapore, they have two separate regimes for the good reason that they state as follows:

> A closer involvement by the local courts in domestic arbitration is desirable, both for the development of domestic commercial and legal practice and for a closer supervision of decision which may affect weaker domestic parties. It is appropriate that the (local) court be able to reflect public policy considerations and national interests involved in purely domestic disputes.

I have, however, thus far refused to be a member of a tribunal whose chairman is not, or legally cannot, be a High Court or Supreme Court Judge, and further who is not either higher in rank than that of a Chief Justice of High Court or senior to me as a judge.

One example of such refusal by me can be found in the case

of *You One Maharia vs National Highways Authority, (2007) 7 SCC 704* of India in which Hon'ble Justice C.K. Thakker—one of the most respected judges of the Supreme Court—referred to this aspect but very rightly refused to grant the petitioner the relief of appointing a chairman at variance with the written agreement about selection of chairman's rank or position.

I have also been appointed conciliator/mediator by consent of parties or by order of court in several disputes. One important matter related to an age-old dispute in the Narang family of Mumbai (owners of Ambassador Hotel in Churchgate, Mumbai), in which the Supreme Court had appointed me as a conciliator/mediator to resolve their unfortunate family disputes within a specified time frame. Despite all efforts, I was only partly successful. The Supreme Court, despite my timely report of partial success, continued my appointment by the following order:

25.01.2005

We have perused the report dated 16.01.2005 received from Chief Justice (Retd.) V.A. Mohta, the Mediator/Conciliator and heard the learned counsel for the parties in the light of the report.

Although some disputes have not been resolved in spite of the commendable efforts made by the learned Mediator/Conciliator, yet we feel that the possibility of finding a solution to the disputes between the parties is not totally ruled out. We request Shri V.A. Mohta to continue with the proceedings in terms of the order dated 11.10.2004 passed by the court.

◆

I regret that despite the best efforts there was no further noticeable success. I believe that the Supreme Court appointed some other mediators also thereafter, but unfortunately they too failed and the disputes continue.

## SOCIAL LIFE POST RETIREMENT

SEARCH: A Registered Society Dedicated to Social Excellence and Justice

SEARCH is a registered society in Delhi dedicated to social excellence and justice. It was founded by the Late Justice V.A. Masodkar, a self-made man from Nagpur who was a judge of the Bombay High Court and after retirement, a member of the Rajya Sabha. Shri G.L. Sanghi, a leading light of the Supreme Court Bar, was elected as its president. Its membership comprises national leaders, judges, lawyers, ambassadors, bureaucrats, university professors, medical practitioners, social workers, etc.

The society holds periodic meetings to which eminent people are invited to deliver lectures on subjects of national and international importance. The major burden of running SEARCH has been, and continues to be, on General Secretary Ranjana Narayan, Supreme Court lawyer and a scintillating speaker in her own right.

The general body of SEARCH unanimously elected me on the sudden and unfortunate demise of Shri G.L. Sanghi as his successor. One of the leading and respected senior lawyers of the Supreme Court, Shri P.P. Rao, approached me for the post, most probably after consulting with the senior members of the organization. On the assurance that my tenure would not exceed two years, I consented to accept the responsibility. During that period, I had the privilege and pleasure of presiding over and listening to the lectures of dignitaries.

His Excellency Shri Mark Sofer, Ambassador of Israel, spoke on the subject of 'Israel–Arab Conflict: Middle East Crisis—What Next?', while Shri H.E. Osama Musa, Ambassador of the state of Palestine spoke on the 'Palestine–Israel Conflict; Prospects for the Future and its Implications for India'.

Justice Zakaria Mohammed Yacoob, judge of the Constitutional

Court of South Africa, gave a talk on the subject of 'Public Interest Law in South Africa'. Dr Shrinivas Rao Sohoni, former bureaucrat and Secretary General, Rajya Sabha, Secretary to the President of India, lectured on 'Secularism in the Indian Ethos', while Shri G. Parthasarthy, former High Commissioner to Pakistan, spoke on 'Indo-Pak Relations in a Volatile Neighbourhood—Energy and Terrorism'.

Shri T.R. Andhyarujina, senior advocate gave a talk on 'Tracing roots of Iranian history and culture', and Smt. Zena Sorabji, international chairperson of the Baha'i House Worship (Lotus temple) spoke on the subject of 'Oneness of humanity—a new framework for moral education'. I learnt much from my very satisfying tenure at SEARCH and was fortunate to receive unstinted support and cooperation from all the members. Although many senior members asked me to continue for one more term, I was not inclined to do so. Since my repeated requests to be relieved were not being considered, I sent a letter of resignation dated 20 April 2008 to Ms Ranjana Narayan, the general secretary, with a copy to the vice-president, Shri M.N. Krishnamani, who is a well-known and popular senior advocate of the Supreme Court and has been the president of the Supreme Court Bar Association. However, I continue to be associated with the organization as a member.

## EUTHANASIA MOVEMENT: INTERNATIONAL CONFERENCE ON EUTHANASIA

I am a strong believer in 'ichha maran'—an age-old philosophy of willing one's own death. It has social as well as legal ramifications. I have been a member of the Society for the Right to Die with Dignity (SRDD), a registered society founded by the famous economist and social thinker, Shri Minoo Masani of Mumbai. I represent SRDD and the Indian Society of Critical Care Medicine in a writ petition under Article 32 of the Constitution pending in the Supreme Court of India for recognition of the right to die with dignity as a part of the fundamental rights within the fold of the right of life or personal liberty guaranteed under Article 21 of the Constitution of India.

The SRDD had arranged a symposium on the subject in Mumbai at Sir Harkishandas Hospital Prarthana Samaj on 21 September 2008, in which eminent medical practitioners of India, social workers, psychologists, religious persons, etc. were invited to participate. Dr Praful Desai, a world-famous oncologist, chaired the symposium. I was invited to speak on 'The Indian Scene—Recent Legal Developments' and referred to the legal aspects and backdrop of the subject with special reference to the pending petition under Article 32 of the Constitution in the Supreme Court of India and the 196th Report of the Law Commission of India.

Thereafter, the Supreme Court of India, in the case of Aruna Ramachandra Shanbaug vs. Union of India and Others, (2011) 4 SCC 454, ruled that passive euthanasia should be permitted in the country in certain situations. It also issued guidelines in the matter that remain operative until Parliament makes the relevant law.

On this subject, I have contributed various articles to journals and dailies and participated in seminars and workshops, the most important being the International Workshop for Development of Policy Statement on Euthanasia held at India International Centre, New Delhi, on 6 August 2011, by the Indian Medical Association and University College of Medical Sciences, New Delhi. It was an extremely well organized and well attended workshop which provided a forum for internationally recognized doctors and sociologists. Five groups—(1) withdrawing/withholding life support treatment; (2) physician-assisted suicide; (3) legalization of passive or active euthanasia; (4) macroeconomics of invasive medical technology for terminal illness; (5) applicability of advance directives and living wills in India—were formed for deliberations on different aspects of euthanasia. I was the group leader on the subject of legalization of passive/active euthanasia. This group comprised about twenty-five delegates, including internationally-renowned activist Shri Phillipe Nitschke. Vibrant discussions and some very relevant paper presentations emanated from the group.

I presented the following paper along with the gist of some judgments and the draft of a living Will as suggested by the SRDD:

The philosophy of willing one's death—'ichha maran'—is not alien to Indian culture and heritage. Even though the ethics of various religions advocate reverence for life, they permit an individual to choose his/her last breath under certain circumstances. Sharbabagna (from the *Ramayana*), who was badly maimed in battle, performed self-immolation. Gandhari, Kunti and Dhritarashtra (from the *Mahabharat*) retired to a forest after performing their death rites; Bhishma willed the day and time of his death; Sant Dyandev chose to relinquish his life at a young age, as he felt that he had served the purpose of his life; and Acharya Vinoba Bhave starved himself to death as he felt there was no longer any purpose to living. In recent times, Ramana Maharshi refused all medicine, food and water and chose to die in samadhi rather than linger on with an incurable tumour.

Yet another example is of Shri Madhu Dandawate, a renowned socialist, national leader and former Union Railway minister, who was diagnosed with cancer in the leg. Ultimately, when it was confirmed that the cancer was incurable and he would to have to suffer life as an invalid, he desired discontinuation of life support. To his son, he said, 'You are my son, aren't you? I don't want simply a biological son but a "logical" one! Do you want me to lead this type of life?' The son had reluctance but he ultimately honoured his father's last wishes. Mahaprasthan is recommended in the *Purana* for incurable diseases. Even according to the *Shastras*, the choice to relinquish life is as basic as the one to live. History records that the ancient Bolivian tribe of Armaya, the Eskimos, the Ethiopians and several other tribal societies conferred such a right upon their members. Often the family participated in the act, with rituals.

This concept never lost its significance, which is evident from the fact that in 1935, intellectual giants such as George Bernard Shaw and H.G. Wells formed a society in England to advocate the concept. Later in 1938, the Rev. Charles Potter, a Christian theologist, established a society in the United States of America. Thereafter, Europe, Australia and Japan subscribed to this concept. The establishment of the World Federation of Societies for Right to Die underlines its global significance. The federation comprises several societies from twenty countries in the world, representing more than five million people. On the same lines, SRDD was formed in India around 1980.

The legal debate on the topic of the 'right to die with dignity' must centre on two sections of the Indian Penal Code, 1860 (sections 306 and 309) and two Articles of Indian Constitution (Articles 14 and 21).

Section 306 IPC deals with abetment of suicide and Section 309 deals with attempt to commit suicide. The distinction between the two can be very well described by referring to Shakespeare's *Hamlet*. Shakespeare had no doubt that Hamlet could consider the question of 'to be or not to be' freely and without fear that he would break any law if he decided 'not to be'. In brief, the question whether a person would like to live or not live was regarded by Shakespeare to be an entirely free, individual decision, without any legal inhibitions. If the offence is complete, the perpetrator is out of the clutches of the law under Section 309; but if the crime is incomplete, the perpetrator will be punished. What an irony of law! This is a monumental exception to basic criminal jurisprudence.

It is rather sad that Section 309 IPC has continued to be on our statute books for about a century and a half, despite a growing feeling amongst thinkers, academicians, sociologists and even judges that this provision has to be erased. Following the French Revolution of 1789, such a law was abolished in Europe. Even Britain, which gave us this law, has abrogated it by enacting The Suicide Act 1961, which decriminalized the act of suicide, though not the act of abetment of suicide. The Swiss Federal Supreme Court, in 2006, held that right to decide on method and time of one's own death is part of guaranteed right of self-determination under Article 8 of the European Convention on Human Rights.

In fact, it must be pointed out that the Law Commission of India in its 42nd Report (1971) recommended its repeal. The IPC Amendment Bill 1978, providing for its omission, was even passed in the Rajya Sabha, but it could not be passed in the Lok Sabha because of the Lok Sabha's dissolution in 1979. Legal scrutiny of Section 309 was made by the Courts in India on the touchstone and Articles 14 and 21 of the Constitution of India. The first decision declaring Section 309 as ultra vires of the Article 14 and 21 was rendered by Bombay High Court in the case of Maruti Shripati Dubal vs. State of Maharashtra, reported in 1986 Mh. L.J. 913. The Supreme Court dealt with this subject for the first time in 1994 in the case of P. Rathinam vs. Union of India, (1994) 3 SCC 394, whereby it upheld the decision of the Hon'ble High Court of Bombay and declared Section 309 violative of Article 21. However, the Supreme Court did not agree with the view that Section 309 violates Article 14.

This decision of the Division Bench of the Supreme Court was overruled by the Constitution Bench in 1996 in the case of Gian Kaur (Smt.) vs. State of Punjab, (1996) 2 SCC 648, taking a view that the right to life does not, as a rule, include the right to die. The Constitution Bench only dealt with the legal question and did not touch upon the desirability or otherwise, of retaining such a penal provision. However, the following observations of this decision are relevant in the debate about the 'right to die with dignity' in general and passive euthanasia in particular.

A question may arise, in the context of a dying man who is terminally ill and in a persistent vegetative state that he may be permitted to terminate his life by a premature extinction of it in those circumstances. This category of cases may fall within the ambit of the 'right to die' with dignity as a part of the right to live with dignity, when death due to termination of natural life is certain and imminent and the process of natural death has commenced. These are not cases of extinguishing life but only of accelerating conclusion of the process of natural death that has already commenced. The debate, even in such cases, to permit physician-assisted termination of life is inconclusive. It is sufficient to reiterate that the argument to support the view of permitting termination of life in such cases, to reduce the period of suffering during the process of certain natural death, is not available to interpret Article 21 to include therein the right to curtail the natural span of life.

The subtle distinction between extinguishing life and accelerating the natural process of death, which has already commenced, was recognised. However, the court did not deem fit to include the same under Article 21 as an essential facet of the right to live with dignity.

The Indian courts had, till 7 March 2011, refused the right to die even during continuous suffering from incurable diseases on the grounds that physician-assisted suicide is not legal in India, despite increasing worldwide support for the concept of euthanasia. Countries such as Belgium, the Netherlands, Sri Lanka, Switzerland, France, Australia, New Zealand, South

Africa, and the states of Oregon, Washington and Montana in the USA, have legally recognized this concept, though the forms are different. Oregon, USA, is the first jurisdiction in the world to permit terminally-ill patients to determine the time of their death. The law is the Death and Dignity Act 1997. The Act was not without challenge in the court but the USA Supreme Court upheld its validity. Under that law, a resident of Oregon can make a written request to a physician for prescription of lethal dosage of medication for ending life, but subject to certain conditions.

A similar Act was enacted in Washington—Death with Dignity Act, 2008. Both these Acts governed the residents of their respective states. The Washington law applies to residents who have less than six months to live. In the Netherlands, Belgium, United Kingdom (UK) and France, the law permits terminally ill patients to refuse treatment in favour of death. Italy has not enacted any such law; however in 2009, an Italian court allowed feeding tubes to be removed from a patient who had been in coma since 1992.

It is well known that a Swiss organization, Dignitas, helps terminally ill patients as well as patients with severe illnesses to die, assisted by qualified doctors and nurses. In Australia, the public advocate of the Supreme Court of Victoria has the power to refuse further nutrition and administered hydration to a patient at an advanced stage of dementia. The Supreme Court of Western Australia has directed that a nursing home in Perth must respect the desire of a middle-aged patient suffering from quadriplegia to starve to death. The Supreme Court of South Australia also granted the right to die by refusing to take food and medication. It was held that a competent adult was under no duty to take life-sustaining medication and therefore a refusal to do so did not amount to suicide. Courts in various jurisdictions worldwide have also pronounced several judgments recognizing this right judicially in appropriate cases.

On 7 March 2011, the Supreme Court, in a landmark decision in the case of Aruna Shanbaug vs. State of Maharashtra, (2011) 4 SCC 454, ruled that passive euthanasia should be permitted in the country in certain situations. In substance, it laid down the following guidelines that will be operative until Parliament makes a law on the subject: A decision has to be taken to discontinue life support either by the parents or the spouse or close relatives, or in the absence of any of them, even a person or a body of persons acting as a friend in place of next of kin, can take such a decision; the doctors attending the patient can also take the decision; however, it should be taken bona fide in the best interest of the patient; hence, even if the near relatives, friend or doctors take a decision to withdraw life support, such a decision requires approval from the High Court concerned as laid down in Airedale's Case. The conditions and procedural aspects to be followed in the matter are also indicated in the judgment.

A private member bill titled 'The Physicians and Surgeons (Indemnity from Civil and Criminal Proceedings) Bill 2005' was introduced in the Rajya Sabha in March 2005. Section 4 of the bill proposes that a person of sound mind should be entitled to make a declaration and also to make a power of attorney regarding the future course of action in case of terminal illness.

Article 21 of Part-III of the Constitution of India deals with the right to life and personal liberty. This right has been widely construed by the Supreme Court to include right to live with human dignity. The question arises as to whether 'life' means: (i) mere undignified animal existence; (ii) compulsion to live under any circumstance; and (iii) does not include the right to choose the method and time of one's last breath.

It may be noted that a writ petition under Article 32 of the Constitution of India, filed by Common Cause (a registered society), is pending before the Supreme Court. It seeks inter alia: (i) declaration that the 'Right to die with dignity' is a Fundamental Right guaranteed under Article 21 of the Constitution of India; (ii) adoption of suitable procedures and methodologies for its effective implementation in the cases of persons of deteriorated health or terminal illness; (iii) recognising 'living wills' executed by them, expressing their desire to terminate life in the above situation, rather than unnecessarily prolonging the agony. The writ petition has been supported by intervention of several institutions including SRDD, Indian Society of Critical Care Medicine (a registered society and the largest non-profit association of Indian physicians, nurses, physiotherapists and other allied healthcare professionals involved in the care of the critically ill) and the Delhi Medical Council.

In March 2006, the Law Commission of India submitted its 196th Report on 'Medical Treatment to Terminally-ill Patients (Protection of Patients and Medical Practitioners) 2006', along with a draft bill. Although several clauses in the said bill seem to be controversial, what is important is the debate and open-mindedness on the subject.

The Law Commission of India submitted to the Government of India its 210th Report recommending effacement of Section 309 from the statute book because the provision is inhuman and outdated. To complete the story, it must be mentioned that after the decision in Gian Kaur (Smt.) vs. State of Punjab by the Supreme Court, the then Law Commission had submitted its 156th Report in 1997 recommending retention of Section 309.

The basic question that haunts such a bill is the possibility of misuse. This possibility cannot be ruled out totally. However, it has to be noted that in most of the cases all over the world, the requests for withdrawal of life support had come from the closest family members, such as parents and spouses. It will not be out of place also to mention that so far not a single case of misuse has been reported anywhere. Of course, this does not mean it cannot happen in future. There is no law and/or power known to mankind which is incapable of misuse. However, that cannot be the justification for not having a proper law. What is crucial is that the law has to be resistant to misuse.

The most detestable form of euthanasia is 'active euthanasia'. This is not a new concept in India. Concept and practice of 'active euthanasia' existed and continues to exist in both Jainism and Hinduism. In Jainism, it is called 'santhara' and in Hinduism it is called 'prayopravesh'. It must be remembered that 'love and compassion' are the main core values of euthanasia—both passive as well as active. Compassion emerges out of the depth and intensity of suffering and it overtakes the desire to retain the company of a loved one. It is a matter of common knowledge that sometimes, occasion arises when permitting and/or assisting the dying is the kindest thing to do by those responsible for the care of loved ones. It was the compassion of Pinki Virani that made her seek relief for Aruna Shanbaug. It was also the compassion of staff of KEM Hospital who opposed it. There are cases where compassion not only justifies but also demands active euthanasia. In fact, voices in its favour are being heard even in India. No doubt, the possibility of misuse of active euthanasia is higher than the misuse of passive euthanasia. Public opinion in India is not likely to be in its favour today. But who knows how the wind will blow tomorrow.

It may be mentioned that the writ petition under Article 32 of the Constitution was recently heard by a bench of three Hon'ble Judges of the Supreme Court. After considering the submissions of the petitioner, the interveners and the Union of India, the matter was referred for final hearing to the Constitution bench of five judges for final hearing, which has been completed.

## CONCEPT OF BASIC STRUCTURE OF THE CONSTITUTION

The Institute of Social Sciences, New Delhi, and Forum of Federations had arranged a seminar on 'Federalism, Governance and a Conflict of Views between the Supreme Court and the Constitution'. The former prime minister of India, Shri I.K. Gujral, inaugurated this seminar at which I was privileged to be invited to participate. Though consensus was in favour of the validity of 'basic structure', I belonged to the minority that advocated a contrary view. I had written an article on the subject titled 'Basic Structure of the Constitution: Where is it? What is it?' for the souvenir published by the Bar Council of Maharashtra and Goa for the State Lawyers Conference at Akola on 24 February 2013, which reads thus:

### Basic structure of the Constitution: Where is it? What is it?

The question of the ability to amend the Fundamental Rights in Part III of the Constitution was considered directly for the first time in the case of Shankari Parasd, 1952 SCR 89, and it was held by a unanimous verdict that they were amendable. This view was reiterated, even after thirteen years, in the case of Sajjan Singh, 1965(1) SCR 933. However, in the case of I.C. Golak Nath & Ors. vs. State of Punjab & Anr, 1967 (2) SCR 762, there was a difference of opinion on the subject and by majority it was held that the Fundamental Rights cannot be abridged in view of Article 13 of the Constitution. This led to the 24th Amendment to the Constitution in the year 1971, which introduced Article 13 (4) saying that nothing in that Article shall apply to any amendment to the Constitution made under Article 368, which in turn was suitably amended.

For a long period, no voice was raised against these judgments by any member of the Constituent Assembly, many of whom were then still alive, or anyone else. Although during the process of framing of the Constitution, which is a product of exhaustive study and deliberations, this concept was not contemplated.

In the case of His Holiness Kesavananda Bharati vs. State of Kerala, 1973 (4) SCC 225, Golaknath's case was overruled by a narrow majority of 7:6. It was held that Article 368 itself had the power of amendment of the Constitution and that the word 'law' in Article 13 (2) did not include amendment under Article 368 and that does not enable Parliament to alter the Basic Structure of the Constitution. However, it was not made clear as to what constituted the basic structure. It thus remained an open question. By the Constitution (42nd Amendment) Act, 1976, Clauses 4 and 5 were inserted in Article 368 with the object of diluting the limitation of the basic structure to Parliament's amending powers.

However, the 'basic structure doctrine' was reaffirmed by the Supreme Court in the cases of: (i) Smt. Indira Nehru Gandhi vs. Raj Narain, 1975 (Supp) SCC 1; (ii) Minerva Mills Ltd. vs. Union of India, 1980 (3) SCC 625; (iii) P. Sambamurthy & Others vs. State of Andhra Pradesh, 1987(1) SCC 362; (iv) Kihoto Hollohan vs. Zachillhu & Others, 1992 Supp (2) SCC 651; (v) Raghunathrao Ganpatrao vs. Union of India, 1994 Supp (1) SCC 191; (vi) S.R. Bommai vs. Union of India, 1994 (3) SCC 1; (vii) L. Chandra Kumar vs. Union of India, 1997 (3) SCC 261; (viii) State of UP vs. Dr Dina Nath Shukla & Another, 1997 (9) SCC 662; (ix) All India Judges' Association vs. Union of India, 2002 (4) SCC 24; (x) T.M.A. Pai Foundation & Others vs. State of Karnataka & Others, 2002 (8) SCC 481; and (xii) more recently in the case of I.R. Cohelo vs. State of Tamil Nadu (2007) 2 SCC 1.

In these cases, concepts such as 'democracy', 'free and fair elections', 'separation of powers', 'secularism', 'Judicial review', 'jurisdiction of Supreme Court under Article 32 and High

Courts under Article 226 and 227 of the Constitution', 'certain objectives in Part III', 'non-appointment of sufficient number of judges', and 'Preamble of the Constitution' have been held to be non-amendable features of the Constitution.

The case of Minerva Mills Ltd. vs. Union of India, 1980 (3) SCC 625 was decided on the basis that the Constitution had conferred only a limited amending power on the Parliament which cannot be enlarged into absolute power. It is difficult to locate any such limitation in the Constitutional scheme. A close examination of the catena of the case law on the subject will reveal that there has been no judicial unanimity on the identification of the Basic Structure. There is no foreclosure of the list of basic features which means they are not crystallized or identified.

Moreover, in Indira Gandhi vs. Raj Narain (1975) Supp (1) SCC 1, the Supreme Court observed that the theory of 'basic structure' has to be considered in each individual case, not in the abstract but in the context of concrete problems. It would, thus, be seen that the Supreme Court itself has not identified the basic structure of the Constitution in a clear and succinct manner. Indeed, there are differences of opinion on the concept, which ex facie, are vague and to be determined by the Court on the basis of the circumstance in each case.

Uncertain basic structure by its very nature has become higher than the identified fundamental rights. Basic structure is unknown, not only to ordinary people, but to many of the legal eagles also. A law-abiding citizen would not know in advance what the law is. His action would be determined by the law to be identified sometime in the future and that too, to a varying degree. The Fundamental Rights are known, but the higher concepts of basic structure are not known to the public for whom alone the Constitution is made. Judicial individualism and uncertainty will have the growing potentiality of creating havoc, and would leave people bewildered about their rights and duties—a situation that is not in the public interest.

The doctrine of basic structure of the Constitution is a judicial invention made after nearly two decades of the making of the Constitution. It is not a product of a legislative exercise but of a judicial one. Under our Constitution, Courts are only mandated to *declare* the Constitution made by the Legislature. They are not authorized to *make* it.

The Constitution, as a whole, is the basic law of the land. It is difficult to divide it into the category of 'basic' and 'non basic'. Dr Ambedkar's words on this subject are significant:

We divide the articles of the Constitution under three categories. The first category is the one which consists of Articles, which can be amended by Parliament by a bare majority. The second sets of Articles require two-thirds majority. If the future Parliament wishes to amend any particular Article, which is not mentioned in Part III or Article 304, all that is necessary for them is to have two-thirds majority. They can amend it.

The incorporation of specific basic features in the Constitution has been a legislative exercise in some countries such as Nepal. The Indian Constitution has been described by some as a 'scissor-and-paste operation' from various Constitutions in the world. That may or may not be so, but the point of relevance is that the basic feature has been neither incorporated in the Indian Constitution nor was deliberated—even whispered— in the exhaustive and high-level debates in the Constituent Assembly by the high-level sections of Indian elite, national leaders and Constitutional experts during the framing of the Constitution. Moreover several amendments were made in the Constitution in its earlier period, which were judicially examined. Even in those decisions, this concept was not considered or elaborated.

This should legitimately lead to the conclusion that the persons in charge of making the Constitution did not want any provision of the Constitution to be absolutely unamendable. Sovereignty vests in the people of India for whom the Constitution is intended. If the beneficiaries of the Constitution, through their representatives, are considered powerless to make the desired and needed changes, who else can?

While dealing with the dangers of an absolute Bar against the ability to amend the Constitution, Nehru said:

'And remember this, that while we want this Constitution to be as solid and as permanent a structure as we can make it; nevertheless there is no permanence in Constitutions. There should be certain flexibility. If you make anything rigid and permanent, you stop a Nation's growth, the growth of living, vital organic people. Therefore, it has to be flexible.'

Thomas Paine, an English-American revolutionary and a defender of French revolution, in his classic *Rights of Man* (1791), said:

'There never did, there never will, and there never can, exist a Parliament, or any description of men, or any generation of men, in any country, possessed of the right or the power of binding and controlling posterity to the 'end of time', or of commanding for ever how the world shall be governed, or who shall govern it; and therefore, all such clauses, acts or declarations by which the makers of them attempt to do what they have neither the right nor the power to do, nor take power to execute, are in themselves null and void. Every age and generation must be as free to act for itself in all cases as the ages and generations, which preceded it. The vanity and presumption of governing beyond the grave is the most ridiculous and insolent of all tyrannies. Man has no property in man; neither has any generation a property in the generations, which are to follow. The Parliament of the people of 1688 or of any other period, had no more right to dispose of the people of the present day, or to bind or to control them in any shape whatever, than the Parliament or the people of the present day have to dispose of, bind or control those who are to live a hundred or a thousand years hence. Every generation is, and must be, competent to all the purposes, which its occasions require. It is the living and not the dead that are to be accommodated. When man ceases to be, his power and his wants cease with him; and having no longer any participation in the concerns of this world, he has no longer any authority in directing who shall be its governors, or how its Government shall be organized or how administered.'

There is no *practical alternative* to make the required changes in the Constitution [other] than by its amendment, which in the case of basic features, is rendered impossible. Three alternatives are suggested in certain circles. These are: (i) revolution; (ii) Parliament converting itself into a Constituent Assembly; or, (iii) referendum. The first alternative is outside the Constitution, the second is ruled out in view of the decision in the Minerva Mills case, which has taken a view that the limited nature of amending power is also a basic feature of the Constitution and the Parliament cannot enhance its powers by converting itself into a new Constituent Assembly. The third alternative does not seem to be practical in an illiterate country like India, apart from the highly debatable power to make a referendum. A static system of laws is the worst tyranny that any Constitution can impose upon a country. The net result would be that even a unanimous vote of 1,000 million citizens or their representatives cannot bring a change in future by any legal means and the deadlock could, if at all, be resolved only by revolution. We cannot even imagine that such consequences were intended by the framers of the Constitution since the Constitution is meant to endure.

An open-ended/uncertain doctrine of basic feature is a judicial innovation introduced seventeen years after the adoption of the Constitution. The provocation behind this was the spate of Constitutional amendments and apprehension of misuse of powers by the majority party in the Parliament. Who can deny that there has been such misuse? Constitutional amendments brought about to nullify a judicial decision in an election dispute in the case of Prime Minister Indira Gandhi, was an example of the misuse of Constitutional power. But there is no human institution immune to misuse of power. Yet the possibility of misuse of power cannot by itself determine the legality, or otherwise, of that power, although the actual abuse of power can be struck down by the Courts, on the well-established ground of malafides.

Possession of power is one thing; its exercise is another. This is a well settled proposition of interpretation of statutes. The division of powers and functions is the hallmark of our Constitution. No institution is superior to the other. Only the Constitution is superior to all. The Legislature, Judiciary and Executive are our three wings of governance. War against several of our ills, such as poverty, illiteracy and gross inequality, is to be fought through the rule of law; and to fight any successful war, all wings of governance must coordinate although they must not trespass on the demarcated lines, except where there is mala fide or gross inaction.

It is necessary for everyone to keep in mind Harold Laski's dictum: 'When arguments loose [sic] strength, strength become [sic] arguments'.

Who can deny that strength is increasingly becoming the argument in India?

## INDIA INTERNATIONAL MAHESHWARI SOCIETY

The Akhil Bhartiya Maheshwari Mahasabha is an age-old institution of the Maheshwaris (the community to which I belong). My father was closely associated with it. The Mahasabha holds conferences annually. In 1994, a conference was arranged at Jaisalmer (in Rajasthan), from where my ancestors had migrated to Vidarbha. I was asked to accept chairmanship of the reception committee by community leaders such as Shri Ram Gopalji Maheshwari, founder of the famous *Nava Bharat* group of newspapers of Nagpur, and other office bearers. I had no personal connection with Jaisalmer and hence was not really qualified for that post, but at the request of leaders of the community I agreed to hold the post but not the responsibility. The reason was simple. Living in Mumbai, it was not feasible for me to contribute to the management and preparation of this huge gathering of approximately six to seven thousand delegates from all over India. The conference was a grand success. It was inaugurated by His Highness the Maharaja of Jaisalmer. I delivered the welcome address. The small but world-famous tourist town of Jaisalmer had never before witnessed such a gathering. I was gratified to receive a gracious and appreciative letter from Shri Ramgopalji Maheshwari after this event.

There was also a registered society in Delhi called the India International Maheshwari Society, the founder members of which resolved to request me to accept presidentship of the society by their resolution dated 30 April 2000. Hon'ble Shri Justice R.C. Lahoti introduced that society to me and persuaded me to accept the responsibility for a period of five years. I complied and was fortunate to receive the active cooperation of all the members of the general body and the executive committee, including Secretary General Shri T.R. Maheshwari—an IAS officer who was devoted to the cause. During my tenure as the society's president, several new eminent members from different parts of India, as well as the world, joined the society. Justice Lahoti was subsequently appointed as Chief Justice of India, which made the community not only happy but also proud. Towards the end of my tenure, I requested the executive committee to initiate the process of electing a new president. The executive committee as well as some members of the society requested me to continue in office for another term, but I was reluctant and ultimately submitted my resignation on 29 August 2005. On 5 September 2005, I received a communication informing me that the managing committee in its meeting dated 4 September 2005 had resolved not to accept my resignation. Some members contacted me on the phone, others came to my house to persuade me to continue for one more term, but I declined with deep gratitude for the confidence they reposed in me. To the good fortune of the institution, Justice Lahoti graciously accepted the office of president after his retirement from the office of Chief Justice of India and added value to the organization.

I firmly believe that every self-respecting person occupying a public chair must always mentally carry his undated resignation letter in the pocket. One does not know when the need to take a call can arise. I strongly believe that only those who are ready to kick the chair, if the occasion arises, can occupy it with dignity. I can proudly claim that I did carry such letters in my pocket. Similarly, self-respect also lies in the ability to leave public office on the expiry of the designated term and not crave its extension. In that also lies dignity of the occupant. People should miss you when you leave.

## FOREIGN VISITS

I have travelled to many countries of the world including the erstwhile USSR, UK, Belgium, France, Switzerland, Italy, USA,

Japan, China, Thailand, Hong Kong, Australia, New Zealand, Egypt, Sri Lanka, Pakistan, Bhutan, Nepal and Kenya. Kamla accompanied me on my visits to UK, Europe, China, Thailand and Hong Kong. The trip to USA was an official one in connection with an accident involving an Indian Airlines flight as I have mentioned earlier, while the China visit was semi-official being a study tour mainly comprising chief justices and judges of high courts led by Hon'ble Shri Justice R.P. Sethi, judge of the Supreme Court. Our trip to China was from 14 to 27 May 2001 and our itinerary included the cities of Guangzhou, Guilin, Xi'an, Beijing, Shanghai and Hangzhou. The group was received in China on behalf of the Indian embassy in Beijing. At that time, Shri P. Shivshankar Menon was the Indian Ambassador to China. We witnessed the working of some trial courts and on 21 May, even visited the Supreme Court of China in Beijing, specially opened that day for our visit. The Supreme Court of China does not necessarily function every day. A sitting Supreme Court Judge received us and we had an interesting discussion with him. On that day there was a demonstration led by a lady in front of the court. Shri Menon had arranged a lunch in our honour at an Indian hotel in the central part of Beijing. Interestingly, though I admit it is a bit of trivia, the dessert menu of the restaurant had masala tea as one of the items. This was immediately popular and almost all of us ordered it!

Our journey inside China was very well planned. We travelled mostly by train so that we could see the interiors of China to the maximum extent possible. Noteworthy on that journey was the cleanliness of the platforms, tracks and the lavatories in the train. Use of lavatories was banned as the train slowed down to pull into a platform and the lavatories would be locked to prevent use at this stage. As the train left the station, the lavatories were unlocked and could be used again. We were all impressed by this thoughtful rule, which was perhaps the main reason for cleanliness especially in the platform area. Sometime in 2002, I was invited as a guest to a function at the railway divisional headquarters in Nagpur, where high-level officials of the Indian railways were also present. I narrated the above experience of China, which I thought was worthy of following. The officials also liked the idea and told me that they would broach the subject with their seniors in the administration. I don't know what happened thereafter.

The most memorable figure on our tour was Smt Sethi—an affectionate elderly lady who took good care of us all. Food, especially vegetarian food, is a real problem in China. Smt. Sethi had thoughtfully carried semi-roasted Indian rotis and pickles of different varieties. Train journeys were mostly of about twelve to eighteen hours at a stretch. The ladies, led by Smt. Sethi, would heat the rotis on the electrical irons that were operable during the train journey. What a unique idea!

In September 2007, the 15th Commonwealth Law Conference was held in Nairobi, Kenya. A group of senior lawyers of the Supreme Court decided to attend the conference and, more importantly, on that pretext to visit the world famous Masai Mara game reserve, which is to the south of Nairobi on the boundary with Tanzania. The details and plans for the trip were finalized by our common friend Shri K.N. Bhat, senior advocate and former Additional Solicitor General of India. When we reached Nairobi, the group found it difficult to visit all the places of interest within seven days and hence most of us decided to skip the conference. We visited Samburu National Reserve, Mount Kenya National Park, Lake Nakuru National Park and Masai Mara National Reserve. It was fascinating and thrilling to be in the company of African lions, leopards, elephants, other wild animals and a host of exotic birds moving freely or flying just in front and above us. The journey from Nairobi to Masai Mara was on a rough road and was made in the heavy vehicles specially meant for such trips. I became sick in Masai Mara but was looked after very well by

Smt. Nighat Ahmed, wife of my close friend Shri Altaf Ahmad, senior advocate and former Additional Solicitor General of India, whom we unfortunately lost recently.

My trip to Egypt held great relevance for me since in that country one could get glimpses of the early period of human civilization, see the world's longest river, the Nile, and visit the city of Alexandria, on the Mediterranean Sea, where Alexander the Great had died.

## CELEBRATIONS

*Completion of Fifty Years of Togetherness with Kamla, Celebrated by Our Children*

In 2003, on completion of fifty years of our marriage, our family had arranged a grand and memorable function over two consecutive days at Nagpur. The planning for this event started early and elaborate and detailed preparations were made. For over a month, long practice of dance and music numbers took place early every morning. Video and detailed scripts of our life's journey showing and narrating significant incidents were thoughtfully prepared, based on old photographs collected from various sources and old records. There was no doubt that the whole exercise was a product of united and untiring efforts by my family. Each of them participated in the display and narration turn by turn. Kamla and I were touched by this loving display. References to past incidents in our life were presented in a variety of dances, replete with significant songs in which my grandchildren and other relatives also participated. Only close relatives and friends were invited and almost all of them generously responded to the invitation. It was an unforgettable event, which the family, friends and relatives remember till this day.

*My Completion of Seventy-five Years of Life Celebrated by the Family*

My wife Kamla and our family had arranged a function in Delhi to celebrate the completion of seventy-five years of my life. This was widely attended by members of the Supreme Court Bar, seniors as well as juniors, sitting and retired judges of the Supreme Court and high court. Shri T.R. Andhyarujina (a very respected and astute lawyer of the Supreme Court and Solicitor General of India at Delhi and past Advocate General at Mumbai), Shri Ram Jethmalani, my friend Justcie B.N. Naik (who was my colleague on the bench and presently also in the Bar in the Supreme Court) made fond and generous references about me. My eldest daughter-in-law, Surekha, wife of Anoop, representing all my daughters-in-law (Dr Ujwala, wife of Narendra, and Archana, wife of Sanjay), spoke fondly about both of us. Ram Jethmalani, who has always been kind to me, came especially from Mumbai to attend the function after taking leave from the court in an ongoing matter and delivered a speech in his usual scintillating style, certain references in which were quite partial and also embarrassing for me. But who can stop Ram?

It was a matter of great satisfaction for me that my schoolmate Professor P.D. Mandaogane, president of the Akola Education Society, not only fondly remembered me but also penned down some features of my life journey from my early childhood in Akola until that day, which was published in Akola dailies in the second week of April 2008. Following is the English translation of what he wrote in Marathi:

### Shri Justice Vallabhdas Mohta (Retd)—At a Crossroads

The name of Hon'ble Shri Vallabhdas A. Mohta, the illustrious former Chief Justice of the Orissa High Court and currently senior counsel in the Supreme Court of India, is well known in the corridors of Indian law and judiciary. There are many in this field whom we hold in awe for their erudition and scholarship. Others we respect for their legal acumen and expediency, but here is one whose devotion, wisdom and vision, wakes in us a personal affection. There is a special reason for the people of Akola to rejoice because Shri Mohta is a son of the soil, bred and brought up here, having won the unique honour of being the first-ever citizen and member of the Akola Bar, as also the first-ever lawyer from the mofussil area to be made judge of the High Court and then elevated to chief justice. As a judge, he has earned the reputation of being most upright and as a lawyer his contribution to the development of law is well recognized. The reason to recollect this is that this doyen of the legal profession is completing seventy-five years of an eventful life on 26 April 2008.

Like all great men of law and judiciary, Shri Justice (Retd) Mohta has a great measure of versatility. There is in him a judge and a lawyer, a creative thinker and an expert adviser, an author and a speaker, a social and cultural activist and an active participant in national and international conferences: a many-sided personality, in whom all these stand merged into one.

Shri Mohta did his schooling in Akola, graduation in Kanpur and LLB in Nagpur. Gifted with an artistic bent of mind, he holds a certificate in drawing from the JJ School of Art, Mumbai. In his early years, he didn't get much parental guidance. But his late father, to whom his monumental work *Arbitration and Conciliation* has been dedicated, has all along been a real presence. However, in actual life, this want was supplied to a great extent by the late Advocate A.S. Athalye alias 'Kakasaheb', who ever remained a father figure and inspiration for the young lawyer and whose photograph has a permanent niche in Shri Mohta's study. He always wanted to be in the legal profession and had his first lessons of legal practice under the guidance of Kakasaheb. Shri Mohta attributes his legal knowledge, practice and profession to Shri Athalye, who instilled in the young learner integrity and devotion to work. Shri Mohta often recounts with great pride and reverence how the late Shri Motilal Setalwad, the former Attorney General of India, once complimented Shri Athalye as a perfectionist in drafting. The old man was very kind and loving to his junior. If he used any harsh words, they were only a concern of a senior for his junior.

In the professional career a lawyer has to face three phases of practice: (i) no work, no earning; (ii) more work, less earning; and (iii) less work, more earning. Shri Mohta faced them all with patience and equanimity. At an early stage of his practice, he was tempted to accept the post of judicial magistrate first class, which would have been safe and secure, but his senior prevailed upon him to abandon his plan because he considered it to be a wrong decision. So he stayed on. Later on when the appointment as a High Court Judge came his way, there was a sharp division in his family and he was in two minds: to be or not to be a judge! Ultimately he accepted the invitation, what a piece of dramatic irony! When he was eager to be a junior judge, he was dissuaded from entering judiciary and now when he hesitated to be a High Court Judge, no less a person than the Chief Justice prevailed upon him to give up his lucrative practice and become a judge. It is indeed a warm tribute to a warm human powered by values and wisdom. Honest advice and concise arguments were always and continue to be his landmarks.

The twin personality of a lawyer and a judge brought a rare clarity and maturity to the oral and written expression of Shri Mohta. The book *Trade Mark, Passing off and Franchising*, of which Shri Mohta is the author, is an eloquent proof. However, his major contribution to legal literature is the book *Arbitration and Conciliation*. In a short period, the books earned a well-deserved reputation as classics and got him a place in the 'Who's Who in the World' and 'The Cambridge Blue Book'.

The second edition of this book titled *Arbitration, Conciliation and Mediation* has been co-authored by his worthy son Shri Justice Anoop Mohta, of the Bombay High Court; a passing on of the legacy! A further crystallization of his thought and expression can be seen in the number of articles on various subjects contributed to several national and international journals, addresses at conferences and seminars, the landmark report that he produced within the allotted time limit and that too at less cost, about the air crash at Aurangabad, which was accepted and endorsed by the Government of India in toto; a rare event in the notorious record of delayed reports in India.

But this is not all. The making of a good and reliable lawyer and judge was discernible in him soon after his start. Unanimous acceptability seems to be the chief characteristic of Mr. Mohta's versatility. There was total unanimity when he became the President of the two premier academic institutions of Vidarbha: RDG College for Women and BGE Society, Akola, and vice-president of the Bar Council of Mahatrashtra.

When asked about the secret of his success as a senior counsel at the Supreme Court, Shri Mohta replied, 'Maximum matter in minimum words.' But bring him to the company of friends and colleagues, he is a different advocate in manners and temperament, because here he has so much to say. With his large expressive eyes and cheerful look, Shri Mohta often attracts the young and old around him and regales them with his reflections and conclusions on men, and matters and situations that he has encountered during his life's journey. He likes fun and prefers a three-hour escape to the theatre to especially watch Marathi and Gujarati dramas, to beat the stress of the routine.

The picture that emerges of Shri Justice V.A. Mohta (Retd) at seventy-five is that of a man of ideas, the study of law and widespread range of personal friends irrespective of their positions in life. In and through him, the city of Akola salutes the first-ever son and citizen who was elevated to such a high stature as the Chief Justice of the Orissa High Court, and yet retained his basic identity as a son of the soil.

On 26 April 2008, Shri Mohta completes seventy-five eventful years of life and marches on to the century. We greet him and his family on this occasion, and would like to ask for the blessings of the Almighty to be showered upon him.

My fiftieth wedding anniversary and seventy-fifth birthday were momentous occasions in my life. Kamla and I were fortunate to be showered by the love, affection and kindness of our family, friends and my colleagues from various walks of life and the reaffirmation that came from each one of them of all the good fortune with which I have been blessed.

## MY COMPLETION OF EIGHTY YEARS OF LIFE CELEBRATED BY THE BAR COUNCIL OF MAHARASHTRA AND GOA

The Bar Council of Maharashtra and Goa had arranged the State Lawyers Conference 2013, on the theme of social justice. It was held in Akola on 24 February 2013 in the newly constructed massive hall of Punjabrao Krishi Vidyapeth, which has a seating capacity of about 2,500. Delegates from all over Maharashtra and Goa packed the hall to capacity. Hon'ble V.S. Sirpurkar, a former judge of the Supreme Court and the chairman of the Competition Commission of India, inaugurated the conference. It was also attended and addressed by sitting judges of the Bombay High Court, namely, Hon'ble Shri Justices Bhusan R. Gavai, Anoop V. Mohta, Bhushan P. Dharmadhikari, Madan T. Joshi and Hon'ble Smt Justice Sadhana S. Jadhav. All sitting members of the Bar Council were present.

The chairman of the Bar Council, Shri Motisingh G. Mohta, past chairmen Shri B.K. Gandhi and Shri G.B. Lohiya, all from Akola, some other members of the Bar Council, and president of Akola Bar, Shri P.S. Wakhre, also addressed the conference. The Bar Council had decided to honour me at this conference since I was about to complete eighty years of life.

The reasons must have been twofold, namely, that I had a long association with the Bar Council as a member as well as vice-president and because I belong to Akola where the conference was being held. I was touched by the fond and general references made about me by several speakers including the chief guest, Hon'ble Justice V.S. Sirpurkar, all High Court Judges present and friends from Akola. Young and promising advocate Shri Shriniwas G. Khot alias Raju Khot, son of my very dear friend late Shri Ganesh Khot, contributed the following write-up on me to the souvenir:

### 'Jewel of Bench and Bar'

Ideals are like stars in the heaven, we never reach them, however like the mariners of the sea, we chart our course by them.

No need to tell, he is an ideal for Bench and Bar. He is not only an ideal guide, ideal friend, ideal teacher, ideal father, ideal path-shower but also an ideal human being. Like Eklavya in Mahabharata many consider him as their Dronacharya, a true and ideal teacher, and follow the way he is. In Mahabharata Dronacharya asked for the thumb of Eklavya, but in this era our modern Dronacharya has not even demanded a single favour but in reality has given a lot to the bench and bar. He is at the pinnacle of fame, still he is down to earth.

As regards his unbeatable contribution to the judiciary from 1979 up till now everybody knows that he cared for social justice and had given landmark decisions. He was a member of the committee for implementing the Legal Aid Scheme formed by Government of India that was headed by Chief Justice of

India. He was appointed by the Government of India to conduct a Court of Inquiry (under the Aircraft Rules), to investigate into the causes of an accident to an aircraft at Aurangabad, and in that connection visited Boeing in Seattle, and NASA in San Francisco, USA. He was delegate in a Soviet Cultural Society study tour of USSR. He was delegate at the SAARC Law Conference in Sri Lanka, Pakistan, and Bhutan and undertook a study tour of China in a delegation headed by Supreme Court Judge. He has been writing articles on various subjects of public importance that have appeared in national and international journals. It is a matter of immense pleasure, that he is a member of Akola Bar Association. Born on 26 April 1933 at Akola he received school education in New English High School, Akola, he was elected member of Bar Council of Maharashtra and Goa in 1968 and in 1973 for the second time and was Vice-Chairman of the said council in 1974.

My father Advocate Ganesh Khot, and Advocates Balasaheb Kulkarni, Ram Dixit, Niwane, Bhaiyasaheb Pimparkhade and Bhaskarrao Palhade were his very good friends. I can never forget his parental touch with me. Since my childhood there are great impressions on me about him. He is my ideal in life. Really his mannerisms are fantastic. His way of hospitality, his way of greeting the people, his killer smile and his overall personality are unmatched. Really, I am blessed to have had such a personality in my life during my childhood.

Once when he was chief guest of our college, he was encouraging students to join the legal profession. I remember his words, he said this is the profession from which you can earn fame, money as well as discharge your duties towards society and can discharge a pious obligation. Just in jest during the lecture, he said that, in this profession initially there is neither work nor money, in the second stage there is only work and no money, and in the third stage money and little work.

Really, he is a great orator. That is the reason that he was and is an eminent advocate.

He is an ideal parent, his eldest son Anoop is a High Court Judge. Second son Dr. Narendra is a doctor and youngest son Sanjay is a big entrepreneur. All live successful lives. Indeed! He is a real patron, stalwart and dynamic. He contributed the lion's share towards strengthening the judiciary. He is the best example of purity, patience and perseverance. He proved an ideal judge.

He has completed eighty years of age. We termed it as 1000 full moons were witnessed by him. It is a matter of pleasure no less than a joy to have this golden jubilee function celebrated at this occasion.

May god bless him with all happiness and health. I wish him best regards and pay my gratitude for his versatile personality and outstanding work for Bench and Bar.

In my speech of thanks I referred to my association with the town of Akola, the Bar Association Akola and my respected senior Shri Kakasaheb Athalye. All advocates who had completed fifty years of practice were felicitated at the conference. They included old friends Sarvashri V.V. Bhadang, G.A. Pimparkhede, B.G. Palhade, G.B. Lohiya, R.B. Agrawal, R.C.Bang, V.R. Agrawal, S.N. Lohiya, V.H. Jaltare, and N.M. Chopde. I was delighted to meet many old acquaintances, old lawyer friends and newcomers. Every moment of the conference was greatly pleasurable and exciting. The president of the Bar Council, Shri Motisingh Mohta and his entire team, the president and members of the Akola Bar Association, wholeheartedly and unitedly worked hard for the grand success of this conference.

## MY OFFICE IN AKOLA AND DELHI, AND JUNIORS

Initially, my office in Akola was on the ground floor of our residence in Tajnapeth. After a few years, I shifted it to rented premises in the medical market near our house, where I continued until my elevation. I had the benefit of being assisted by several sincere and hard-working juniors in the office. First and foremost was my younger brother, Laxmansingh (who is now practising in Nagpur), as well as A.S. Bajaj and R.R. Mantri (presently leading lawyers in Aurangabad), K.N. Mohta (who retired from a high managerial post in a leading company), Ashok Lohia (practising in Pune), Birjmohan Gandhi (presently practising in Akot after laying down office of the president of Akot municipal town), D.D. Tulsan (a leading industrialist and merchant in Akola) and S.R. Malviya (one of the leading lawyers of the Akola Bar). Each of them was of considerable assistance to me and, until this day, they keep in touch with me. Tulsan never forgets to greet me on Guru Purnima day.

My Delhi office was established in one room of our residence, though a few years ago I moved my office to another independent flat within Priyadarshini Society where I live. Luckily with me in Delhi I have two grandsons—Anoop's son, Devansh, and Sanjay's son, Nakul—who are also lawyers. Devansh's wife Shweta and Nakul's wife Misha are also lawyers. Consequently, I am in the company of lawyers not only in the court but also in the house.

A young, sincere and dependable junior lawyer, Nilakanta Nayak, who hails from Odisha, looks after my Delhi office. I am happy to note that he has started his own independent practice. I have no doubt that his intrinsically dependable character and capacity for hard work will make him a successful lawyer.

I had three clerks in the office in Akola, the senior-most being the late Shri Shankarrao Joshi, a very experienced person. The other two were Shri Abarao and Shri Prahlad Shirale. All of them served me very well in their respective ways. Prahlad belongs to a Scheduled Caste and is a brilliant and hard-working person with a keen interest in law. Realizing this, I had encouraged him to undergo a law course. He has now become a lawyer and is at present a busy practitioner of criminal law in Akola, having specializised in the Negotiable Instruments Act. He educated his children very well and the fruit of this is evident in the fact that one of his daughters has been selected as civil judge and judicial magistrate. It gives me great satisfaction to note his and his family's progress. He makes it a point to meet me whenever I go to Akola and sometimes speaks to me on the phone, even about personal matters.

## LAW AS A CAREER

The first occasion at which I had to publicly express myself on the subject of law as a career was at the centenary celebration of the Akola Bar Association held on 27 June 1981. Hon'ble Shri Justice Y.V. Chandrachud, Chief Justice of India, inaugurated the grand and memorable function over which Hon'ble Shri Justice V.S. Deshpande, Chief Justice of the Bombay High Court, presided. The organizers asked me to contribute an article for junior lawyers in the souvenir published on the occasion. It reflects my thoughts on the subject and reads thus:

### A dialogue with the Junior Bar

Akola Bar has completed a century of its existence. Undoubtedly, it has been a fruitful existence with good traditions. The process of stocktaking is inevitable in centenary celebrations and indeed is one of its objects. Stocktaking is, in any case, a human weakness that provides the opportunity to revel in history and past glory. What after all is time? Nothing but a threefold present—the present, as we experience it; past, as present memory; and future, as present expectation. Reference to the past has importance only because it can guide the future. The younger generation is the present expectation and therefore, this dialogue with them in the background of the present memory. People hate to receive sermons. I abhor giving them. These are not sermons.

Nothing is more important in life than one's own self-respect. Respect of the profession to which one belongs is equally important. Literature of almost every age has treated the profession of law rather unfairly and unkindly. In *Henry VI*, Dick the Butcher says, 'The first thing we do; let us kill all the Lawyers.' According to Disraeli, 'The legal mind chiefly displays in illustrating the obvious, explaining the evident and expatiating on the commonplace[...]' Charles Dickens wrote in *Bleak House*, 'In a long matted wall of Court, you might look in vain for truth at the bottom of it.' Chaucer said of a lawyer, 'There was nowhere anyone so good as he in feathering his own nest.' Dean Swift in *Gulliver's Travels,* observed, 'Lawyers are a society of men brought up from their youth in the art of proving by words multiplied for the purpose, that white is black and black is white according as they are paid.' Even today, this class is a butt of the same criticism. But, I do not think, the charges are seriously made. Every profession has black sheep. Similarly, every profession must reflect the general standard prevailing in a society. This profession is noble and it does not cease to be so only because some of the professionals may not be noble. There is no other profession which has contributed more public men of repute everywhere in the world. The nasty comments made about the profession reflect only vague impressions. In this regard Abraham Lincoln's following observations are apt, 'There is a vague popular belief that lawyers are necessarily dishonest. I say vague because when we consider to what extent confidence and honours are reposed in and conferred upon lawyers by the people, it appears improbable that their impression of dishonesty is very distinct and vivid. Yet, the impression is common, almost universal. Let no young man choosing the law for a calling yield to the popular belief.' (*Speeches and Letters of Abraham Lincoln* 1832–1865, Ed. Merwin Roe, E.P. Dutton & Co. 1912).

Take Abraham Lincoln seriously and assume that you have chosen one of the finest professions known to mankind. Similarly don't be scared by the picture of overcrowding in the profession presented to you. This complaint is heard by every generation of lawyers.

Success is the result of a combination of luck and effort. Luck is beyond one's control, so, there is no use bothering about it. Effort is one's own. Therefore, one must concentrate on it. Every man's capacity is different for no two men are equal. A person must explore his/her own capacity to the fullest. There is no short cut [sic] to hard work, generally in life and more so in this profession. Famous instrumentalist Paderewsky gave his enchanting performance before Queen Victoria. She paid tributes to him and called him a genius. 'Perhaps, but before I was a genius I was a drudge,' was the reply honestly given. Thus, those who have no capacity to work hard should not join this profession and if by mistake they have joined, sooner they leave, it is better for them. Red and blue pencil must always be with you, though its use should not be made indiscriminately. Only exceptional personalities like K.N. Katju could keep the briefs 'in a state of virginity', as his friends used to describe light heartedly. Mere effort without proper planning and without use of proper tools does not yield optimum results. Command over language is as important as the thought, which is why the relationship between law and literature is well known. A lawyer without a good command over language is a mechanic, a mere working mason. To construct a beautiful structure on a well laid plan, one must be an architect and for that command over medium of communication is extremely essential. This is not to suggest even indirectly that Law Court is a public platform and it is necessary to be oratorical or sonorous.

'How to argue a case effectively?' was the question put to Lord Moulton. 'Play chess with it,' was the reply. Someone asked Abraham Lincoln, 'How long one's legs should be?' He answered, 'Long enough to reach the earth.'

'Ex facto jus oritor' or 'the facts make the law' is a well-known maxim. Law is not academic but endemic. Take care of facts and law will look after itself. Similarly, take care of weak point. Strong points have inherent strength to assert themselves. There is a golden rule of advocacy. 'Stand up, speak up, shut up.' It is as important to close at the appropriate time as to begin effectively. A junior was conducting a case. Judge was clearly with him but, the arguing counsel did not attempt to realise this. A more experienced lawyer was sitting by his side. The judge was about to lose patience when the senior wrote a note and handed it over to the over enthusiastic junior. Somehow, this did not escape the attention of the judge. He called for the note. The junior became nervous and feared some complications but the judge insisted on getting the note. When it was handed over, he read it and then asked the junior whether he had read the note. The answer was in the affirmative. 'Then why not act accordingly,' asked the judge, and read the note aloud in court. It only contained the following line: 'Stop it, the old bastard is with you.'

Our whole judicial system suffers from procedural dominance and is getting crushed under the burden of conflicting case law, as a result of which the substance of the matter is a casualty. Although cases are rarely decided on the basis of precedents, there is a fashion to cite quite a good number of them. Check that temptation. In any case, Court room [sic] is not the place for either studying the precedent or reading it in full. Remember for ever [sic] that no two cases in the world are ever similar in all respects, as no two fingerprints of two men are identical. We often hear about the learning of

Judges and Lawyers. Time has come when homage should be paid not to learning but to ignorance; for the part it played in interpreting the law, especially the Constitution, in the early period without aid of precedents. This universally applies to all countries. Justice Miller of United States of America, an erstwhile medical graduate and subsequently a lawyer, who was invited to join the Bench once remarked, 'One of the factors for the high standard of early American Law was the ignorance. Judges had only the Constitution and the Debates. They were apt to do the right thing. Their successors with several volumes of Law Reports cannot be sure.' To the same effect is the view of another great Judge, Justice Jackson. He said, 'When the Supreme Court moved to Washington in 1800 AD, it was provided with no books which probably accounts for the high quality of their opinion.' It is necessary to know not only what is law but also why it is the law. Once it is located, its application will be easier and quite clear and reduce the chances of getting lost. It is easier to get into thick jungles, but very difficult to get out.

Amongst many factors leading to uncertainty in law, is the individual factor of a Judge. Judges are of all varieties. They are learned as well as ignorant, witty as well as serious; hardworking as well as casual; technical as well as non-technical; over confident as well as doubting; patient as well as impatient. This factor is unavoidable in any human system. The human race has yet to produce a perfect individual. The Judge generally does not know the case better than a lawyer and it is well-nigh improbable for him to study each case thoroughly and to hunt out the right section, rule or precedent. Nothing is more refreshing to him than good and relevant arguments from both sides. These arguments are no doubt one-sided. A thorough and searching one-sided view from each side is the only guarantee that nothing worthwhile has been missed. Judges know very well that there can be no good judgment without good arguments. He needs and welcomes assistance but he is likely to react adversely to an overdose. One can safely proceed on the assumption that a Judge has a desire to do justice and to arrive at a correct conclusion according to his conviction. Treat him with courtesy but never be browbeaten by him. In no case, tolerate an insult especially if it is intended. Learn presence of mind and the artless art of repartee. A lawyer, known for his shabby appearance, once put on a new coat. The Judge asked him sarcastically whether he had won a lottery. 'No, my Lord, that your Lordship wins every month,' was the reply. A Lawyer once prayed for sympathy saying, 'after all I am a widow'. The Judge remarked, 'You mean the widower.' Came the prompt reply, 'Widower in my own right, but widow as representing the client.' An immature Junior was once surprised at the obviously wrong proposition of law coming from the bench. The junior said, 'I am amazed.' The Judge felt insulted and started browbeating the lawyer. A senior came to his rescue saying, 'My Lord, he is an inexperienced young man, excuse him. After gaining some experience of this Court, he will not be surprised by anything that your Lordship says or does.'

Education is an eternal debt which maturity owes to youth. Seniors perform that sacred duty. One must respect every senior and particularly one's own senior. Every man has defects. It is most improper for a junior to ridicule his senior in public or in the Bar room. People may enjoy listening but no person worth the salt will respect such a junior. It is every man's duty to invest some time in building-up [sic] a profession to which he belongs. Help building the strength of the profession and its proverbial unity. Each person is entitled to his own views in all walks of life but do preserve the proverbial and felicitous brotherhood at the Bar, especially when the cause is of the profession. Even Shakespeare, who was a great critic of this profession, complimented its brotherhood. In the *Taming of the Shrew* he wrote, 'Do as adversaries do, in law; strike mightily but eat and drink as friends. Of course, the advice about 'drink' should be taken in the proper perspective and not literally.

The greatest tragedy of this profession is that in it there is a place only at the top. Either you have to do killing work or there is no occasion to work. 'Work is hard; no work is harder' is a Cypriot proverb. Let there be a sincere effort not to suffer from the greatest ordeal in life, that of no work. A lawyer's life has three stages, in the first stage, there is neither work nor money; in the second, there is only work and no money and in the third there is no work and there is only money. There is a constant clash of personalities in this profession, which calls for the best in the man. Try your best, leaving ultimate success to the Almighty. Remember Tolstoy's wisdom when he says, 'There is only one way of serving mankind. That is, to become better yourself.'

Very recently, the Nagpur High Court Bar Association invited me to address the juniors in the high court. The young and popular president of the Bar, Shri Anand Jaiswal, arranged this well-attended lecture, which was presided over by Hon'ble Shri Justice Ambadas Joshi of the Bombay High Court. The basic substance of the address was not, and could not be, much different from the above article. I did remember to add ancient Chinese philosopher Confucius' pithy injunction to 'Choose a job you love and you will never have to work a day in your life.' While emphasizing that real pleasure and satisfaction lies in doing one's best, I cannot negate the fact that success does give pleasure even if it is not a result of effort or performance.

I had concluded my speech by reading the following motivating passage from the writings of famous filmmaker Shri Satyajit Ray:

The studios in Calcutta show their hallowed past in every tatter on the canvas that covers the ceiling. Some of the families of rodents that inhabit the rafters have lived there ever since the foundation of the industry. The floor is pitted, the camera groans as it turns, the voltage begins to drop after sundown, the general air of shabbiness is unnerving. And yet, I do not mind these as hindrances. After all, we have the essentials to make a film, and it is within us to make it badly or well. It is bareness of means that forces us to be economical and inventive, and prevents us from turning craftsmanship into an end in itself. And there is something about creating beauty in the circumstances of shoddiness and privation that is truly exciting.

There was a free and frank dialogue with the younger lot of the Nagpur Bar. To be in the company of young friends is always refreshing. I not only thoroughly enjoyed the event, but visiting the Bar Association after about a decade and a half was itself a great pleasure. Justice Joshi gave some excellent tips of practical importance to the juniors. The events along with the substance of the addresses were widely reported in the following day's local press.

## BACK TO THE BEGINNING: FAMILY STORY

> 'You must know the story of your culture and be
> proud of your ancestors.'
> —Romana Banuelos[8]

In old age, interest in one's ancestors intensifies whereas a youth's interest lies primarily in his/herself. Immediate ancestors, grandparents and sometimes even great-grandparents are generally

---

[8]The thirty-fourth head of the US Treasury and the first Hispanic person to hold that position.

known, although I fear that even that level of interest is fading in the modern generation. Eighty is certainly old age and I have achieved it. My recent new status of becoming a great-grandfather, I feel, adds to my venerable stature. I recently started to research my roots, ancestors and their backgrounds and have had some results. In the first place, I discovered that 'Mohta' is a title in Rajasthan and not a surname. Our real surname is 'Taori'.

As mentioned in the very beginning of my story, my ancestors belonged to Jaisalmer, Rajasthan, which was then a barren land. They migrated to the Vidarbha region in eastern Maharashtra to conduct their business. The business started well and it expanded in the towns of Akola, Khamgaon and the villages of Undri, Pipalgaon/Nimgaon, etc. My grandfather looked after that part of the business and agriculture that was in Pipalgaon. However, when partition of the family business took place in 1896, my grandfather was allotted the business and properties in Akola, Khamgaon, Nimgaon, etc. as his share. He, his two sons and one daughter shifted to Akola, which became the headquarters of his business. The business prospered and within a few years of shifting to Akola my grandfather built the first three-storied house in Akola. The façade of that massive house had huge wooden carved pillars about twelve feet high. I remember being told in my childhood that the villagers from nearby areas used to come to see that house.

My grandfather had three sons—Manmalji, Aidanji (my father) and Tolaramji and a daughter Ratni Bai. Unfortunately Manmalji died at the young age of three. My father and my uncle Tolaramji were known in Akola as a pair of siblings like Ram and Laxman, because of their intense love for each other. My father started the business of exporting cotton bales to Japan and also acquired a great reputation in the social circle. My uncle Tolaramji was adopted by Brijpalji, the son of a granduncle.

My father had four sons—Khusalsinghji, Vithaldasji,

Vallabhdas (me), Laxmansingh and two daughters—Kesharbai and Gulabbai. Khusalsinghji was our step-brother given in adoption to our uncle Tolaramji. When father died in 1941, my sisters were married, my elder brother Vithaldasji was about twelve years old, I was eight years old and my youngest brother Laxmansingh was a toddler.

I married Kamla, daughter of Shri Laxminarayanji and Smt. Ayodhayabai Innani of village Tamsi, district Washim, about 50 kilometres from Akola, on 20 June 1953 at the age of twenty. This was a late marriage according to our family convention. Unfortunately, after a prolonged illness of two years, Kamla left us for her heavenly abode on 18 January 2012, creating a great void after nearly sixty years of happy married life. She was an accomplished hostess and a devoted wife and mother who single-handedly discharged the heavy responsibility of looking after the family and its affairs, leaving me completely free to pursue my career in Akola and subsequently in Nagpur, Mumbai, Cuttack and Delhi. In 2010, my second son Dr Narendra (MS) and his wife Dr Ujwala (MD) shifted Kamla from Delhi to Nagpur as she was suffering from several diseases, mainly of the heart and kidney, for which they wished to give her their personal care and much-needed perennial medical attention. Illness did not dampen Kamla's spirits. She continued with her family duties, social obligations and hobbies such as singing, drawing, reading and playing cards. The valiant battle against her serious diseases—fought by Narendra and Ujwala and their team of medical friends, supported by sincere and loving staff members and the constant attention and care of my son Sanjay and his wife Archana, who were in Nagpur—was ultimately lost. My eldest son Anoop and his wife Surekha who were in Mumbai would visit her intermittently. She breathed her last in the presence of her entire loving family, including her brothers and sisters.

Kamla was a master in Reiki, which is a Japanese technique

of harnessing 'universal life-force energy'. She had acquired the highest qualification in Reiki and was qualified to teach it. She opened the Chaitanya Reiki Centre. She was extremely fond of Marathi books and her special interest was *Dasbodh* written by Swami Samarth from Sajjangarh, situated in the western mountain range of Maharashtra. Using a correspondence course prescribed by Shri Samarth Sevamandal, she passed certain examinations about the teachings of *Dasbodh* and received many appreciative certificates for *Dasbodh* parichay from that institution. She was also a social worker and was much sought after for social functions in the ladies' circles. She had a sonorous voice and often sang at public functions. Bhajans were her favourite. She had a team of co-singers and musicians in Nagpur and some of their programmes were broadcast on television and radio. But all her many accomplishments aside, I can only say of Kamla that I was truly blessed in my life-partner and soulmate.

I have three sons—Anoop, Narendra and Sanjay. Anoop, born in Akola on 4 December 1955, is the eldest and led all the kids of the family in activities ranging from cricket and kite-flying to festival celebrations and social activities. He is a movie buff and has a special liking for music. His all-round personality was the reason he was adjudged the best Leo Secretary of Maharashtra in the 323 District Conference of the Lions Club. He is an MALLB and practiced law successfully mainly in Nagpur (from 1981 to 1993) and Mumbai (since 1989 to 2003), starting his practice at the Nagpur Bench of the Bombay High Court from where he shifted to Mumbai when my departure for Odisha became imminent. He has appeared in the Supreme Court on numerous occasions. He and I have co-authored two books titled *Arbitration, Conciliation and Mediation* and *Trade Marks, Passing Off and Franchising*. Anoop was elevated to the position of a judge of the Bombay High Court on 14th November 2003. Despite his busy schedule, his love for cricket endures. He won an award for best bowler of the cricket tournament held between the senior counsel and sitting judges of the Bombay High Court. Anoop's strength lies in his hard work, calm nature, perseverance and keen analysis and balance.

Anoop's wife is Surekha, daughter of late Shri Kashinathji Toshniwal from Nasik, who was a great social worker, manufacturer of Ayurvedic medicine and a known astrologer. She was president of the Maheshwari Kishori Mandal and won many trophies in chess, badminton, table tennis and sports. She was also a professional Kathak dancer. Surekha acquired the qualification of MCom, LLB after marriage but chose not to practice law in view of her husband's position as a judge. She is a diploma holder in alternate dispute resolution (ADR) mediation from Bombay University and also possesses a diploma in naturopathy. She is a life-fellow member of the International Council of Complementary Medicine. They have two children, son Devansh and daughter Aditee.

My second son is Narendra. He was also born in Akola, on 4 November 1956. He holds an MS in urology and andrology. In 2003, he constructed a five-storied hospital-cum-residential complex in Ramdaspeth, Nagpur, and established in it the 'Kamal Institute of Andro Urology', named after Kamla. It is a prestigious medical facility, unique in many ways and the first of its kind in central India. Its operation theatre complex is equipped with state-of-the-art surgical equipment and gadgets, largely imported from Germany. The institute caters not only to Indian but also to foreign patients coming from distant countries such as the UK, USA and the African continent. Narendra has served as president of several professional and social institutions such as the Academy of Medical Sciences, Nagpur Urological Society of Central India and the Rotary Club of Nagpur-East. He was the assistant governor Rotary District 3030 and director of the Institute of the Urology and Research Centre Pvt. Ltd. He was recently elected as the president of Urological Society of Central India. His hobbies are reading and painting. Narendra's strength lies in bringing friends and family together.

Narendra is married to Dr Ujwala, daughter of Smt. and Dr T.B. Rathi from Amravati. She has an MD in anaesthesiology and practises in Nagpur. She helps Narendra in the management of the institute, while striking a perfect balance between her professional and domestic life. They have two children, a son Kartik and a daughter Apoorva.

Sanjay, my youngest son, was born on 29 June 1958 at Tamsi in Washim. As a youth from a business family, I had no thought of a future in the profession of a lawyer. Similarly, Sanjay as a youth from a professional family had no thought of business, but time and chance led him down that very path. With a degree in commerce, Sanjay has proceeded to run a successful business as a pharmaceutical distributor under the banner of M/s S.M. Pharmac. This business was a new venture as no one in the family had any experience in the pharmaceutical trade. Yet, his brilliance, entrepreneurship, hard work and devotion have enabled Sanjay to single-handedly establish not only a successful business but also a high reputation in the market. Within seven years of starting the business, he was elected as the president of Nagpur Pharmaceutical Association. He has also been a joint secretary of the Maharashtra Chemists and Druggists Association, executive committee member of the All-India Association of Chemists and Druggists, and a member of the Nagpur-Vidarbha Chamber of Commerce.

Having been a witness to the collapse of a colossal family business in my younger days, I feel happy to witness the return of success in the family.

Soon after he started the pharmaceutical venture, our tenant returned our family cinema theatre in Khamgaon. The additional responsibility of managing another new venture, operating a theatre, also fell to Sanjay because although the family owned a theatre, the business of running it had not been handled by anyone in the family before. Sanjay, albeit reluctantly, agreed to bear the burden—mental as well as physical. Mental, because he was a novice to that venture, and physical, because of the distance of 300 kilometres between Nagpur and Khamgaon. The main relieving factor in this endeavour was the help and guidance of my brother-in-law, Rameshchandra Innani of Washim, who was and is an established cinema-owner and operator. Sanjay managed the new show quite successfully for about five years. That period was the most tiring part of his life, but he fulfilled it ably and earned a reputation even in that venture. He travelled by road/rail transport to Khamgaon regularly. After I purchased our first new car, a Maruti-800, he used it for his travel. Once while returning to Nagpur late at night, the car, driven by our driver, Bandu, met with a serious accident. Both Sanjay and Bandu were seriously injured, but considering the magnitude of the accident, the Almighty was kind. Eventually, we sold that theatre.

Sanjay is devoted to the Rotary movement and has also been intensely connected with the Jaycees Club. He was president of Rotary Club of Nagpur Ishanya, district director of membership development in the Rotary and vice president of the Orange City Jaycees. He has received much recognition in these movements and has been conferred the New Jaycee award, best Jaycee Week award and Rotary international Significant Achievement award. He is fond of music, cricket and reading. His strength lies in leadership in social and business life.

Sanjay is married to Archana, daughter of Smt. and Shri Nandkishoreji Bisani of Narwar, Gwalior. She is a graduate and a devoted homemaker. She is connected with several social and women's organizations of Nagpur in various capacities. She is president of Trinayan Maheshwari Mahila Sagathan Nagpur. She has also helped Sanjay in his business activities. They have two children, a son, Nakul and a daughter, Pooja.

I am a lucky and proud grandfather of six talented grandchildren Devansh, Aditee, Kartik, Apoorva, Nakul and Pooja. The recent happy additions to the family are my great grandchildren: Yashveer and Sashwat, sons of Devansh, and Riansha and Anvaya, daughters of Kartik.

Devansh, our oldest grandchild, was born on 16 November 1981 at Nagpur. A lawyer by profession, he is BLS, LLB from Government Law College, Mumbai, and has been practicing law in Delhi since 2007, mainly in the Supreme Court. He also practices in the Delhi High Court and various statutory tribunals and forums. His preferred branch of law is arbitration and conciliation. He was attached to the chambers of Shri Gopal Subramanium, Solicitor General of India. After earning his law degree in 2005, he had his initial legal training at M/S Desai and Diwanji, advocates and solicitors of Mumbai and thereafter he joined the chambers of Shri Iqbal Chagla, senior advocate of Mumbai. He has done judicial clerkship under Hon'ble Shri Justice Arijit Pasayat, Judge, the Supreme Court of India. He was not interested in practicing in Mumbai since his father became a judge of the Bombay High Court and hence shifted to Delhi. He was research assistant for our two books *Arbitration, Conciliation and Mediation*, and *Trade Marks, Passing Off and Franchising* authored by Anoop and myself. Devansh is a scintillating orator who has won many trophies for his incisive arguments and convincing deliveries. He was awarded the Best Student Trophy in the Government Law College and represented the college as a speaker in the All-India Moot Court Competition held at Ernakulum, in which his team won the 'Best Team and Best Memorial' award. He represented the college as a speaker in the Justice P.N. Bhagwati Constitutional Law Moot Court Competition held by National Law School, Bengaluru, and he was adjudicated as the Second-best Team. He also represented the college as a speaker at the All-India Inter-

Collegiate Competition, Cochin University. He presented a paper on 'Obscenity on the Internet' in the 40th LAWASIA International Conference, Goa. His other interests are music and reading. He has built an excellent home library comprising legal as well as non-legal books. He is a brilliant, well read, mature and highly dependable person. Devansh's strength is his straightforwardness, foresight and analytical skill.

Devansh is married to Shweta, daughter of Smt. and Shri Shishir Majmudar of Delhi. Shweta is a BA, LLB and is a practicing lawyer in Delhi. She is a talented and loving person and strikes an excellent balance between her professional and home life. She and Devansh were blessed with two sons, Yashveer, on 22 March 2013 and Sashwat on 26 December 2015.

Aditee was born on 3 February 1987 at Nagpur. She is a BCom, LLB. She obtained a diploma from Welingkar Institute of Management in public relations and is at present working as a corporate lawyer in a leading corporate firm in Mumbai. She is involved in the Rotary movement and was a part of Rotaract Club of Church Gate for five years, as secretary of the club, joint secretary of R.I. District (3140) Mumbai, and has won many awards including Best Rotaractor of the Year and Outstanding Secretary of the District of the Year. Her main interests are singing, dancing and elocution, which led to her selection as a house-captain in school. She recently performed her arangetram in Bharatnatyam at Birla Matrushri Kendra in Mumbai after seven years of learning the dance form. Aditee has many talents but her self-confidence and maturity are her most outstanding features.

Kartik was born on 17 September 1986 in Nagpur. He has been a meritorious student throughout. Holding a M.S.E in robotics from Pennsylvania University, USA, he went on to pursue a PhD in robotics from the same university. He has done BTech in electrical engineering from IIT Mumbai and was selected in the team of five students to represent India at the International Physics Olympiad

(IPHO) held in South Korea in 2004, in which he got a silver medal. He and his team were felicitated at the august hands of the president, Dr A.P.J Abdul Kalam, in Rashtrapati Bhawan. He was awarded the Institute Citation for contribution to technical activities at IIT Mumbai. His other interests include Formula 1 racing and cycling, but his principal interest is in computers. Kartik is quiet, focused and dedicated. Although not an extrovert, his warmth and sincerity engage those who make the effort to know him. What he does not even endeavour to convey are his extraordinary achievements. His modesty is mind-boggling. He is married to Dr. Vandana, M.S (ENT).

Apoorva was born on 20 March 1989, in Nagpur. She did BE (information technology) from Nagpur University and MS (information management) from Syracuse University, Syracuse, New York. Her research paper 'Intelligent Path and Speed Tracker' was published in the *International Journal on Computer Applications*. She has organized and participated in several department-level festivals as technical head. She is a diploma holder in soft skills and personal development and obtained merit certificates for these. Her interests are reading, gadgets and technology and adventure sports. She has passed three levels of tabla exams and has performed in school concerts and competitions. Apoorva, a girl of few words and strong will, is a voracious reader.

Nakul was born on 03 September 1986 in Nagpur. He holds an LLB (Hons) from Amity Law School, New Delhi, and has been practicing law in Delhi since 2010. He also practices in the Supreme Court, Delhi High Court, National Consumer Dispute Redressal Commission, Telecom Dispute Settlement & Appellate Tribunal and Debt Recovery Tribunal. He was attached to the law firm M/s Agarwal Associates of Delhi. He holds a diploma in cyber law from the Asian School of Cyber Laws and GLC, Mumbai. He has done judicial clerkship under Hon'ble Shri Justice C.K.

Thakker, judge, Supreme Court of India. He was an associate in Agarwal Law Associates from 2009 to 2013. He participated in the V.M. Salgaonkar Moot Court Competition held in Panaji, Goa, in 2005 and the Kerala Law Academy's All-India Moot Court Competition held in Thiruvananthapuram, Kerala, in 2008. He was the vice president of Amity Law School Students' Academic Committee (ALSAC) and during his tenure conducted an Annual National Seminar on 'Alternative Dispute Resolution in the Era of Globalisation'. Nakul is intelligent, sharp, firm in his views, has a great sense of humour and is a friendly person. Nakul got married to Misha, daughter of Smt and Shri Himanshu Rohtagi of Delhi. She is BA, LLB and is practising law in Delhi. She is an intelligent, hard-working and loving person.

Pooja was born on 16 October 1990 in Nagpur. She is my youngest grandchild. She acquired her CA and BCom degrees in 2012. She has a great interest in social as well as academic activities and is an active member of the Rotaract Club, Nagpur Ishanya. She writes very well and two of her articles have been published in the popular Nagpur daily *The Hitavada*. One was titled 'Scary New Year' and the other 'Actions Define Priorities'. Her paper on 'Risk Management' for the twenty-first all India CA students conference was selected for presentation. She was selected to be a part of the five-member youth brigade Nagpur and participated in 'I lead India', an initiative of *The Times of India*. She completed her post graduate diploma in management from Goa Institute of Management. She has won various skating competitions. Her interests are social issues, environmental issues, writing poems and articles. She is extremely fond of nature in all its forms. She has studied various bird and animal species though her greatest interest is in dogs. Pooja, my youngest grandchild, is the most affectionate and natural person in the family and her core strength is her genuineness.

This family story will remain incomplete without short

references to my two brothers, Vithaldasji and Laxmansingh and two elder married sisters—the late Kesharbai, wife of Yudhisthirji Vidyarthi of Gorakhpur (UP) and late Gulabbai, wife of Jethamalji Dangra of Mohagaon (Nagpur). My sisters and brothers-in-law are no more and their families are well-settled in their respective homes. We all badly miss them especially on Bhau-beej and Raksha Bandhan days.

Vithaldasji was my elder brother whom we lost recently. He was married to Smt Geetadevi, who is a devoted housewife. They are blessed with one son, Ajay, who is a busy legal practitioner in Akola, and two daughters—Saroj and Sarita. These three children of Vithaldasji have two children each, all of whom, grown up and settled in their respective lives. The six grandchildren respectively are Shyam and Giriraj; Ashwini and Swapnil; and Rahul and Mehul. Shyam (a lawyer practicing in Nagpur) is blessed with a daughter, Vedika, and a son, Vedant. As a result Vithaldasji has become a great grandfather. Giriraj is a qualified company secretary practicing in Pune and has a daughter, Kaira. Vithaldasji was bedridden for a long time and was very well looked after by all his family members.

Laxmansingh is my youngest brother and is practising in Nagpur. Before shifting to Nagpur he was practising in Akola. He is a very social person and has a large number of friends. He is married to Smt. Sushiladevi who is a busy acupressure and reiki practitioner and also a devoted social worker. They are blessed with a son—Dr Rajiv, a well-known paediatrician practicing in Nagpur; and two daughters—Shaila and Swati. All three children are married and well-settled in their respective homes and have talented progeny: Dr Rajiv has a daughter, Richa; Shaila has a son Aditya and a daughter Shreya; and Swati's child is Hunar. They are all young now.

## BLESSINGS AND TOUCHING LETTERS

During my morning walk in Nagpur, I met an advocate Shri M.B. Parate, who fondly reminded me of his appearance before me in the High Court at Nagpur and introduced me to his companions as a kind-hearted judge who used to encourage junior lawyers. During these embarrassing moments, he also told me that one of his clients, Shri Bhagwat from Pratap Nagar, Nagpur, serving in the forest department, has hung my photograph in his small house. I guess the gentleman must have succeeded in a case that was crucial for his life. It is not unusual in a judge's life to give a decision that is of great importance to someone, but hanging a photograph was a touching gesture, and I cannot check the temptation of mentioning this. What an invaluable return just for doing one's duty!

Throughout my life I have been the lucky recipient of goodwill from a large and loving circle of relatives as well as personal and professional friends and admirers, some of whom remain unknown to me till this day. I have preserved that valuable treasure. I mention the following: (i) a handwritten inland letter sent by a 'well-wisher', which I used to receive regularly for a number of years during my years as a judge in Nagpur; and (ii) a plaque received by me at the time of my appointment as Chief Justice. I have added some of them as appendices for those who would like to read them.

## LOOKING BACK

The mighty peepul tree grows from a tiny seed, spreading its shade far and wide. But no matter how far it spreads, it cannot survive without its roots remaining always firmly grounded. My roots remain in Akola where I grew up and learnt my first invaluable lessons in life under the benevolent guidance of my senior and always with the heavenly hand of my father on my shoulder. Life has been good. I have achieved some professional recognition, financial security and walked always with my head held high but my feet firmly on the ground. My loving wife and family have been my anchors and my strength. I may not be remembered fifty years from today. I may not have left a mark that will carve my name in the annals of judicial history. But, with material comforts and social vibrancy, there have been many blessings for me to count. Yet the greatest blessing of all, that which makes me a son of fortune, is the love and support I have received at every point of my life from family, seniors and well-wishers, respect and affection from juniors and the goodwill of many whose lives have brushed with mine in the course of my eighty-three years and more.

Can fortune be kinder?

# Appendix 1

ADDRESS OF THE HON'BLE SHRI JUSTICE NARESH H. PATIL, THE ACTING CHIEF JUSTICE, HIGH COURT OF JUDICATURE AT BOMBAY, AT THE FULL COURT REFERENCE TO LATE SHRI JUSTICE VALLABHDAS AIDAN MOHTA, FORMER CHIEF JUSTICE OF ORISSA HIGH COURT AND FORMER JUDGE OF THE BOMBAY HIGH COURT ON THURSDAY 27$^{TH}$ SEPTEMBER, 2018 AT 10.30 A.M. IN THE CENTRAL COURT.

My esteemed sisters and brother judges

Shri Anil Singh,
Additional Solicitor General of India, for
Bar Council of Maharashtra & Goa

Dr. Milind Sathe, President,
Bombay Bar Association

Shri V.A. Thorat,
Senior Advocate & Member of Ad-hoc Committee,
Advocates' Association of Western India.

Mr. Kaiwan Kalyaniwalla, President,
Bombay Incorporated Law Society.

Justice Anoop V. Mohta & Members of the Bereaved family

Learned Senior Advocates,
Members of the Bar
Ladies and Gentlemen,

Today, we have assembled here this morning to mourn the passing away of Shri Vallabhdas Aiden Mohta, distinguished former Chief Justice of Orissa High Court, a former judge of the Bombay High Court and Senior Advocate of the Supreme Court of India, who breathed his last in the evening of 3$^{rd}$ July 2018 at Nagpur at the age of 85 years.

Justice V.A. Mohta was popularly known as "Vallabhbhai". His entire career as a Judge, as Chief Justice and also as Senior Advocate of the Supreme Court was one of dedication and deep devotion to the cause of justice.

Justice Mohta was born on 26$^{th}$ April 1933 at Akola in Maharashtra. His father Aiden Sangidas was a well-known businessman in Vidarbha Region and his mother Smt. Hirabai Aidan Mohta was a housewife. He was married to Kamladevi on 20$^{th}$ June 1953.

Justice Mohta had school education in New English High School, Akola. He graduated from D.A.V. College, Kanpur. He passed LL.B. Degree from Law College, Nagpur in the year 1958.

After enrolment as an Advocate on 22$^{nd}$ March 1960 with the Bar Council of Maharashtra & Goa, Justice Mohta initially started practice at Akola and thereafter, shifted to Nagpur.

Justice Mohta had not only acquired reputation as an outstanding Advocate but also took keen interest in social activities. He took keen interest in other subjects like literature, music, education and writings. In 1966-1967, Justice Mohta was elected as the President of Rotary Club of Akola. In 1968-1969, he was appointed as the Governor's Group Representative for Akola, Amravati, Khamgaon, Bhusaval and Jalgaon.

Justice Mohta was a founder President of Radhadevi Goenka Women's College, Akola as well as a President of Berar General Education Society, which runs four colleges and a school in Akola and Karanja. He was President of the "India International Maheshwari Society, New Delhi", and President of SEARCH – a

Society dedicated to Social Excellence & Justice.

He was twice elected as the Member of Bar Council of Maharashtra and Goa, first in 1968 and again in the year 1973. In 1974, Justice Mohta was unanimously elected as the Vice-Chairman of the Bar Council of Maharashtra and Goa.

He was a Member of Authors' Guild of India. He was associated with the Euthanasia movement for recognition of Right to Die with Dignity in India and was invited to lead a group in the International Workshop held in New Delhi for Development of Policy Statement on Euthanasia.

In recognition of the outstanding reputation and knowledge of law, Justice Mohta was elevated to the bench on 27$^{th}$ April 1979 as an Additional Judge of this Court and Permanent Judge on 15$^{th}$ October 1982.

Justice Mohta, by nature and temperament, was most courteous, very cool, helpful and generous. He was a guiding source for many junior members of the Bar.

Justice Mohta known for quick grasp and command over the facts and the law, would precisely pin-point the issue involved in the matter. He was an ideal judge. During his tenure of 15 years at the Bench, Justice Mohta delivered a number of landmark judgments in various branches of law and also endeared himself to the Bar and the colleagues on the Bench. As per the data available on the legal software, there were 475 reported judgments including 17 Full Bench Judgments to his credit. He had authored 14 Full Bench Judgments.

During his tenure as a judge, he was appointed by Government of India to conduct Court of Inquiry to investigate into causes of accident involving an Indian Airlines Aircraft, at Aurangabad. In a study tour of USSR, he was a delegate of the Indo-Soviet Cultural Society. He was also delegate in the SAARC Law Conferences in Sri Lanka, Pakistan and Bhutan. Justice Mohta undertook study tour of China in a delegation headed by a Supreme Court Judge.

He was a member of the Committee for Implementing Legal Aid Scheme (CILAS) formed by the Government of India, which was headed by the Chief Justice of India.

Justice Mohta had authored two books (1) *Arbitration and Conciliation* and (2) *Trade Marks, Passing Off and Franchising* published by the All India Reporter. Both books are now in the Second Edition. The First Edition of *Arbitration and Conciliation* was released in 2001 and the Second Edition was released in 2008.

Justice Mohta was appointed as the Chief Justice of Orissa High Court on 28$^{th}$ September 1994 and retired on 25$^{th}$ April 1995. During the said period, he delivered several landmark judgments on the various important law points. As per the data available on legal software, Justice Mohta had authored 22 reported judgments including 7 Full Bench Judgments.

After his retirement, he started active legal practice as Senior Advocate in the Supreme Court of India and also continued to write and publish books and articles on important subjects in law.

His name was included in *Who's Who in the World* an American Publication of 2002 by Marquis and in *The Cambridge Blue Book* an English Publication by International Biographical Centre, Cambridge, for contribution in the field of Arbitration Law. His articles on various subjects have appeared in national and international journals.

I knew Justice V.A. Mohta and I had met him on few occasions. He was a well known respectable leading Senior Advocate practicing in the Supreme Court of India. He made a mark even while practicing in the Supreme Court.

A glorious innings of Justice Mohta at the Bar for last 60 years, unfortunately, came to an end. In his death, we have lost a dedicated lawyer, distinguished judge and wonderful human being of multi-faceted qualities. His contribution to the administration of Justice will be remembered forever. His memory is carved out in the hearts of all of us and those who knew Justice Mohta.

He is survived by his three sons namely; Justice Anoop Mohta, a former distinguished judge of the Bombay High Court, Dr. Narendra and younger son Shri Sanjay. His younger brother Shri Laxmansingh Mohta is a practicing lawyer at Nagpur.

On behalf of my colleagues and myself, I pay humble tributes to Justice V.A. Mohta with the words: -

Life's race, well run;
Life's work, well done'
Life's victory, won
Now cometh rest

May his soul rest in eternal peace.

# Appendix 2

REFERENCE IN THE MEMORY OF LATE SHRI V. A. MOHTA BY HON'BLE SHRI DIPAK MISRA, CHIEF JUSTICE OF INDIA

Late Shri V.A. Mohta, coming from a small township of Akola, transcended his beginnings to become an established lawyer widely known throughout the State of Maharashtra. His commitment to legal services and his humility made him one of the most revered and loved lawyers of the State. The goodwill, respect and confidence in his leadership was shown by the fraternity by electing him twice as a member of the Bar Council of which he became the Vice-Chairman in 1974. His analytical method of presentation in the Court brought admiration and adoration from the members of the Bar. Frown did not crease his forehead nor did anger cloud his mind.

Recognizing his talent and legal acumen, Shri Mohta was elevated as a judge of the Bombay High Court in 1979. After completing assignment of inquiring into the causes of the accident of an Indian Airlines aircrafts at Aurangabad, he was appointed as the Chief Justice of Orissa High Court on September 28, 1994. His contribution to the field of law is reflectible from many a pronouncement. In Minoo H. Mody v. Hemant D Vakil, Shri Mohta dealt with intricate questions of procedure concerning an appeal under the then Section 10F of the Companies Act, 1956 against the orders of the Company Law Board passed under Sections 397 and 398 of the Act. Examining the distinction between appeals and petitions in a remarkably precise judgment capturing the original and the appellate side of the High Court, he led the Bench in declaring that no appeals could be filed as petitions. This ended an issue that was causing great confusion in the High Court for quite some time.

As the Chief Justice of the Orissa High Court, his judicial skill resolved a complex issue of lawyers' arguments on the distinction between a proviso, an exception, a saving clause, a non-obstante clause and an explanation. Presiding over the Full Bench in Laxminarayan Saw Mill and Anr. v. State of Orissa, he upheld the constitutional validity of the Orissa Saw Mills & Saw Pits (Control) Act, 1991 and the interpretation of the proviso creating a total ban on the operation and establishment of private saw mills and pits within ten kilometers of a reserved forest in an extremely analytical manner. He ruled that what has to be examined is the substance, not the form adopted by the legislature. The principle of safeguarding environment and the forests intellectually impelled him to treat the restriction valid. He was also careful to point out that whether a restriction is to be permanent or temporary is a decision for the legislature and not for the courts. He opined that the area of the restriction is a matter of policy so long as the same is not absurd or more drastic than is necessary.

His devotion to judicial work went hand in hand with his contribution to the society. After his retirement from the Orissa High Court on April 25, 1995, he started his practice in the Supreme Court. His gentle yet forceful argument was very persuasive. I knew him quite closely and I must admit that he was always optimistic and felt proud that he had become a great grandfather. He was affectionate to juniors and his smile was contagious. Shri Mohta also had a strong penchant for academic scholarship. This is evident from the two books that he authored on arbitration and trade mark laws. He remained active till the end as a lawyer. We are left to recall Shri Mohta as a warm and dear human being when his personal memoir *Time and Chance*, now under publication, comes into our hands.

Shri Mohta's wife Kamladevi predeceased him. He is survived by his three sons, Shri Anoop Mohta, a former Judge of the Bombay High Court, Dr. Narendra Mohta, and Shri Sanjay Mohta, an engineer. Two of his grandsons, Mr. Devansh Mohta and Mr. Nakul Mohta are practitioners in this Court.

I, on behalf of my brother and sister judges, extend our heartfelt condolences and pray to the Almighty to bestow peace upon the departed souls. May their souls rest in eternal peace.

# Appendix 3

Fwd : HAPPY FRIENDSHIP DAY BABUJI

From: "Pooja Mohta " <poo famoh ta @qmail.com>
**Date** 07-Aug-201610:30 AM
Subject: Happy Friendship Day Babuji To: <vamohta@hotmail.com>

Hello Babuji.
You must have read the newspaper and in it you might have seen loads of advertisements about 'Friendship Day'. I guess even friendship, one of the basic relationships living beings develop, is now getting so lost that we need a day to appreciate it. Makes me wonder where are we headed w.r.t to the larger purpose of life. We are all busy earning money which we won't carry to heaven, and gaining power which will be lost when we leave for heaven. Why the fuss then? Momentary happiness? I find myself as well sometimes getting drawn to this rat race, it's getting harder to resist. But I don't think I'll succumb. After all I'm a 'Mohta'. We don't do the ordinary. :)

Babuji, you are my greatest source of inspiration to stick to my values, and act honourably. My professional career has just started and I'm already feeling the pressure of competition, but winning a race is one part, being a good player is another. Being both, that's something to be aimed for. Just like you, Babuji.

Thanks a lot for being my inspiration. Loads of love.

Pooja.

# Appendix 4

On the occasion of his 75th birthday

सितारो से आगे और भी है
कामयाबी के निशान और भी है
बीत गये 75 वर्ष कामयाबी की सीढ़िया चढ़ते-चढ़ते
परिवार और स्नेही जनों के साथ चलते-चलते 25 साल और
बीत जायेंगे
आसमान की बुलंदिया छू जायेंगे
बहुत कम होते है, ऐसे बिरले
जो आसमान से टकराते है
पर अपने पैर ज़मीन पर टिकाय रखते है
उचाँइयों के बुलंदियो पर भी शालीन रहते है
खुशनसीब है हम, कि हम जुड़े है आपसे
आपकी छत्रछाया में रहते है प्यार से
आपके आर्शीवाद के आज भी हकदार है हम
खुशनसीब है हम आप हमारे साथ है।

सुरेखा
25.7.2008

# Acknowledgements

This is my fifth book. The previous four were on legal subjects. This is personal—a story of the long journey of 84 years that started from Akola, a small town in Vidarbha region of Maharashtra.

Every story has back stories. The journey has been fascinating, brimful with love and support of not only close family members, but also of a large number of near relatives, dear friends, and well wishers. Most of them are easily noticeable in the book. Some are unknown. Without them this long life would have been a drudgery. Their contribution in my life is invaluable. I find myself short of words to express my gratitude to them. In fact gratitude can never be adequately expressed.

The idea of this book is not originally mine. It was of some of my close family members expressed through my grandson Devansh, a practicing lawyer in Delhi. This book could not be written just by stretching my memory. The period was long, events and turns were many. They had to be selected and organized. This inevitably led to tracing, searching and examining old records, files, correspondence, photographs, etc. This could not be done single-handedly. To complete the tedious process of collating the notes, my two grandsons Devansh and Nakul, and their wives Shweta and Misha—all practicing lawyers in Delhi—helped me a lot. They made valuable suggestions about some additions and deletions. My associate Nilakanta Nayak also rendered great help in the process.

Praveen Mohta, my close relative from Akola, performed the difficult task of researching the old family tree.

In the making of this book, Shri Ram Jethmalani, my senior and a well wisher from Akola days (1970s) and my close friend from Delhi, Shri K.N. Bhat, Senior Advocate of the Supreme Court and former Additional Solicitor General of India (a scintillating writer of articles on important and controversial topics, legal as well as general, that have appeared in national-dailies), rendered valuable suggestions. I am grateful to them.

The editor of this book Ms. Neena Thomas made invaluable contribution. She took personal interest in the book and has given valuable suggestions not only about inclusion and exclusion of some topics, but also about their contents. Her interest in the book was not just professional. There was a noticeable personal touch. Many thanks, Neena.

Hon'ble Justice M.N. Venkatchalaiah, former Chief Justice of India and Chairman of Human Rights Commission—whom doyen of Indian Bar Mr. Fali S. Nariman often rates as one of the best Chief Justice of India—has made value addition to this book by inscribing a generous and touching foreword. How do I express my gratitude to him? I have no words.

I am very happy that this book is being published by Rupa— a well-known publisher of books in India. I thank Mr Kapish Mehra, its Managing Director, and especially Ms Elina Majumdar, for taking personal interest in the book.